FLOWERS IN
THE BLOOD

FLOWERS IN THE BLOOD

THE STORY OF OPIUM

BY JEFF GOLDBERG WITH DEAN LATIMER

INTRODUCTION BY WILLIAM BURROUGHS

Skyhorse Publishing

Skyhorse Publishing books may be purchased in bulk at special
discounts for sales promotion, corporate gifts, fund-raising, or
educational purposes. Special editions can also be created to
specifications. For details, contact the Special Sales Department,
Skyhorse Publishing, 307 West 36th Street, 11th Floor, New York, NY
10018 or info@skyhorsepublishing.com.

Skyhorse® and Skyhorse Publishing® are registered trademarks of
Skyhorse Publishing, Inc.®, a Delaware corporation.

Visit our website at www.skyhorsepublishing.com.

10 9 8 7 6 5 4 3 2 1

Library of Congress Cataloging-in-Publication Data is available on file.
ISBN: 978-1-62636-540-7

Printed in the United States of America

CONTENTS

PREFACE, 2014
THE AYATOLLAH'S OPIUM

While this book was being written in the winter of 1979, the Shah of Iran fell and the sinister hawk-like face of Ayatollah Khomeini, in his black turban, white beard and scowling gray eyebrows, sent a Pavlovian shudder down the nation's spine. He was the Imam America loved to hate. So, it was especially intriguing when that same sinister face was pictured in the December 15, 1979, *New York Post* beside several big baggies of opium, that most sinister drug.

Earlier in the month, customs agents at Kennedy Airport had discovered four kilos of opium concealed in four hollow portraits of the Ayatollah, arriving from Shiraz on the way to the West Coast. In Canoga Park, near LA, Drug Enforcement Administration agents arrested three Iranians, and seized thirty-five pounds of opium and eleven more portraits of Khomeini. The next day, they proudly displayed the stash for reporters, and the image of the Ayatollah and his opium was beamed straight to the hateful heartland.

Neither the DEA nor anyone else puzzled over why anyone in his right mind would smuggle thirty-five pounds of smelly, oozy, bulky opium to America, in portraits of the Ayatollah, in the middle of the fifth week of the hostage crisis. Did these guys want to get caught? It seemed likely.

The DEA issued grave warnings that a tidal wave of Iranian junk was heading for America. And. indeed, over the next six months, suitcases full of black opium and an influx of heroin hit the New York streets.

The Iranian connection? Maybe. Law enforcement officials were quick to attribute a record 680-ton opium harvest in Iran to Khomeini's Green Revolution, but it didn't make sense. Since opium in Iran is planted in the fall and harvested in the spring, the bumper crop had to be in the ground before the Shah left the country. Was the Ayatollah's opium really the Shah's opium?

Such is the winding trail of the Dragon.

In the thirty-five years since *Flowers in the Blood* first appeared, some things have changed for the better—in the United States, finally, an emphasis on drug treatment, based on the disease model of addiction, has largely replaced the criminalization and condemnation of addicts as moral weaklings and nervous waste cases [see Chapter 8]. Other things haven't changed at all. In 2012, HSBC, the very same Hong Kong Shanghai Banking Corporation that financed the Opium Wars [see Chapter 6], plead guilty and was fined $1.9 billion on charges of laundering money for Mexican drug lords and terrorist organizations including Al Qaeda. At the same time, the yellow peril of the inscrutable Chinaman [see Chapter 9] and threat of cocaine-crazed Negroes [see Chapter 10] were in the process of morphing into Mad Muhammadans. From the Ayatollah Khomeini to Osama bin Laden to the Taliban,[1]* all have been portrayed as the sinister face of the dope trade.

But if you really want to know who started it all, go back to Hassan-ibn-Sabbah, the legendary Old Man of the Mountain, who lived in Persia (Iran) in the early twelfth century and was the leader of the Assassin Order, perhaps the most efficient terrorist organization in history.

Like Khomeini and ninety percent of all Iranians, Hassan-ibn-Sabbah was a member—in fact, an early champion—of the Shiite movement, which since its inception has fought for the

---

1   However onerous the Taliban, under their control opium production in Afghanistan dropped to 185 tons in 2001. It has increased to over 5,800 tons since the US invasion.

civil rights of non-Arab Moslems, the minority Aryan Moslems who live mainly in Iran.

When the Turkish Sultan of Rum invaded Persia, Hassan's Assassins, all innocence and blood in their white tunics and red turbans, staged guerilla raids that systematically killed him and all his adult successors, leaving a child on the throne.[2]

According to Marco Polo, the secret of Hassan-ibn-Sabbah's power over his Fedayeen was dope. In Polo's account of his travels, he wrote that Hassan erected a pleasure garden, where fountains of wine, milk, and honey splashed and "the most beautiful damsels" sang and danced. The garden was a veritable Paradise, the original vision of Coleridge's Kubla Khan [see Chapter 5].

> Now no man was allowed to enter the Garden save those whom he intended to be his ASHISHIN... He would introduce them into his garden, some four, or six, or ten at a time, having first made them drink a certain potion which cast them into a deep sleep. When therefore they awoke, and found themselves in a place so charming, they deemed that it was Paradise in very truth... So when the Old Men would have any prince slain, he would say to such a youth: 'Go thou and slay so and so! And when thou returnest my Angels shall bear thee into Paradise, and shouldest thou die, natheless even so will I send my Angels to carry thee back to Paradise.'

The fact behind the fairytale was uncovered by the linguist and orientalist Silvestre de Sacy, who argued that the word "assassin" originated in the word "Hashishiyah"—"hashish-eater" or, simply, "dope-fiend"—for in Hassan's day, "hashish" was not distinguished from other drugs: hashish was cannabis, opium, and a wide variety of herbs; e.g., "dope."

It seemed quite possible to de Sacy that Hassan did initiate his troops with a drug (most likely a combination of cannabis and opium), to provide them with a vision of Paradise. Yet, even the

---

2   Hassan-ibn-Sabbah died in May 1124, uttering his last words: "Nothing is forbidden. All is permitted."

sinister Hassan-ibn-Sabbah was not the true historical source of the Iranian connection. Opium came to Persia from the West, after being introduced in the third century AD by Alexander the Great. The Persians passed the poppy's painkilling secret to their Arab neighbors, who were less enchanted with the magical substance. In fact, they were downright suspicious. Why? Because it was a white man's drug.

Undoubtedly, Marco Polo heard the legend of Hassan from Arabs who associated dope with those low-life Aryan Iranian Hashishiyah, who picked up the evil monkey from those insidious white Romans.

Now, whose monkey is it? And who's the monkey?

—Jeff Goldberg, 2014

INTRODUCTION
GOD'S OWN MEDICINE
BY WILLIAM BURROUGHS

Poppy field on screen . . . the petals fall like snow in the wind . . .

Commentator's voice: "The opium poppy has been cultivated for thousands of years and opium extracted from the ripening seed pods." As he says this we see workers emptying little scoops of opium into a cauldron of water.

"The juice drained from the pods is boiled and filtered to remove impurities, then processed into raw opium."—Blocks of opium on screen—"And for thousands of years opium has brought relief to suffering humanity—suffering from the pains of sickness . . ."—persons in various costumes from togas to suits take opium in one form or another for coughs, colds, lumbago, toothache, leprosy, etc.—"The pain of old age . . ."—Old Chinese smoking opium—"The pain of grinding poverty . . ."—Indian farmers in a hovel wash down opium at dawn—"Or the pain of simple boredom."

Eighteenth century gentleman in chemist's shop.

Chemist: "Shocking night out sir."

Gentleman: "Yes indeed. Need a spot of laudanum."

Chemist: "Certainly sir. How much?"

Gentleman: "A liter. Taking to my bed for the winter you know."

Chemist: "Of course sir. Very sensible of you sir."

Commentator continues: "Armies have marched on opium from Vietnam to Asia Minor a thousand years ago." A soldier in Vietnam leans his M-16 against a tree and takes a shot ... same soldier in Turkish dress washes down his ration of opium, dates, and brown sugar.

"But long before the poppy was brought under cultivation and man learned to extract the opium, some intrepid experimenter must have eaten an opium pod, discovered its medicinal properties, and passed this knowledge along to apprentices. Here are the Unglings, a Cro-Magnon tribe 30,000 years ago. Homo sapiens like you and me—or the folks next door."

The prehistoric Unglings are in animal skins, carrying stone axes; one is old, suffering from rheumatism, hobbling along with the aid of a staff. They come to a field of opium poppies. The petals have fallen, and the pods are ripe and yellow. The old man can go no further. He sinks down among the pods. One hand rolls a pod in his fingers; there is a speculative look on his face. He bites into the pod, sucking the juice. He gets up and throws away his staff. Vigorously he directs the others as they gather pods.

"Throughout the long cold winter the Unglings take refuge in a cave, cooking the pods into a thick black brew. It is a bitter potion, but somehow it makes it easier to endure the cold, the hunger, the endless search for food."

The Unglings pass around a gourd of opium solution. They shudder at the bitterness but then smile as the potion takes effect, and go vigorously about their tasks.

"But unexpected things were happening..." A female Ungling, hands on hips, stands over a young male. She breaks into vituperative words. "What is she saying? Well I think we can all guess. ... And now something else: as spring comes on and the last of the pods have been used, the Unglings are suddenly very sick. What is this mysterious illness that afflicts not only the old but also the young? Can nothing be done? The wise old Ungling has an inspiration. There must, he thinks, be some connection between the lack of pods and the illness. Young Unglings are dispatched. They return with pods. And soon the old man's wisdom is manifest."

Over the years countless millions were to confirm the findings of the wise old Ungling, and to learn that opium affords relief from pain, discomfort, illness and fatigue, but exacts over a period of time the price of dependence. Four to six months' daily use establishes addiction, and the sudden withdrawal of opium then brings on a spectrum of incapacitating symptoms: stomach cramps and diarrhea, watering of the eyes and nose, sneezing fits, restlessness and insomnia, weakness and prostration, hypersensitivity, spontaneous orgasms, and nightmares.

Yet at the same time there is a feeling of renewal and increased health. Cocteau likened withdrawal symptoms to the spring flow of sap into the trees. And the author Thomas De Quincey wrote:

"Jeremy Taylor conjectures that it may be as painful to be born as to die, and during the whole period of diminishing opium I had the torments of a man passing from one mode of existence to another. The issue was not death but a sort of physical regeneration, and a restoration of more than youthful spirits." We all experience during our lives the comfortable stasis of habit, and the feeling of renewal and rebirth as a habit of mind or body is laid aside.

This book covers the subject of opium from the earliest historical references to the present time. The recent discovery of opium receptors in the brain, and the body's own painkiller endorphin, suggests that there is a preaddiction metabolism related to endorphin deficiency. The addict needs to supplement a vital substance insufficiently produced in his body much as the diabetic needs insulin. So the absurdity of penalizing a metabolic deficiency is now manifest. The writers are careful not to take sides. By simply presenting the evidence, they demonstrate the futility and wasteful folly of the police and jail approach to addiction.

"Those who are ignorant of the past will suffer its repetition."

Prohibition did not stop people from drinking but it did deliver this country into the hands of organized crime. Undeterred by the dismal and expensive failure of Prohibition, reformers are still trying to legislate narcotics out of existence. The predictable result is thousands of addicts, a huge uncontrollable black market, and casualties from overdoses, hepatitis, infections, and poisonous street dope. And the attempt to enforce these unenforceable laws is costing the taxpayer billions of dollars. Methadone maintenance was the first glimmer of sanity in the antidrug hysteria that gripped America in the fifties and sixties under the able propagandizing of Harry Anslinger. And still newspaper editorials cite the growing number of addicts as reason for continuing with measures as unsuccessful as they are expensive. They are citing the failure of drug laws as reason to continue and amplify such laws. If something doesn't work why go on doing it? *Flowers in the Blood* provides a fascinating documentation for a sane approach to opium and opiates.

PREFACE
FLOWERS IN THE BLOOD

My imagination was once so kindled by the perusal of a little book called the **Opium-eater** *that I resolved to put its pleasing assurances to a practical test...*

My portion stuck fast as original sin; and I shortly lapsed into a disturbed slumber, in which appeared to me that I retained my consciousness entire, while visions passed before me...That one time I was soaring on the pinions of an angel among splendors of the highest heaven, beholding at a glance the beauty of their unveiled mysteries, and listening to harps and choral symphonies over which time, sorrow, and death have no power; and then my presumption was checked, my cleaving wings, like the waxen plumes of Icarus, were melted away, and I fell down, down, till caught in the bosom of a thunder cloud, from which I was again hurled, linked to its fiercest bolt upon the plunging verge of a cataract, that carried me down, frantic with horror, into the lowest depths of its howling gulf...

Still I floated upon the frightful verge...till coming around near the north pole...an iceberg with its mass of frozen torrents came rolling in, and catching me in one of its dripping shelves, bore me through seas lashed by the hurricane...

Being benumbed and paralyzed by the stiffening ice I fell from my trembling lodgement, and descending through the sea was carried by the wave of the submarine current quite within

*a little grotto... where a mermaid was gently kindling a fire,
beneath whose reviving ray I soon felt each frozen vein and
limb slowly tingling back to life—when as if to reclaim my
bewildered thoughts, and sooth their delirious excitement this
daughter of the deep raising her harp, struck one of those soft
strains whose liquid flow melts into the heart like fragrant dew
into the bosom of the folding rose.*

*But scarce had the last note of this sweet minstrel died away
into the listening stillness of peace, when a call loud as the
summoning trump of the archangel, sent its rending thunder
through the hollow caverns of the astounding ocean, and the
rent tombs of the shaking earth, starting even death itself from
his sleep. The sheeted dead went up from their watery graves
to stand on the sea, while the earth, from precipice to plain,
from shore to mountain's brow, was covered with the shrouded
myriads that had left their couches of clay.*

*The sun with a changed, despairing aspect disappeared, leav-
ing a huge darkened chasm in the heavens; the moon spun
round and round and slowly receded from view, leaving another
fearful blank in the blue vault; the planets fell from their places,
and were quenched as they sank into the lifeless void beneath;
and darkness in a thick palpable mass filled all space... The
curling wave lay half broken on the shore; the torrent ceased
to plunge from its wave-worn steep; the war-horse kneeled down
and died; the monarch in his capital discrowned, stood pale
and speechless; the peasant in his field called aloud on his
forgotten God; while the imploring shriek of nations went up
like the last wail of the ruined world.*

Rev. Walter Colton, 1836

*After two pipes I felt a certain drowsiness, after four my mind
felt alert and calm—unhappiness and fear of the future became
like something dimly remembered which I had thought important once. I, who feel shy at exhibiting the grossness of my
French, found myself reciting a poem of Baudelaire to my
companion. When I got home that night I experienced for the
first time the white night of opium. One lies relaxed and wake-
ful, not desiring sleep. We dread wakefulness when our*

thoughts are disturbed, but in this state one is calm—it would be wrong even to say one is happy—happiness disturbs the pulse. And then suddenly without warning one sleeps. Never has one slept so deeply a whole night-long sleep, and then the waking and the luminous dial of the clock showing that twenty minutes of so-called real time have gone by.

Graham Greene, 1951

We've been on heroin a week now, Stuart and I. Seven days of voluntary illness. And how ill we feel...My personal view at present is just one made gray and utterly grim by heroin. The extraordinary thing is that it brings no joy, no pleasure. Weariness, above all. At most, some hours of disinterest—the world passing by while you just feel untouched. Even after the injection there is no sort of thrill, no mind-expansion nonsense, no orgiastic heights, no Kubla Khan. A feeling of oppressed breathing, a slight flush, a sense of strange unease, almost fear unknown...You doze, see a daft scene where someone throws something, jump with a sort of panic, and doze again. Hypnagogic hallucinations, they're called. Itching and itching, you scratch and turn. Why should people take this stuff—not for joy. Only for an hour of sudden shafts of panic and itching.

Dr. Ian Oswald, 1968

A nineteenth century itinerant preacher on an eye-opening visit to Constantinople, a famous novelist doing fieldwork in Saigon during the Indochina War, and a young doctor laden with EEG wires and skin-conducture leads in a research lab in London: three different people, three different times, three different settings, and three distinctly different opinions of what it *feels* like to take opium—or, in the case of Dr. Oswald, opium's potent derivative, heroin. Three distinct experiences, but all equally profound.

How can a minute quantity of dried sap from the head of a poppy affect people in such disparate and powerful ways? Scholars, sorcerers, scientists, and poets have been seeking the answer to opium's mystery for three thousand years at least. Fables and myths about opium began at the dawn of history, but the reasons for its strange effects on the mind and body have only come to light recently.

By the early seventies, a handful of researchers scattered around the world had come to a startling conclusion: opium, and a wide variety of other drugs from LSD to aspirin, worked by mimicking endogenous chemicals—*substances already in the body*. Tiny shifts in the balances of these molecular human components govern not only how we feel physically, but also our mental state—who we are—at any given moment. And since the balance of chemicals inside the body can vary from moment to moment and person to person, drugs which mimic them naturally may produce widely variant experiences.

Both LSD and psilocybin, the active ingredient in psychedelic mushrooms, mimic serotonin—a hormone that promotes wider connections between cells, a psychic explorer that carries long-range messages over the intricate time, space, and feeling networks of the brain. When tripping on LSD, the brain cells connected by serotonin transmission—particularly those clustered in the limbic system, the brain's emotional boiler—are firing crazily, presenting a lot more pictures, information, and feelings at a much higher pitch.

By far the greatest excitement in scientific circles, though, surrounds one group of body drugs, the endorphins (from endogenous morphine), natural substances with the same pain-relieving properties as opium and morphine. Dr. Avram Goldstein, a pioneering neurobiologist working at Stanford University, first speculated that such things existed in 1972. It took him and four other research teams in England, Sweden, and the United States three years to find them. He based his reasoning on then-recent discoveries about how nerve cells transmit messages.

At the synapses (the microscopic clefts between nerve cells), chemical messages are exchanged in the form of minute bursts of four main impulse transmitters—norepinephrine (NoR), serotonin (5-HT), dopamine (dopa), and acetylcholine (ACh)—and about thirty auxiliary transmitters. These tiny pieces of protein are fired from one nerve cell across the synapse, and they fit like molecular keys into protein keyholes on the next cell. After turning the key these neurotransmitters either return to the mother cell for reuse or are broken down by enzymes. Increasing or decreasing levels of these transmitters forms an internal code that translates into consciousness as the primal signals friend/foe, fight/flee, pain/pleasure, sex, and intuition; at the same time they modify blood pressure, body temperature, heartbeat, nausea, and a host of other physical phenomena. The rate of fire of synaptic transmitter systems at any given moment pretty much determines what mood you're in. Since opiates in particular decidedly modify a person's moods, Dr. Goldstein suggested that "the places in the brain cells where morphine and similar molecules combine must be shaped to accommodate the morphine exactly as a lock accommodates a particular key."

But Dr. Goldstein and his colleagues also wondered aloud about the "bizarre coincidence" that keyholes should exist in the human nervous system for a chemical derived from the sap of the poppy. Clearly, some substance already in the body could produce the same effects. Where was it and what was it made of?

Specific receptor sites for opiates—the morphine keyholes—were located in a pig's brain at Johns Hopkins University by Dr. Sol Snyder and Dr. Candice Pert in 1973. The next major discovery took place in Scotland. At the University of Edinburgh in 1975, Dr. John Hughes vasectomized a few hundred mice and centrifuged a few hundred pigs' brains into a thin soup. It seems the vas deferens, the tube that in male mammals conducts sperm from the testicles to the penis, is a structure that, unlike any brain structure, contains opiate-receptor sites *only*. (Biochemists are still puzzling over this.) Since morphine is a capital anticonvulsant, Dr. Hughes caused convulsions in the isolated mouse vas deferens tissue through electrical stimulation; then he dropped portions of pig-brain soup onto them, one-by-one, speculating that any that quelled the convulsions would be endogenous opiates. Results were inconclusive.

And there it might have stayed but for a truly weird fluke. "About six months after we suspended the project," recalls Dr. Hughes, "we came to clear out the deep freeze, and the technician asked me if we should throw the old hormones away. And I thought, well, perhaps we'd better just check them again. And a couple of the bottles that had proved negative before turned out this time to be positive." Eureka! The body's own morphine.

Well, not quite. Hughes coined his own term for the substance, enkephalin (meaning "brain produced"), and sent a few precious micrograms down to Cambridge to have their chemical structure checked out, electron by electron. A young technician named Howard Morris had just perfected a mass-spectrometry technique to do just that. He was able to determine that the pig-brain substance alleged to have opiate properties was broken into two peptides (constellations of amino acids, just a few connections short of being whole proteins). Just three months later Morris was looking at another batch of amino acids with *exactly* the same molecular structure, only these had come out of *human* brains. No question about it. These were the body's own opiates.

Meanwhile, back in the States, independent corroboration of Dr. Hughes' findings was emerging rapidly. At the University of California Dr. Huda Akil was trying electroacupuncture on rats and found that, yes, it *could* markedly raise their tolerance for pain. Suspecting further that this might be due to enhanced endorphin activity in the animals, she then treated them with naloxone, an opiate antagonist.

Naloxone has been used for years to bring heroin-addicts out of overdoses; thirty seconds after a shot of naloxone all the effects of heroin disappear, to be immediately replaced by violent withdrawal symptoms: sweats, cramps, vomiting, even spontaneous orgasm. If acupuncture stimulates endorphins, and if endorphins work anything like opiates, then a shot of naloxone into Dr. Akil's rats ought to have reduced their pain thresholds to normal, or even below. This it definitely did.

Still, pain relief is only one of the many powerful experiences reported by opiate users. What would explain the wide range of other sensations, seemingly contained in this age-old drug? As research continued, scientists thought they had the answer.

Endorphins are very complicated. There are at least three different kinds, each with different effects, and opium interacts with them all in subtle ways. Met-enkephalin seems mainly responsible for short-term pain relief. Beta-endorphin, a longer chain of amino-acids, seems responsible for long-term pain relief and some components of euphoria. Gamma-endorphin, on the other hand, heightens sensitivity to pain and promotes aggressive, suspicious behavior.

The pituitary is the gland at the base of your brain that regulates your automatic body processes—heartbeat, sweating, sexual arousal, excretion—and your higher emotional and voluntary motor functions. We still don't know a lot about it, except that it produces endorphins, among other hormones.

In 1964 Dr. C. H. Li, researching the causes and treatment of obesity at the University of California at San Francisco, suspected that the roots of both compulsive overeating and plain genetic obesity lay in malfunctions of the pituitary gland. (He was proved correct.) In the course of his work, Dr. Li happened onto a class of pituitary hormones that appeared to have opiatelike effects, and another batch that produced precisely *opposite* effects.

By 1972 Dr. Li had isolated a class of chemically similar pituitary hormones that he called lipotropins, meaning "affects fat." One of these, beta-lipotropin, appeared to have conspicuous painkilling properties. Then Dr. Li's work stalled. He was getting his beta-lipotropin from the pituitaries of camels, animals that enjoy a notorious indifference to pain of any sort. Still, Dr. Li had to mash up the brains of two thousand camels to get one milligram of beta-lipotropin, which was methodically awkward to say the least.

But what about those *nonopiate effects* referred to by Dr. Li in his fat research?

In 1976 Dr. David Kasten at the Veterans Administration Hospital in New Orleans began giving lipotropins to lab rats and observed some most unexpected effects: the lipotropins augmented the animals' attention and increased their activity in low doses. Unscientifically speaking, the animals seemed to get smarter. Floyd Bloom at the Salk Institute in La Jolla, California, reported that in *high* doses rat reactions bordered on the supernatural: "We were totally amazed. The animal was doing absolutely nothing. Its sole behavior was an occasional wet-dog shake, an occasional sniffing of the air, and then lapsing into this vacant stare." At the same time, though, the rat's electroencephalogram (EEG) was scribbling wildly, "his head absolutely generating an entire village's worth of electricity. The EEG pens were just wrecking off the paper, ink splattering everywhere. We just couldn't believe that so much was going on in the head."

Simultaneously, researchers from all over began to report that their rats were learning things more quickly on endorphins (or enkephalins or lipotropins), retaining learned responses longer, and actually improving their appetites and their memories. In the Netherlands, Dr. Henk Rigter broke off a piece of beta-lipotropin that he found had the property of eradicating amnesia; and this piece, under mass-spectrometry, turned out to be molecularly identical to the pituitary hormone ACTH (adrenocorticotrophic hormone), known for years as a memory stimulator.

The known properties of ACTH, which is conducive to alertness and hair-trigger reactions, are almost diametrically opposed to those of opium. It's so much the mirror image of beta-endorphine that it can only be described as the body's own speed.

It turns out that endorphin and ACTH both emanate from the same elemental source. The source, as described by Dr. Dorothy Kreiger and Dr. Anthony Liotta, is a complete pituitary protein, a galaxy of a molecule they've dubbed pro-opiocortin. From bottom to top, here's how it's built: beta-lipotropin for appetite, melanocyte-stimulating hormone for skin complexion, met-enkephalin for short-term pain relief, beta-endorphin for pain relief and euphoria, and ACTH for attention, retention and response to environment. All these things appear to come out of pro-opiocortin in the pituitary and then are disseminated into the brain and the bloodstream, to perform their various functions.

Even more curious, however, was the observation by Drs. Kreiger and Liotta that, in fact, these substances work so subtly that the *time of day* at which they're administered to animals and humans can totally disrupt the results, as can the time of year. This may explain why Dr. Hughes' enkephalins were inert the first time he tried them out on his mouse sperm ducts. Most tellingly, it is now obvious that the researcher's own frame of mind—his or her expectations as the experiment is undertaken—can and does deeply affect the results.

This explains wonderfully why opium can produce widely diverse experiences in different individuals, but it throws brain research into the same muddle in which particle physicists have been floundering for the last decade or so. When you're dealing

with matters as ineffable and evanescent as these subtle proteins—when the lab environment, the circadian rhythm, the immediate state of the organism or issues under observation, and
the observers themselves can't *help* but influence the study's
results—then you're caught in what's called the Heisenberg uncertainty principle.

At this point, researchers have to start from scratch, rethinking
their hypotheses, restructuring their experiments, turning their
methodologies inside out and praying they get a little further on
the next expedition before it all falls apart again. "The brain's
so complex," Floyd Bloom concludes, "we might be able to
figure it out by the year 3050."

One can only marvel at this vision of body and mind as a vastly
complex chemical equation, interacting uniquely with the chemicals in plants like the opium poppy. We've been linked sym-
biotically, on a molecular level, man and poppy, endorphin and
opium, since the first days of creation. "We all carry within us
something folded up like those Japanese flowers made of wood
which unfold in water," Jean Cocteau wrote in 1924. "Opium
plays the same role as the water. None of us carries the same
kind of flower." This being literally true, it's only natural that
opium has played a dramatic and varied role in the history of
mankind—inspiring religious veneration, scientific exploration,
the bitterest rancor and the sweetest ecstasies. We all have flowers
in the blood, and this surely has everything to do with the story
of opium.

ONE
LEGENDS

...in a Pagan land, supposing it to have been adequately made known through experimental acquaintance with its revolutionary magic, opium would have altars and priests consecrated to its benign and tutelary powers.

Thomas De Quincey
Confessions of an
English Opium-Eater

Opium: The three syllables *sound* oriental. They conjure up images of six-inch Mandarin fingernails rolling black balls of gleaming dope, and dark cellars lined wth narrow bamboo racks inhabited by hollow-eyed coolies in various states of torpor and coma. But this is opium legend à la Hollywood and old-fashioned dime novels: villainous, slant-eyed and absolutely without historical foundation.

Real oriental opium legends, like those current today among the Lisu and Lahu peoples on the Burma-Chinese border, are peculiar among myths. In one Shan State opium tale, a beautiful young woman, who had remained unmarried because she smelled bad, died, and an opium poppy grew from her grave. Others say it was an ugly, old woman who gave birth to the eerie flower. In either case, the opium-generating woman had been tainted, at one time, by contact with foreign men, specifically westerners:

and that's how opium-child came to the Burmese highlands. So culturally speaking these are *new* myths. Opium arrived in East Asia relatively recently, around A.D. 300, brought from Persia and India by Arab merchants. (It had been brought to Persia and India no earlier than 330 B.C. by Alexander the Great.) And its notorious endemic use in the Orient didn't begin until the 1700s, when industrious European mercantilists turned a modest native herb trade into the most profitable big business in the history of commerce up to that time (see Chapter 6). The opium poppy is botanically native to the Mediterranean region and it is from this part of the world that the *real* opium legends originate.

Consider, for example, a certain ceramic opium pipe that was recently unearthed on the island of Cyprus off Turkey, where archeologists estimate it had been buried for some three thousand years. Cyprus in 1200 B.C. was largely populated by the Peoples of the Sea, the old Greek sea-kings and their people, who fled south from a great barbarian invasion of the Peloponnesus. The people who smoked opium out of this pipe were the blond and blue-eyed legends Homer sang about, the Philistine giants Samson slaughtered with the jawbone of an ass in the Book of Judges, the grandfathers of Goliath. Consider as well two Bronze Age Cypriot vases, two thousand five hundred years old, housed at the National Museum of Naples. Both are painstakingly hand-crafted ceramic capsule-heads of *Papaver somniferum* at the culling stage, detailed precisely with incision slashes; so detailed, in fact, that it's obvious the Peoples of the Sea were employing surgical-quality culling knives to harvest their opium before 1100 B.C. They were not only smoking opium before the fall of Troy, but cultivating and *trading* it in their poppy-shaped vases.

Nearly *twice* as far back, opium was known by the Sumerians of the Euphrates delta (in modern-day Iraq), as "Hul Gil"—the "joy plant"—and they used it to mend their ills. The Sumerians bequeathed the plant of joy to the Assyrians, who gave it the less poetic name of "lion fat." Assyrian cuneiform tablets, circa 700 B.C. describe how, "Early in the morning, old women, boys and girls collect the (poppy) juice, scraping it off the notches with a small iron blade, and place it within a clay receptacle." Seven hundred years later, Dioscorides, herbalist and personal physician to the emperor Nero, detailed the same poppy-culling process:

> For opium, slit the seeds with a small knife after the dew is well dried. The knife must be drawn around the crown without piercing the fruit within: then the capsules should be incised on the sides near the surface, and opened a little. A drop of juice will ooze forth onto the finger sluggishly, but will soon flow freely.

And twenty centuries later the culling process still remains substantially unchanged, wherever opium poppies are grown. It's still all done by hand, each poppy one by one, with the peasants crab-walking backward along the poppy rows, bent over double and slicing each capsule round about and up and down, capsule after capsule. They wear masks so they don't get dreamy from the fumes. And when they finish a row, they go over it again, one by one, finger-drawing the white opium-ooze into clots. After it turns brown and tacky, they go through the rows again, crab-walking backward, doubled over, rubbing it into balls, capsule by capsule...

The sheer labor of it all undoubtedly explains why there was no opium problem before the nineteenth century. Until canny Europeans devised plantation management schemes to more efficiently produce the drug, it was just too much hard work to foster anything like an addiction epidemic.

The Babylonians also learned the art of poppy-culling from the Assyrians, and they passed it on to the Egyptians, who sent their loved ones to the spooky animal-headed magistrates of the netherworld with Cypriot-style poppy jars full of *shepen* or *spenn*, the better to argue their cases before the disorienting eye of Horus. The Egyptians cunningly started growing a powerful cultivar of it for themselves, *Papaver rohas*, and selling the prepared gum to the Phoenicians and Minoans, who moved it across the Mediterranean Sea to Greece, Carthage, and probably into Europe. The superior Egyptian product, *opium thebaicum*, was cultivated far upriver at the capital city of Thebes. The thebaicum trade boomed in the thirteenth century B.C., during the very peak of classic Egyptian culture—the reigns of the conquering Thutmose IV, the visionary Akhenaton, and the boy-king Tutankhamen—and continued long after they had joined the shades of their

"The Poppy Goddess, Patroness of Healing."
Archeologists speculate that this female deity,
crowned with poppy pods, presided over an opium-
smoking cult on ancient Crete 3,500 years ago.

ancestors. The tombs of pharaohs from the Eighteenth to Twenty-sixth Dynasties (1600–600 B.C.) were decorated with paintings of opium poppies, mandrake, and the blue water-lily.* Egyptian doctor-priests included opium in their *materia medica* for a variety of ailments. A particularly poignant example occurs in the Ebers papyrus (1500 B.C.), in a chapter entitled "Remedy to Prevent the Excessive Crying of Children," wherein they recommend:

> ... the grains of the *spenn*-plant, with the excretions of flies found on the walls, strained to a pulp, passed through a sieve, and administered on four successive days. The crying will stop at once.

So began the venerable tradition of dosing bawling babies with opiates—whether *spenn* and fly-specks or "Street's Infant Quietness"—which continued uninterrupted from the time of the pharaohs to the reign of Queen Victoria.

It's clear that opium was known and revered by the ancients of the Nile. Egyptologists are puzzled, however, by a certain "oleaginous ointment" found in the tomb of an Eighteenth Dynasty nobleman: The ointment contained not opium, but morphine.**

Yet, it was the ancient Greeks who first incorporated opium into their legends and mysteries. To them the poppy was a magical plant, inspiring a rich folklore long before it was used as medicine; a sacred plant to which were consecrated altars and priests, as De Quincey so perspicaciously intuited nearly a century before the first archeological evidence surfaced to support such a view.

Since then, illuminating scraps of pottery, poetry and painting have surfaced which suggest that some of the first Greek dieties to emerge from primordial chaos brought opium along with them.

---

*This species of lily contains an analogue of the drug apomorphine, a fiercesome emetic and dysphoric hallucinogen. Similar plant-drugs have been used by Mayan witch doctors to attain states of divine madness. Curiously, in our own century apomorphine has been used to treat the insane and as a cure for heroin-addiction.

**If you think that's strange, Pharaoh Ramses II (1292–1225 B.C.), appears to have been chewing tobacco. Biochemists recently ran a full autopsy and bioimmune assay, and his mummy turned up a wad of tobacco in his tummy, and nicotine in his body tissues. This was so *extremely* long before Sir Walter Raleigh turned Queen Elizabeth I on to tobacco that there's just no puzzling over it. You can bet Ramses II didn't puzzle much over it: to go by his other grave-goodies, he was a stone opium-head.

Nyx (Night), and her son Thanatos (Death), were very appropriately portrayed wreathed in poppies and bearing poppies. Lucian of Samosata, who embellished on these spooks in the second century A.D.—before that, it would have been deemed profane to do so—presented Nyx and Hypnos sharing a rustic bungalow, surrounded by poppies. At dusk they would ramble about the countryside, followed by a flock of dreams, with jars of poppy-juice to drop in the eyes of sleepy mortals. Hypnos (Sleep), another of Nyx's offspring, characteristically reclined on his couch in a dark misty cave on the island of Lemnos, brooding over the infinite variety of his sons, the dreams. One of these sons was Morpheus, after whom was named morphine.

Greek heroes used opium for heroic purposes. Heracles, having murdered his family and been driven insane by the Erinyes, was ritually purified with opium, prior to beginning his Labours, by the semihistorical Eleusinian witch doctor Eumolpus. On the "Lovatelli" urn commemorating the event, housed at the Museo Nazionale Romano, Eumolpus is seen pouring wine over a sacrificial pig while holding a platter of poppy capsules. Theseus, slayer of the Minotaur (who also slew Eumolpus' son Kerkyon, to become king of Eleusis and neighboring Athens), pacified Cerberus, Hell's watchdog, with poppy-juice on his aborted raid to kidnap the spring-princess, Persephone, from her lover, Hades. Jason of Thessaly was an adept herbalist—the name translates as "healer"—well-acquainted with opium. He used it as a kind of Mickey Finn, sprinkling it on the eyes of the serpent guarding the Golden Fleece. And the fire which Prometheus stole from Zeus is described metaphorically by Aeschylus as both flower and drug. Prometheus concealed the "fire" in the customary manner of Greek herb-gatherers—in a hollow fennel stalk—and stole it from Zeus at a place called *Mekone*, which translates literally as "poppy town."

Opium is not really a drug of heroes, though. A tricky, subtle agent not very appropriate for butchery and rapine—and only efficacious in the treatment of illnesses when properly gathered, prepared and administered with exquisite craft—it was generally identified in the prehistoric world with women.

Women appear to have presided over European culture for some five thousand years between the recession of the great glaciers and the institution of writing. The major accomplishment of women—in what is actually a remarkably brief span of time—was the accomplishment of this epoch: They developed the craft of clocking the seasons and growing live things, which included in time various plant-drugs. Earth goddess cults and female mysteries evolved naturally out of this nexus. People were already putting up mysterious windowless shrines to female deities along the Danube before 7000 B.C.: two-story temples for a typical waterbird goddess in Yugoslavia were lifted up on leg-like stilts, and were entered through rooftop passages shaped like swans' necks.

Toward the end of this epoch, the Minoans of Crete were honoring the Mother in multiple forms, from goats to snakes to plants. One of her effigies, dug up in the 1930s, was primly dubbed "The Minoan Goddess With Uplifted Hands" by her excavator, S. Marinatos—resolutely overlooking the three salient and robust poppy capsules sprouting out of her tiara.* Three feet high, sublimely eyeless with a Mona Lisa smile, the lady was found in proximity of a tubular, ceramic opium pipe in a windowless shrine furnished with nothing but a charcoal firegate. Devotees climbed in through a rooftop passageway.

This primordial Cretan opium den owes its preservation to the tons of volcanic ash and earthquake debris that securely buried it around 1500 B.C. when the island of Thera, just over the Aegean horizon, blew itself to bits in a long dreadful series of fiery catastrophies. The prevailing southerly winds, carrying sulfurous death, almost entirely annihilated the Mother-worshipping Minoans, and carried in a grand invasion of Greeks from Mykenae on the Peloponnesus Peninsula, where Father Zeus presided. The Father seems not to have been entirely ill-disposed toward opium, since poppies begin appearing in Mycenaean ceremonial ware around this time.

When the renowned Graecophile Tsountas dug up Mycenae in the 1880s, he found among the ladies' baubles preserved there an assortment of poppy-headed needles fashioned of bronze,

---

*She has since been renamed more appropriately "The Poppy Goddess, Patroness of Healing."

which he took for brooch-pins. Most of them being a good deal long for fixing hair or clothes, the needles were regarded with puzzlement for quite some time, until P. G. Kritikos, a pharmacognosist at the University of Athens, happened to look at them. Yen-hoks, he declared, was what they were, just like the old mandarins used thirty centuries *later*: you pierced a wad of opium on the sharp end, and twiddled it over the charcoal fire until the smoke bloomed. Some of the poppyheads were hollow, with twist-off tops, suggesting that the opium was most likely concealed inside them. Questions over whether the smokers were concealing their stash from *somebody*, or whether this paraphernalia accessory was invented purely for convenience, remain unanswered. The practice disappeared over the next two centuries, and Tsountas' Mycenaean brooch pins are the last persuasive indication that anyone smoked opium for the next three thousand years, until the Europeans in the Orient rediscovered the practice.

People more commonly ate opium in Greece, or drank it in various sacramental and medicinal concoctions. This practice continued traditionally in honor of the Mother, whom they called Rhea, Amalthea, or Gaia. Even Zeus-fanciers universally recognized her as the original source of life, and all the gods and heroes and plants and animals and people were in *her* womb before they were conceived or born. One of her more delightful manifestations was the love-goddess Aphrodite, conceived and born in the pearly surf of Cyprus—site of the opium paraphernalia described above. On Cyprus, they called her Kythera, and said she played on a sort of lute which we call a "zither."

Another accomplished zither-player was Helen of Troy—generally held to be Aphrodite in her formal roles of witch, sex object, and maker of cuckolds. After Troy fell, around 1200 B.C., and King Menelaos of Sparta, the cuckold, reclaimed her from her ravisher Paris, Helen settled down domestically as zither-player and herb-healer in Menelaos' palace. Ten years later, Telemachos, son of the long-missing Odysseus, arrived there in a state of profoundest depression. To brighten things up a bit, says Homer (*The Odyssey, c.* 700 B.C.) :

> ... it entered Helen's mind to drop into the wine that they were drinking an anodyne, mild magic of forgetfulness. Whoever drank this mixture in the wine bowl would be incapable of tears that

day—though he should lose mother and father both, or see with
his own eyes a son or brother mauled by weapons of bronze at
his own gate. The opiate of Zeus's daughter bore this uncanny
power. It had been supplied her by Polydamna, mistress of Lord
Thon, in Egypt, where the rich plantations grow herbs of all kind,
maleficent and healthful; and no one else knows medicine as they
do, Egyptian heirs of Paian, the healing god. She drugged the
wine, then, had it served . . .

Homer is describing opium, or *nepenthe* as the Zeus-born Helen
called it, and the name surfaces elsewhere in myths as a magic
draught conferring easiness of mind, general disinhibition, and
a calm, airy reverie of benevolence toward all the world.*

Helen was clearly a minister of the primordial All-Mother,
who by Homer's time had acquired the name of Demeter. She
presided over perhaps the greatest religious tradition ever, flourishing unbroken from before the Homeric Age to around A.D. 400,
when the Christians finally wiped it out. It was called the Eleusinian Mysteries, a complex scheme of seasonal rites, feasts,
fasts, anointments and shrivenings that filled the calendar with
special significance.

The central occasion was the "ravishment" every autumn of
Persephone, the daughter of Demeter, by Hades, Lord of the
Underworld. This happened near the beginning of November.
The lady was swept away by Hades while out gaily gathering the
"hundred-headed *narkissos*," associated in Greek herb-lore with
narcotic plants in general. Every November this would happen,
causing All-Mother Demeter in her bereavement to blight the
earth with killer-cold, so that all froze, nothing grew, and misery
reigned everywhere. All winter she'd wander the earth seeking
surcease of sorrow, and every winter on a dim, depressing day

---

*At Menelaos' table it gave every indication of being profoundly therapeutic. Helen,
customarily formal in public, lets her hair down and relates a spicy encounter with
Odysseus ten years before in Troy, which tickles Telemachos no end. Menelaos the
cuckold, far from getting huffy, spins the oft-told yarn of the night in the Trojan Horse,
when it had been dragged past the gates, and the Greek chiefs inside were surrounded
by suspicious Trojans; and forsooth hadn't the witch Helen walked around it three times
in a circle, calling out to each man within in the ventriloquistic voice of his much-missed
wife. "Odyseus fought us down," Menelaos recalls nostalgically, "despite our craving."
Presumably he bore Helen no grudge for this treachery, after ten years of her nepenthe.

in early February, she would find it, magically, in the form of an early-blooming poppy. Or so her devotees firmly believed. On that day, every year, they would gather at Agrai near Athens to eat a little *opos*—congealed poppy-juice—and by heaven, things not only *looked* better, they *got* better. Within a couple of weeks the first balmy rush of spring breezes would always eddy down brightly out of Thrace. Demeter's opium fete at Agrai also featured a special ritual in which the male congregants would pretend to give birth to effigies of babies. And what became of this sublime orthodoxy? Christian censorship was brutal and efficient. Opos-day is now celebrated as Groundhog Day.

The Mysteries of Demeter also involved, once each autumn, another ritual drug called *kykeon*, the source of the ultimate illumination: a solution of pennyroyal mint and water, sprinkled with a purple grass rust, *claviceps paspali*. *Paspali* is closely related to the rye rust *claviceps purpurea*, from which Dr. Albert Hofmann in Switzerland first derived LSD-25 during the Second World War; in 1976, at the suggestion of mycologist Gordon Wasson, Hofmann tried a few micrograms of *paspali* and rated it about one-twentieth as potent as LSD, affording a four-hour trip that would have been sublimely suited to the purposes of the Eleusinian Mysteries. Having journeyed deep into their earthly selves on *opos* in the winter, the fall *paspali* ritual must surely have provided Demeter's followers with a most cogent experience of rebirth.

By around 600 B.C., though, a change of consciousness was fulminating in ancient Greece, toward reason and away from magic altogether.* This change was exemplified in a second tradition which eventually overshadowed the magic of the powerful poppy goddess. This was the tradition of male medicine, and it began with the mythical leech, Aesculapius.

---

*It was around this time that the venerable institution of the *pharmakos* was discontinued in ancient Greece. As late as 600 B.C., every sizable city maintained on the municipal budget an assortment of crippled, imbecilic, leprous, or otherwise useless wretches in a shed by the main gate. Whenever a great common affliction arose, like a plague or famine, one of these degraded souls was selected as the *pharmakos*, to be stoned to death in the marketplace by able-bodied citizens. From this sacrificial cure for plague, peril and pestilence our own word pharmacology—the science of drugs, their preparation, uses and effects—was derived.

*Depicted here holding a bouquet of poppy capsules,
the mythical healer Aesculapius was the avatar of a cult
of doctor-priests who dosed their patients with opium
and henbane and diagnosed illness on the basis of dreams.*

His story takes us again to Agrai, where the opium fair of Demeter was annually celebrated. Agrai was also the hunting preserve of the goddess Artemis. She was a virgin, immortally, a fact that didn't seem to faze her handsome mortal consort, Hippolytus. He loved nothing more than hunting, or, more aptly—since Agrai is a place curiously bereft of animals but richly abundant in herbs—taking drugs with Artemis, and he spurned the love of mortal women. This enraged Aphrodite, who inspired his stepmother with a fierce passion for Hippolytus. When he rejected her, she committed suicide and left a note telling his father King Theseus that Hippolytus had "ravished" her. This so enraged Theseus that he prayed to *his* father, Poseidon, to avenge the alleged obscenity. So one day, when Hippolytus was driving his horses near the sea, a giant bull charged out of the water, the horses bolted, Hippolytus was toppled out of his chariot and dragged to his death.

Enter Aesculapius, persuaded by Artemis to bring Hippolytus back to life, using the magical simple shown him by a serpent in a cave on Thessaly. This he did, which so outraged Zeus that the All-Father zapped the meddling leech with a thunderbolt, dispatching him forthwith to Hades.

Similarities in setting and action between this tale and the earlier myth of Demeter, Persephone, and Hades are everywhere apparent, only here the dead soul is restored to life not in the symbolic belly of a woman, but through the healing arts of a doctor. No specific formula for Aesculapius' magic bullet is offered. It is, rather, *the* Drug, that which alchemists would later call the *elixir vitae*, the "water of life," whose formula no man would ever know, as it was beyond all knowing. Yet there must have been someone, perhaps a zealous student of Aesculapius, who was sure he knew the formula, just as centuries later alchemists and then doctors were *sure*: the universal panacea was opium. This deduction was well supported: statues of Aesculapius were crowned with poppy capsules.

Aesculapius became the avatar for a cult of doctor-priests, touted as the best in ancient Greece. At shrines honoring him, the first ethical sanitaria were built. One at Epidamos was constructed underground, with the interior designed like a mole hill—

apparently in literal homage to Aesculapius, whose name translates as "mole." His most famous hospital, however, was on the island of Cos. There, on the first night of their stay patients were given an infusion of opium—probably garnished with belladonna—and then retired to the main ward to stretch out on the bloody skin of a freshly-slaughtered ram, to sleep and dream. On the basis of their dreams the doctors would prescribe the proper course of diet, baths, massage and drugs to make them well.

Without changing their basic procedure, the Aesculapians by the fifth century B.C. had evolved and recorded a remarkably sophisticated body of medical knowledge, incorporating the common-sense benefits of good diet, sleep, exercise, cleanliness and a healthy sex life, as well as treatises on surgery, and the identification and preparation of plant drugs.

In deference to his widespread influence, these various writings of the Aesculapian faculty are generally attributed to one avatar, Hippocrates, the father of modern medicine. Called by Plato the "Aesclepiad of Cos," the original Hippocrates was born around 460 B.C. in the shadow of the Cos sanitarium, the son of a humble doctor Herakleidos, but heir to all the healing magic of the mythical Aesculapius himself. Between travels to Thessaly and Thrace, Egypt and Libya, he delivered lectures at Cos beneath an old gnarled plane tree, in which he explained how, under planetary influence, the Four Humours—blood, phlegm, yellow bile, and black bile—give rise to the Four Tempers—sanguine, phlegmatic, choleric, and melancholic. He urged his students to carefully observe their patients—"Those with physiques that are fleshy, soft and red, find it beneficial to adopt a rather dry regimen"; to carefully examine their excreta—"Urine, stools, sweats, by the manner in which they supervene, show whether the disease will have a difficult crisis or an easy one"; while amusing them with such pithy clinical observations as—"Eunuchs neither get gout nor grow bald"*; and instructing them on the use of plant-drugs, including the poppy:

*The kidney dysfunctions which give rise to gout proceed from imbalances in adrenocorticotrophic function characterized by an abundance of "male" hormones produced by the testes; likewise, baldness.

For sleep, opium, the dose of one round Attic lekiskion . . . Grind the juice of the poppy with a little water, filter, and kneading with flour bake into a cake. This is rinsed with boiled honey and . . . served to the dropsical. Well-diluted sweet wine or hydromel should be taken immediately after. You may collect the poppy plant and preserve it for medical emergencies.

To Hippocrates, opium was less a magical drug than a nutritional supplement, a food of sorts, that would restore balance to a body whose humours were out of proportion. He distinguished between white, fire-red, and black, and unripe, ripe, and baked poppies, specifying opium's usefulness as a narcotic and styptic in treating internal diseases, diseases of women, and epidemics.

Throughout the Roman Epoch, the Aesculapians of Cos remained the most famous of physicians. There, as in Greece, hospital shrines were erected to Aesculapius, but the sanitarium at Cos remained the state of the arts. Cos was the birthplace of the physician Xenophon, who broke his Hippocratic oath to poison his patron Claudius. The Emperor Nero favored Cos as a drying-out spa; the place so pleased him that he had several statues of the venerable leech recarved in his own megalomaniac image.

Opium is the strongest of the drugs which numb the senses and induce a deadening sleep; its effects are produced when it is soaked in boiling water, taken up on a flock of wool and used as a suppository; at the same time some can be spread over the forehead and in the nostrils.

The last of the great Aesculapiads was Galen, to whom are ascribed these instructions on the correct application of an opium suppository. Galen was schooled at a shrine to the mythical healer in far-off Mysia in Asia Minor sometime around A.D. 140. Today, he is often mentioned alongside Hippocrates as a forefather of modern medicine, but five centuries separated the two men, and they were very different. The old physician of Cos bequeathed "rational" common-sense medicine to the world, despising the notions of magic; Galen bequeathed "scientific" medicine to the world, and opened the doors of magic again.

On the surface, Galen's life was quite conservative. An apt student, he worked hard learning his healing skills, often mending wounds and setting bones far into the night. (There was always plenty to do: His shrine's high priest kept a stable of gladiators.) He journeyed to the great center of learning at Alexandria in Egypt, to specialize in the anatomy of the African monkey. Numerous simian vivisections led to his first great discovery: Blood, not air, flowed in the veins. His prospects assured, he returned to Mysia as a team-doctor for the high priest's gladiators; traveled to Rome in A.D. 161, cured the old philosopher Eudemus, developed a wealthy clientele, and was admitted to the illustrious court of Marcus Aurelius.

Yet this is also Galen: crouched over a smoky cauldron, muttering gibberish incantations, glaring at dusty maps of Heaven and Hell, scratching kabbalistic symbols and cryptic notes in a ponderous yellowed book, absolutely convinced that by these means, soon, very soon, the magical drug that the serpent gave to old Aesculapius, the *elixir vitae*, would be his.

Galen the alchemist began the science of combining plants and other substances, according to a carefully prescribed set of principles, in an effort to enhance their properties; today we call this science pharmacology. These compounds, or "galenicals," were developed on the basis of a universal law which he derived by lining up Hippocrates' Four Universal Humours—phlegm, black bile, yellow bile, and blood—alongside Aristotle's four Universal Elements—earth, air, fire, and water—and thumb-shuffling a bit with the four Universal Qualities—dry, wet, hot, and cold. This was not guesswork. This was solid, deductive, *scientific*, irrefutable. But however sophisticated the thinking behind it, Galen's Universal Law simply amounted to this: "Contrary cures contrary."

Using this system Galen classed opium as a cold, earthy drug which worked by impairing the vital heat of the heart and blood. Its operation on the brain was secondary. Galen called the action of opium "frigorific," because it "congealed" the vital heat. Hence, it would be most effective for those with too much hot, expansive blood (we might call this condition high blood pressure today), and those with a surfeit of choleric humours (from a hairtrigger tendency to fly into rages; or from cholera, a disease for which opium remained the best specific until the twentieth century).

Sometimes, though, it worked too well at congealing the vital heat. Among his case studies, Galen wrote of a patient reduced to the last stage of Coldness by an overdose of opium, whom he had saved with an emetic, followed by "a strong light-colored fragrant wine." This worked better than anything else before the opiate-antagonist naloxone was invented in the 1960s (see Chapter 12). The same technique was used to save the love-struck Hector Berlioz in August 1833, when he gobbled a deliberate laudanum overdose in the presence of one Harriet Smithson to convince her of his affections. Subsequently he composed his "Symphonie Fantastique."

Opium appears in numerous galenicals. Galen was the first in a long line of scientists who would try, by rational, logical, step-by-step means to purify, improve, and boost the powers of poppy-juice; to make magic based on man's native genius, not on the whims of any fickle deity. A great many scientific discoveries of astounding import—the discovery of endorphins to cite but one notable example—have been made, coincidentally, in the course of this quest; but the primary goal of this research—to transform the easeful draught of Demeter into the *elixir vitae* of Aesculapius—has proved extremely elusive, at times downright dangerous. It has led inevitably to the isolation of morphine, the synthesis of heroin, and the invention of the hypodermic syringe, all irrefutably vast improvements, rendering opium better, more effective and safer—but which inevitably made it more proble-matical.

TWO
DRUGS OF
GOOD AND EVIL

*It destroys the mind, cuts short the reproductive capacity, pro-
duces elephantiasis, passes on leprosy, attracts diseases, produces tremulousness, makes the mouth smell foul, dries up the
semen, causes the hair of the eyebrows to fall out, burns the
blood, causes cavities in the teeth, makes the limbs inactive,
causes a shortage of breath, generates strong illusions, dimin-
ishes the powers of the soul, reduces the modesty, makes the
complexion yellow, blackens the teeth, riddles the liver with
holes, inflames the stomach, and leaves in its wake a bad odor
in the mouth as well as a film and diminished vision in the eye
and increased pensiveness in the imagination. It...generates
in those who eat it laziness and sluggishness. It turns a lion
into a beetle and makes a proud man humble and a healthy
man sick. If he eats, he cannot get enough. If he is spoken to,
he does not listen. It makes the well-spoken person dumb, and
the sound person stupid. It takes away every manly virtue and
puts an end to youthful prowess. Furthermore, it destroys the
mind, stunts all natural talent, and blunts the sharpness of the
mental endowment. It produces gluttony, making eating the
addict's preoccupation and sleep for him a characteristic situation. But he is remote from slumber, driven out of Paradise,
and threatened with God's curse unless he gnashes his teeth
in repentance and puts his confidence in God.*

The classic Islamic stance on recreational drug use was characteristically uncongenial, as this catalog of the evils of hashish demonstrates. In this summary of physical and moral horrors, compiled circa 1350, the sober Islamic judge Muhammad az-Zarkashi has brilliantly compressed every slander that ever has or will be heaped on any psychoactive drug: arrests physical development, destroys resistance to disease, defiles the appearance, annuls the sex drive, spits in the face of God Almighty. The drug-user is victim, clown, pariah, enemy, *junkie*. His composite profile in 1350 is precisely the same as modern newspaper and television caricatures of the heroin addict. The accepted image of the dope fiend is preexistent in all its minute lineations, an archetype that altered not a jot between the times of az-Zarkashi and Harry Anslinger, who was the United States narcotics commissioner in the 1950s. Only the drug has changed. In America, the pariah drug was and still remains opium (and its derivatives morphine and heroin); in Medieval Islam, hashish was uniquely ordained for this purpose.

Mind you, the Arabs did have opiates, and, as we shall presently see, were perfectly aware that they were addictive. Yet no comparable anathema against opium appears anywhere in their literature. And this disregard of opiates in a hyperpaternalistic society given to wholehearted condemnation of any sort of deviant, hedonistic behavior is puzzling at first sight.

The lineage of opium in the Middle East is far more august than that of hashish. Before 3000 B.C. the Sumerians were already calling it their "joy plant," and by 1300 B.C. it was a limited but profitable trade item, being moved into Egypt from the Babylonian kingdom of Hammurabi and his successors. The Egyptians venerated, consumed, and cultivated at Thebes the most powerful, consistently effective cultivar of the drug in the Middle East, *opium thebaicum*.

As recently as A.D. 1248, according to the Muslim annalist Abdallah ibn al-Baytar, Acquit (formerly Thebes) on the Nile remained the only dependable source in the Middle East of choice black opium systematically produced for medicine. With 3,000 years of experience, the Egyptians were the only people in the medieval world with enough agricultural experience to cultivate the problematical poppy for commercial export. Hence, quantities

were extremely limited, and the drug was too rare and expensive
to be used purely for pleasure by any but the wealthy. And it is
dubious that even they used opium as a recreational drug: What
distinguished the Egyptian product was the unusually high percentage of one of opium's twenty-four alkaloids, thebaine. High
thebaine opium doesn't produce the same subjective euphoria as
other cultivars, as those, for example, raised in India for the
China market at the height of the British opium trade in the
nineteenth century. But *opium thebaicum* was good medicine and
as such it escaped the wrath of medieval Muslim theocrats.

Hashish has a murkier past. To go by Middle Eastern records,
you'd think it was very abruptly discovered around A.D. 1050,
already a full-blown drug menace, becoming within a century the
favorite intoxicant of bums, thieves, berserkers and apostates.

Prior references to cannabis in any Western culture are scarce.
Galen and Dioscorides, in their early *materia medica*, recommend
it for quelling erotic passion, and for the idle amusement of the
rich at society parties, but neither dwell on it. A more intriguing
reference occurs in the *Histories* of Herodotus of Halikarnassus,
concerning its use by the Scythians of the Black Sea region
around 500 B.C.:

> ...on a frame work of three sticks, meeting at the top, they stretch
> pieces of woolen cloth, taking care to get the joins as perfect as
> they can, and inside this little tent they put a dish with red-hot
> coals in it. They then take some hemp seed, creep into the tent,
> and throw the seed on the hot stones. At once it begins to smoke,
> giving off a vapour unsurpassed by any vapour-bath one could
> find in Greece. The Scythians enjoy it so much that they howl
> with pleasure.

This is familiar enough, from the sound of it.* The Scythians
were an abundant and ubiquitous nomadic folk, and from time
to time they migrated south of the Black Sea region, to occupy
vast areas of what came to be al-Islam, as far east as Afghanistan
and west to Syria. By the time of the establishment of the Islamic

---

*Similar techniques for smoking hashish and opium are still used in the Middle East. In
Iran, opium-smokers commonly place their drug on a charcoal grate called a *gailum* and,
huddled under a blanket, whiff the fumes.

realm, around A.D. 600, the Scythians had become various kinds of "Turks," though not the Turkish Turks one thinks of: they were Circassians, Tranoxanians, Bokharans—a multitude of minority ethnic tribes living under the Persian Empire that was later incorporated into the Islamic Empire.

In the one thousand one hundred years since Herodotus wrote about them, of course, much had changed for these Scythian-descended Turks, but it's impossible to tell how much. For all the wonderful things that might be said about subsequent Islamic culture, there's no denying that it was launched with an unprecedented pestilence of cultural genocide. When the Arab tribes burst out of their ancestral homeland on their first global *jihad*, they systematically exterminated every relic or mildest suggestion of the "days of ignorance" before Muhammad. They were so surpassingly thorough that they located the inner mausolea of the Great Pyramid of Khufu, sealed up for the last three thousand years, and righteously scoured them of anything which might interest future archaeologists—and they did it for the *principle*, not the plunder. On the same principle, they leveled the immemorially ancient Persian capital of Ctesiphon, and scrupulously slaughtered all its inhabitants. If they hadn't, it's possible that today we might have more than a few tantalizing glimpses of the Middle Eastern folk religions that preceded Islam. Even so, it is certain that to the people before Muhammad, *cannabis sativa* was rather more than mere rope. Beyond the easternmost fringe of the Islamic conquest, in India, written references to the employment of cannabis for purposes sacred and profane stretch back to 2000 B.C. And in the Middle East, surviving remnants of the obliterated past, like the Sufi cult of the "Green Man," strongly suggest that cannabis didn't just spring out of the ground to confound the councils of the wise, but was an object of religious veneration before the advent of Islam, and thus posed a profound threat to the New Order of God. And the profane practice of smoking hashish and howling with laughter was morally noxious to most elements of the orthodox Muslim clergy.

Yet cannabis is nowhere mentioned in the Holy Qur'an, which was laid down in its final form in A.D. 632, shortly after the demise of the Prophet in Mecca. This has prompted no end of controversy since then, with orthodox Islamic jurists furiously seeking scriptural grounds for banning the weed, and hashish-smoking Sufi heretics countering that God created al-qunnab "that your dense worries may disappear and your exalted minds become polished," and that if He had *meant* to have it banned, then assuredly He would have stipulated that to His Messenger.

Desperate exegetes have stoutly clung to the provision in the Qur'an which specifically condemns alcoholic wine because it "draws a veil over the eyes." Since hashish allegedly does the same—though this is a controversial claim out front—then it is also to be eschewed, legislators have commonly decreed. But a considerable body of Islamic opinion has contended that this interpretation is an impermissibly loose construction of Holy Writ, and the question is *always* up in the air.*

In A.D. 900 hashish was first identified as a vile toxin in *The Book of Poisons* by Muhammad Ali ibn Washiya, side by side with sour oil of vitriol and nitric acid in lethal toxicity.** Subsequent references to hashish in Islamic literature fall into wildly contrary positive and negative categories, evidence that the drug became enormously politicized. True to form in such developments, in the officially-sanctioned record, the drug acquires all the attributes of some supernaturally potent historical evil, spread through the aegis of an infidel enemy, aggressively vitiating the individual, the social fabric, the state and the very integrity of natural physics.

No such exegetical controversy surrounded *afyon*. It has always been regarded in the Middle East as good medicine, a solid, unchallenged element in the pharmacopoeia, much in use long before all the memories of the days of ignorance were cast down and obliterated by the first Muslims, and still there in the ninth century when they set about reformulating their medical practices. The site was Damascus, where the magnificent Kaliph Harun al-Raschid set up his capital, in A.D. 880, and fostered trade and

---

*The Sayings of the Ayatolla Khomeini, 1979: "Wine and all other alcoholic beverages are impure, but opium and hashish are not."

**He identified it as "Indian hemp," righteously associating it with the non-Muslim races of the wicked East, but the popular name he accorded it was *shartatha*, a venerable term meaning "the plant" in Nabataean, the dialect of the northern Arabian peninsula. Accomplished poisoners fed it to their victims, he charged, mixed with sundry other poisons.

learning with places as exotic as Charlemagne's Europe and Tang Dynasty China. Harun and his son, the Kaliph al-Mamun, instituted a regular university in Damascus (and were afterward much condemned for encouraging Persian heresies there), where a generation of poets, jurists, and translators flourished.

Prominent among them was Hunayn ibn Ishaq, personal physician to al-Mamun. Hunayn set down in writing the pharmacological lore of Dioscorides, Galen and Paulus of Aeginita, with particular reference to their use of opium; and noted that the Syrian doctors had traditionally prescribed it for respiratory illnesses, gallstones, fever, diarrhea, headache, toothache and insomnia. Husayn's Damascene colleague Abulhassan al-Tabari, compiling the first Arabic *Firdaus* (encyclopedia) in 850, added that opium could be given in tablet, poultice and ointment form, and specified a concoction of opium and dandelion juice that effectively silenced cranky infants. The major text on opiates under the Abbasid successors of al-Mamun was the *Ayrabadhin*—"formulary"—of Salih ibn Sahl, 869, which described how to prepare opium in various forms, such as suspensions, suppositories, plasters and ointments.

Clearly the Muslims were perfectly aware of opium's material dangers. Abdallah ibn-al-Baytar describes ten symptoms of overdose with a technical accuracy that suggests it must have been fairly commonly observed by thirteenth century physicians: "lockjaw, lethargy, severe itching, eyes sunken in, tongue tied, extremity and nails discolored, with profuse cold perspiration ejecting opium smell, then convulsions followed by death."

Addiction was noted as early as 1030, and it evidently was nothing new. Abulrayhan el-Biruni commented that pilgrims from more temperate climes tended to overdo opiates if they took up residence in the holy cities of Egypt and the Arabian peninsula:

> People who live in the tropics or hot climates, especially those in Mecca, get into the habit of taking opium daily to eliminate distress, to relieve the body from the effects of scorching heat, to secure longer and deeper sleep, and to purge superfluities and excesses of humors. They start with smaller doses which are increased gradually up to lethal doses.

And it was even recognized that people who became addicted to opium tended to become unwholesomely obsessed with it. As

Abdulla ibn al-Nafis remarked in his *Sharh al-Qanun* around 1250:

> Opium is a strong narcotic, alleviates all pains, darkens the sight as it hardens the spirit, weakens the mind, and degenerates understanding as it corrupts the temperament of the spirit.

This rather formal caveat is followed, though, by a long, detailed description of how best to extract the gum from the plant and mix it into sundry preparations for the *safe* treatment of sundry conditions.

To judge by the dosages which al-Nafis and all other formularists prescribed—usually calling for a couple of dirhams to start with, and progressively augmenting doses until symptoms disappeared—addiction was a decided hazard. Patients with chronic ailments like ulcers, tuberculosis, recurrent malaria and migraine undoubtedly worked up huge tolerance levels.

It was the celebrated Abu 'Ali al-Husayn ibn Sina, whom the uncircumscribed Franks still call *Avicenna*, who came up with the notion of the uniform standard dose around 1010. Having interned at the world-famous "Adui" hospital in Baghdad—the first ever with its own pharmacy and dispensary—ibn Sina was acutely familiar with the symptoms of opium poisoning. In the fifth book of his monumental *al-Qanun fi at-Tibb* ("Canon of Medicine"), the pharmacological section, he indicates that the best overdose therapy is simply to keep the patient walking and talking, between vigorous purges. To help physicians forestall such accidents, ibn Sina counseled that all opium preparations be measured in wholes and precise fractions of round wads the size of chickpeas, a standard still employed by bush doctors from Morocco to Indonesia. A further overdose danger was posed by the widely variable morphine content of opium from district to district of world-girdling Islam; so, as personal physician, diplomatic advisor and ultimately Grand Vizier for Shaws al-Dawlah, the Abbasid governor of Western Persia, ibn Sina thoughtfully tried to standardize cultivation and culling techniques throughout the realm. His directions for slitting the capsule, thumb-squeezing out the gum, and reharvesting the crop are minutely precise, including even the recommendation that the cullers wear masks, so as not to get dreamy and distracted by the opium fumes.

While duly noting in his *Qanun* that immoderate opium intake "thwarts good counseling" and brings on constipation, ibn Sina nevertheless touted it for dozens of ailments and also explored the brief suggestion made by Muhammad al-Razi a century before, that puzzling non-physical afflictions like melancholy and hypochondria might respond to opiates. There are suggestions that he toyed with hashish for the same purpose, which may account for his abrupt imprisonment by Shaws ad-Dawlah, and ultimate banishment from Persia on vague charges of court intrigues. It was dangerous enough for him to be flirting with such Persian notions as the Philosopher's Stone, the Universal Solvent and the transmutation of lead into gold. Hashish was absolutely unthinkable, in the mounting sectarian chaos of Medieval Islam.

THREE
THE STONE
OF IMMORTALITY

They brought before me a knight in whose leg an abcess had grown; and a woman afflicted with imbecility. To the knight I applied a small poultice until the abcess opened and became well; and the woman I put on diet and made her humour wet. Then a Frankish physician came to them and said, "This man knows nothing about treating them." He then said to the knight, "Which wouldst thou prefer, living with one leg or dying with two?" The latter replied, "Living with one leg." The physician said, "Bring me a strong knight and a sharp axe." A knight came with the axe. And I was standing by. Then the physician laid the leg of the patient on a block of wood and bade the knight strike his leg with the axe and chop it off at one blow. Accordingly he struck it—while I was looking on—one blow, but the leg was not severed. He dealt another blow, upon which the marrow of the leg flowed out and the patient died on the spot. He then examined the woman and said, "This is a woman in whose head there is a devil which has possessed her. Shave off her hair." Accordingly they shaved it off and the woman began once more to eat their ordinary diet—garlic and mustard. Her imbecility took a turn for the worse. The physician then said, "The devil has penetrated through her head." He therefore took a razor, made a deep cruciform incision until the bone of the skull was exposed and rubbed it with salt. The woman also expired instantly. Thereupon I asked them whether my services

*were needed any longer, and when they replied in the negative
I returned home, having learned of their medicine what I knew
not before.*

Two wildly disparate approaches to medicine are encapsulated
in this twelfth century anecdote recorded by Thabit during the
Second Crusade. Thabit was a rare exception—a Christian doctor, skilled in the sophisticated dietary, surgical, and herbal therapeutics (including the use of opium), of medieval Muslim physicians. The ghoulish methods of his Frankish contemporary were
far more representative of the state of the arts in Christian medicine.

Throughout the early Middle Ages, Muslim physicians were
esteemed and highly paid in all the princely courts of Europe,
and the high clergy did not hesitate to consult these heathen
doctors, though the Church, in its efforts to blot out the pagan
past, had spawned a medical doctrine of its own. It had originated
with Saint Augustine back in the fifth century. "All diseases of
Christians," he argued, "are to be ascribed to demons." The
recommended course of treatment: exorcism, not drugs or other
unnatural interventions.

For one group of Christian practitioners, this evolved into the
kill-or-cure Frankish system known in time as Heroic medicine.
Their techniques were rooted in the notion that the way to exorcise
one set of afflictions from a patient's body was to subject it to
a considerably more violent set of afflictions. The heroics were
entirely on the part of the patient: for even the mildest ailments,
one could expect to be bled, leeched, cupped, blistered, ampu-
tated, sweated, trepanned, scourged, purged and flayed to a fare-
thee-well. (Opium was, predictably, rejected as lazy by most
early Heroic physicians.) Appalling as these techniques may
sound, they may sometimes have worked—subjected to extreme
and sudden physical stress, the body's immunological systems
are likely to be stirred into overdrive, which could conceivably
counteract low-grade viral or bacterial infections. With no such
thing as antibiotics in the world, Heroic medicine may have been
better than nothing in a small percentage of cases. In most cases
it was useless, of course, and downright lethal in many, yet its
tenets remained broadly accepted for nearly a millennium.

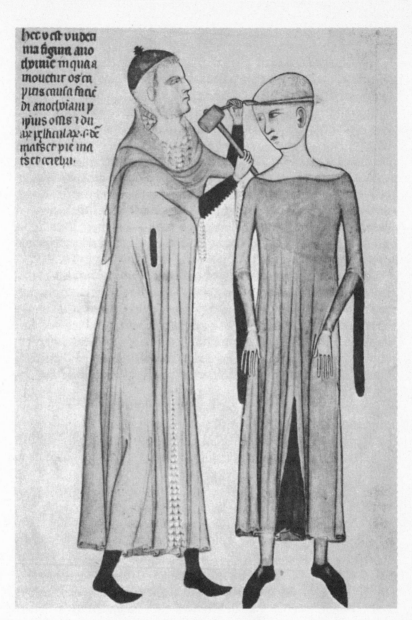

"La dissection du curveau."
**This fourteenth-century painting illustrates a popular
technique of the Heroic school of medicine for banishing
the evil spirits thought to be responsible for senility.**

The other designated Christian healer in the Middle Ages was the priest, and while some priests studied medicine, most did not; their sanctified course of treatment consisted mainly of prayer, fasting and ministrations with holy water and sacred relics. The wood of the cross, blood of Jesus, milk of Mary, and toenails of Saint Peter were purchased from priests in huge quantities by the diseased faithful. During the twelfth century, the cemetary at the Church of Saint Ursula was meticulously picked clean by relic brokers who claimed to have found there the bones of eleven thousand Virgin Martyrs, hailed—despite the fact that many of these bones clearly had belonged to men—for their miraculous curative powers. This of course is faith healing; and it, too, may *sometimes* have worked.

But when the common folk of medieval Europe took sick, they generally turned neither to doctors (unless they were uncommonly wealthy) nor to priests (unless they were dying). Their first choice for medical help was, obviously, the apothecary, barber-surgeon, herbalist, or midwife—all of whom sold herbs, poisons, and love philtres, and offered a rudimentary knowledge of healing techniques and commonsense psychotherapy at a fraction of the cost of a good Muslim doctor.

Opium, when it turned up in the folk remedies of these non-professionals, usually took the form of poppy-straw—poppy-heads mashed into a paste with other ingredients for external use, or brewed into tea—prepared from recipes passed down from ages past. But the psychoactive drug most often identified with this group of practioners was mandrake which, unlike opium poppies, grows wild throughout Europe. Mandrake had a long and colorful history dating from pre-Christian times. Its foot-long root, resembling the body of a man, inspired a rich folklore: the plant was said to scream when it was plucked from the ground, and gathering procedures were complexly ritualistic. Mandrake contains the belladonna alkaloids—hyoscyamine, scopolamine and atropine—and in low doses will alleviate nervous tension and promote sleep.* As such it was recommended as a home remedy for insomnia, and as an aphrodisiac. In high doses, man-

---

*Belladonna, until recently, was the chief ingredient in SOMONEX, the popular sleep remedy, and is still available in CONTAC.

drake will produce prolonged, vivid hallucinations (though virtually paralyzing the user for hours), and was used by mediums whose mutterings while on the drug were said to foretell the future, and in the famous "flying potions" brewed by medieval witches.

Opium was mainly understood and employed by a small but influential group of doctors who derived their techniques from the School of Salerno in Sicily. Originally established by Muslim physicians in the ninth century, the School of Salerno flourished under Frankish occupation, and remained the most respected medical institution in Europe until the twelfth century. Among the remedies touted by its faculty was something called *spongia somniferum*, a gooey swatch containing opium and mandrake—applied orally or as a suppository—for a variety of ailments.

The School of Salerno was eventually eclipsed by the Frankish Schools of Paris (the Sorbonne), Bologna and Montpellier, which graduated some accomplished Christian doctors, rooted in classical medical tradition as well as Heroic techniques. The most famous of these was Guy de Chauliac, the "father of modern surgery," who between 1340 and 1370 was the personal physician to three popes: Clement VI, Innocent VI, and Urban V.

In his *Cyrurgie*—a massive compendium of healing lore drawn from the works of Galen, ibn Sinna, and the School of Salerno—de Chauliac cites opium medications for use in the treatment of morbid swellings of the face and members, wounds, "ulcers of the fondement" (hemorrhoids), diseases of the eye, and among "medecynes that letten the heres to grow ageyne that are pulled up by the rootes." In most cases, though, application of opium was external, in ointment form, following one of de Chauliac's tremendously innovative but often pointless Frankish surgical procedures. There are indications that he used opium as a sedative to prepare his patients for surgery, but he valued the drug chiefly as a calmative after it was over, feeling also that such soothing opium ointments promoted a "laudable pus" and insured healing. He especially recommended it for gout, noting that in treating Pope Clement VI in 1348 for that ailment he had employed with success "the hedes of white popy with the sedes and with the ryndes."

De Chauliac's ministrations may also have kept the Pontiff

from catching the plague that year. As the Black Death swept through Europe Pope Clement, as part of his gout regimen, was virtually quarantined in the cosiest room of his palace, bundled in a pile of blankets and impervious to plague-carrying ticks. Of course, de Chauliac could hardly have guessed this: He and his contemporaries were unshakably convinced that the planetary conjunction of Jupiter, Saturn, and Mars in Aquarius in 1345 had caused the earth to exude poisonous vapours which had precipitated the plague.

If references to opium were scarce before The Plague, they were virtually nonexisent in its wake. Trade with the Arab world had broken down, eliminating the small supply of imported prepared opium. Within fifty years of Pope Clement's gout, moreover, opium had become a very risky subject of inquiry in circles of learning watched over by the Holy Inquisition, which was then in the process of methodically exterminating all manner of heretics, Jews, and witches. Anything from the East was inextricably linked to the Devil. The plague had, after all, come from the East, spreading its raging fever, gangrenous carbuncles, and strangulating buboes along the caravan routes into Europe. Opium was not quite the unmitigated evil that mandrake—with its pagan past, anthropomorphic root and reputation as a flying potion—was in the eyes of the Inquisition, but for two hundred years it virtually disappeared from the historical record. It was not until the late sixteenth century that opium was reintroduced into the medical literature of Europe. And it took a very brave, ingenious, and outrageous man to do it. His name: Philippus Aureolus Theophrastus Bombastus von Hohenheim, known to all the world as Paracelsus.*

On Saint John's Day 1527, Paracelsus, drunk with righteous indignation and with ale, lurched onto the village green in Basle, Switzerland, flourishing a large brass vase and a handful of books and papers. Into the vase he ceremoniously dumped the works of Galen and ibn-Sinna, the latest papal bull, and a fistful of sulphur nitro, Paracelsus' version of Chinese gunpowder. And

*From the words "para"—"better than"—and Celsus, one of the most notable of post-Galenic physicians and alchemists.

striking his tinderbox, he blew the whole lot—Pagan, Muslim, and Christian medical doctrines—to bits. To the crowd gathered around the smoldering debris, he then announced: "You will all follow me, ye professors of Paris, Montpellier, Germany, Cologne, and Vienna: and all ye that dwell on the Rhine and the Danube—ye that inhabit the isles of the sea; and ye also, Italians, Dalmatians, Athenians, Jews—ye will all follow my doctrines, for *I am the monarch of medicine!*"

Had this happened anywhere but in Switzerland, the center of the Reformation, where burning papal bulls and such was a common form of dissent (practiced frequently by Zwingli), Paracelsus would have likely been accused of witchery on the spot. Even in freethinking Basle, where he taught physics and natural philosophy at the University, his performance was shocking, but then so were most things about the man. Herr Professor von Hohenheim thereafter was known to boast of summoning Galen and ibn-Sinna from Hell so that he might chastise them for their wrong-headed doctrines.

Despite his eccentricities, however, the accomplishments of Paracelsus in his short lifetime (1493–1541) were of such an extraordinary nature that he was tolerated, up to a point. Medicine is indebted to him for "chemotherapy," the use of minerals to treat disease. ("Make medicines not gold," Paracelsus counseled aspiring alchemists.) Zinc, one of the many minerals he introduced into therapeutics, remains a most effective remedy for external infection. He recommended iron for "poor blood," invented chemical urinalysis, was the first to suggest that syphillis was communicated by contact, and developed the mercury treatment for it. He rejected Galen's doctrines, and in their place urged that medicines be compounded for *specific* ailments through experimentation not universal law; demanded that the application of excrement and feathers to wounds be abolished, and recommended ether—which he classed as a "sulphur" and named "Sweet Oil of Vitriol"—for anesthesiology fully three hundred years before the practice was widely accepted in surgery.* And

---

*"This sulphur," he wrote, "has such a sweet taste that even chickens will take it whereupon they sleep for awhile and awaken without injury."

In the early sixteenth century, Paracelsus reintroduced opium into European medicine as laudanum—"pills which had the form of mouse turds," and with which, he boasted, he could "wake up the dead."

if these techniques and simples weren't enough, Paracelsus, of course, had:

> ...pills he called laudanum which had the form of mouse turds...He boasted that with these pills he could wake up the dead, and indeed he proved that patients who seemed to be dead suddenly arose.

Though these little black pills, described by a nameless disciple, bore little resemblance to the ruby-red tincture popularized by Thomas Sydenham one hundred years later—and two hundred years later, tippled by De Quincey and Coleridge—there is no mystery about the active ingredient of this laudanum: It was opium.

Paracelsus performed literally hundreds of experiments with the drug. "That which rests or sleeps," he reasoned, "does not, in the course of nature, cause any discomfort." And since "sleep does not necessarily apply to the sufferer only, but may be predicated of the disease itself," an ideal medicine would be one that puts the disease to sleep without putting the patient into a coma. The calm, centered half-sleep of opium fit his model perfectly, and he set to work observing its properties and seeking ways to enhance its effects.

> Take of Thebaic opium, one ounce; of orange and lemon juice, six ounces; of cinnamon and caryophilli, each half an ounce. Pound these ingredients carefully together, mix them well, and place them in a glass vessel with its blind covering. Let them be digested in the sun or in dung for a month, and then afterwards pressed out and placed again in the vessel with the following: Half a scruple of musk and half a scruple each of the juice of corals and of the magistery of pearls. Mix these, and after digesting all for a month, add a scruple and a half of the quintessence of gold.

Paracelsus called this formula the "Anodyne Specific" and boasted that here was a medicine "capable of removing any disease, internal or external," which specifically called for a painkiller—which included, in the sixteenth century, many diseases indeed.

His discovery required little to work besides the first ingredient, opium. The pearls, corals, quintessence of gold, etc. were part of an alchemical credo which stipulated that if the remedy was sufficiently elaborate, "the ailment shall have, or can have, positively no effect on the body." (The pearls, coral, quintessence of gold, etc. also had the practical benefit for the alchemist/physician of making his remedies very expensive.)

Yet, Paracelsus may have stumbled onto something more. He'd most certainly tried *opium thebaicum*, but self-testing the Anodyne Specific he became vehemently convinced that it wasn't just ordinary poppy juice. Why? The answer may be found in those six innocent ounces of orange and lemon juice. Acetic acid (found in all citrus juices), causes subtle chemical changes in opium's principle alkaloid morphine, modifying its molecular bonds to such an extent that the effects when ingested are quite marked. Perhaps it was this extra kick that Paracelsus took as a sign from heaven that he'd found, as he thought, the "Stone of Immortality." Chemists in the late nineteenth century stumbled onto the same formula when they boiled morphine in acetic anhydride, to yield diacetyl-morphine, a compound they touted as the anodyne specific of its day, and named "heroin."

Despite such achievements, Paracelsus was finally forced to leave Basle in the wake of another outrageous performance. He'd invited the University faculty to a lecture in which he promised to reveal the "mysteries of putrefactive fermentation", the greatest secret of medicine. When all were assembled in hushed anticipation, he strode to the lectern holding a large lidded platter, which he uncovered to reveal two actual large turds.

He adjourned to Colmar in 1528, from there to Nurenburg in 1530, and finally to Salzburg, where he died in 1541 at the White Horse Inn, allegedly murdered by a gang of thugs hired by rival physicians.

After his death his myth was magnified. Sects of Paracelsists sprang up in France, Germany and England, spreading his doctrines with the Reformation. While they were responsible for preserving the substantial body of work attributed to him—and advancing a new, revolutionary attitude toward science—the major concern of many of these zealots was the "Stone of Immortality"—*Laudanum Paracelsi*. They took his passionate boastings literally, and ignored his more reasoned doctrines. Opium, in their view, was not a specific to be used selectively on the basis of experimentation, but a cure-all, a panacea. This was the opinion of Oswald Croll in his 1608 *Basilica Chymica*, and of his contemporary Michael Toxites, who touted laudanum as "a medicine beyond all praise... than which nothing more excellent could be found in all the world"; it would cure every disease except leprosy, "and even resuscitate the dead."

By the mid-1600s then, throughout Europe, taboos against opium had been largely dispelled by glowing reports attesting to its medical usefulness. But good publicity was far more plentiful than supplies of the drug itself, and it took another century for opium to really catch on.

In England the most popular panacea of the day was rhubarb. Rhubarb is a splendid laxative and, judging by apothecaries' records, constipation—brought on by an unvaried diet of meats and fish with no green vegetables—was one of England's greatest health problems. Opium constipates—this in fact is one of its chief medical indications, but there was not much use for things that constipate in seventeenth century England. A bill from the apothecary to Queen Elizabeth I includes "a royal sweetmeat made of incised rhubarb" along with two of the day's most highly coveted and expensive quack remedies, bezoar stone and unicorn's horn. Another apothecary bill to one Edward Nicholas in 1633 is even more explicit in its simplicity:

> *A dose of purgative pills, a purge for your son,*
> *A purge for your worship, a purge potion*

Also, though opium had reentered the medical literature, it was still not used much by physicians. When King Charles II suffered a massive stroke while shaving in February 1685, the Royal physician Dr. Scarburgh recorded a virtual compendium of medicines and Heroic techniques used, without success, to bring him around: Opium was conspicuously absent.* Not that it would

---

*The King was bled to the extent of one pint in his right arm; his shoulder was incised and cupped; an emetic and purgative administered, followed by an enema containing antimony, sacred bitters, rock salt, mallow leaves, violets, beet root, camomile flowers, fennel seed, linseed, cinnamon, cardamon seed, saffron, cochineal, and aloes. The King's head was shaved and blistered; a sneezing powder of hellebore root administered; a concoction of barley water, licorice and sweet almond poured down his throat, as well as white wine, absinthe, anise, and an extract of thistle leaves, mint, rue, and angelica. A plaster of Burgundy pitch and pigeon dung was applied to his feet; followed by infusions of melon seeds, manna, slippery elm, black cherry water, dissolved pearls, gentian root,

have been of any real value except to ease the final hours of the dying King—and perhaps that is why his Heroic physicians excluded it. Opium was certainly available to them. As early as 1601, Dr. Turner, an apothecary on Bishop-gate Street in London, was already selling a compound called *Laudanu*, and ships chartered by Elizabeth I in 1606 were instructed to purchase the best Indian opium for transport back to England. But in King Charles's time it appears that the drug was regarded more as a home remedy than as a bonafide medicine.

Opium still wasn't plentiful by any means in the seventeenth century but in 1656, a young Oxford undergraduate was able to acquire enough of it to perform some unusual experiments, providing mankind with the first record of intravenous injections of opiates. The name of the precocious youngster was Christopher Wren, who later rebuilt London after the great fire of 1663. Inspired by William Harvey's newly-launched hypothesis on the circulation of blood, Wren injected a dog with wine and opium tincture, using a bladder and quill device of his own design.

Later that year he repeated the experiment for witnesses. An expansive account, with special emphasis on Wren's precision as a surgeon, is provided by a school chum named Boyle:

> His (Wren's) way was briefly this: first to make a small and opportune incision over that part of the hind leg where the larger vessels that carry the blood are most easy to be taken hold of . . . He made a slit along the vein . . . great enough to put in the slender pipe of a syringe; by which I proposed to have injected a warm solution of opium in sack that the effect of our experiment might be more quick and manifest. And accordingly, our dextrous experimenter, having surmounted the difficulties which the tormented dog's violent struggles interposed, conveyed a small dose of the solution or tincture into the opened vessel, whereby setting

---

nutmeg, quinine, and cloves, and extracts of flowers of lime, lily-of-the-valley, peony, and lavender. When he went into convulsions, forty drops of extract of human skull were administered, followed by bezoar stone when he got worse. Then wrote Scarburgh: "Alas! after an ill-fated night his serene majesty's strength seemed exhausted to such a degree that the whole assembly of physicians lost all hope and became despondent: still, so as not to appear to fail in doing their duty in any detail, they brought into play the most active cordial." After this final ministration—consisting of pearl, julip and ammonia—was forced down his throat by his frustrated doctors, the King obligingly died.

into the mass of blood... it was quickly, by the circular motion of that, carried to the brain and other parts of the body: so that we had scarce untied the dog before the opium began to disclose its narcotic quality, and almost as soon as he was on his feet he began to nod his head and falter and reel in his place, and presently appeared so stupified that there were wagers offered his life would not be saved. I caused him to be shipped up and down a neighboring garden, whereby being kept awake and in motion he began to become himself again; and being recovered but began to grow fat... But I could not long observe how it fared with him; for this experiment and some other trials made upon him, having made him famous, he was soon after stolen from me.*

Wren's brilliant experiments, charged with youthful optimism and near-obsession, were indicative of the exuberant mood of post-Renaissance science. Inspired by the likes of Paracelsus and Harvey, aspiring young men all over Europe were engaged in animated debate and experimentation, claiming almost daily discoveries of elaborate new techniques against which disease would surely stand no chance. And it's not surprising that among these experimenters there should have been a few who set their minds to compounding new opium preparations.

Among them was the English apothecary Thomas Sydenham, who in 1680 introduced mankind to Sydenham's Laudanum: opium compounded with sherry wine, saffron, cinnamon and cloves to mask the bitter taste of the drug. Sydenham's praise for opium was unbounded: "Among the remedies which it has pleased God to give to man to relieve his sufferings," he was fond of reiterating, "none is so universal and efficacious as opium." But mixing it with wine made it even better. By this time it had been observed that people sometimes became sick from too much opium or when deprived of the drug after long periods of steady use, but the addition of alcohol, Sydenham was convinced, purified opium of those contaminants that were harmful.

From such humble beginnings the patent medicine industry

*A somewhat later account of a similar procedure is provided by Samuel Pepys in a "Journal" entry marked 16 May 1664: "With Mr. Pierce, the surgeon, to see the experiment of killing a dog by letting opium into its hind leg. He and Dr. Clark did fail mightily in hitting a vein, and in effect did not do the business after many trials; but with the little they got in, the dog did presently fall asleep and so lay till we cut him up."

was born. By 1700 Sydenham's Laudanum was competing with Venice Treacle, Mithridate, London Laudanum, and Dr. Bates's Pacific Pill. Merchandising of these pioneering compounds, however, was still severely limited by the scanty supply of imported opium. The proliferation of opium-based proprietaries didn't really begin until Dover's Powder, a "diaphoretic" for gout was introduced some twenty years later. But then Dr. Thomas Dover, inventor of this opium and ipecac compound, had unusually good connections with the early seafaring opium traders. He was the very same *Captain* Thomas Dover who had piloted the privateer vessel which rescued the real-life Robinson Crusoe (Alexander Selkirk) from Juan Fernandez Island in 1709. It was shortly after that famous voyage that Captain Dover, at the age of forty, announced his intention to become a doctor. Much to the dismay of the Royal College of Physicians, he also announced that he was far too old to actually study medicine; he simply intended to cure people. And that's exactly what he proceeded to do with his Dover's Powder.

> ...a most delicious and extraordinary *Refreshment* of the spirits upon very good *News*, or any other great cause of *Joy*, as the sight of a dearly-loved Person etc. thought to have been lost at *Sea*. It is indeed so unexpressibly fine and sweet a *Pleasure*, that it is very difficult for me to describe, or any to conceive it, but such as actually feel it; for 'tis as if a *Good Genius* possessed, or informed a Man; therefore people do commonly call it a *Heavenly Condition*, as if no *worldly* Pleasure was to be compar'd with it.

The popularity of opium preparations was greatly boosted by such panegyric: the pleasures of opium as described in 1700 by Dr. John Jones of Oxford in a landmark book, *The Mysteries of Opium Reveal'd*. Jones's *Good Genius* ran to four hundred pages of detailed observations on opium's effects and uses; including a number of lengthy digressions—comparing his achievements to those of Harvey, discoursing on linguistics and on the merits of William of Orange—which scholars have taken as evidence that the *extraordinary refreshment* of opium was not unknown to the author, even as he wrote.

It may not be going too far to suggest that Jones was an addict; he does convey with revealing poignancy (at a time when there just weren't that many opium-addicted subjects available) the utter despair of being without the drug when one has become accustomed to it: "It is as if a Man used to Dance to Excellent *Musick*, were required to do it without *Musick* at all, nor so much as *thoughts* of it, or mumbling it within himself." Clinically precise chapters follow, devoted to the effects of an excessive dose—"Laxity and Debility of all Parts, Loss of Memory, Difficulty Breathing, Nausea"; to the effects of a "long and lavish" use of opium—"Inability to do anything, except it be while Opium operates"; and to the lesser and greater woes of withdrawal, ranging from sweats, chills and diarrhea to,

> Great and even intolerable Distresses, Anxieties and Depressions of Spirits, which in a few days commonly end in a most miserable *Death*, attended with *strange Agonies*.

But why give up opium anyway? Dr. Jones was the most outspoken supporter of the notion that advancing chemistry would render opium completely harmless by ridding it of the nasty "refinous parts," with their tiny "stinging points." The addition of alcohol, he noted, had already gone far in doing so. And in a glow of optimism, he went on to catalog the hundred-fold benefits of a "moderate" regular dose of opium which, in addition to freedom from pain and anxiety, included: "Serenity... Alacrity and Expediteness in Dispatching and Managing of Business... Assurance... Ovation of the Spirits... Courage... Contempt of Danger... Magnanimity... Euphory... Easie undergoing of all Labour... Satisfaction... Acquiescence... Contentation, and Equanimity." Opium, swore Jones, was good for what ailed you, be it mental or physical—gout, dropsy, catarrh, ague, asthma, voiding of the stone, fever, nausea, colic, measles, rheumatism, cancer, pox, plague, *anything*.

Lunacy, perhaps, but in at least one respect, inspired lunacy. Jones contended that the drug worked not by virtue of its being Cold or Earthy, as the ancients professed, nor, as his contemporaries believed, by "fumes, vapours, auras or effluviums rising from the stomach to the brain." No, he argued, opium worked by imitating a substance already in the body, Sal-Volatile-Oleosum or fatty, stimulating salt.

> It cannot be much wondered at, considering our Active principles are a Sal-Volatile-Oleosum and that *Opium* is such, and that we

naturally carry an *Opiate* within us, that in some cases our ordinary Sal-Volatile-Oleosum... being by some accident exalted towards the Nature of *Opium*, may have the Effect of an *Opiate* upon us.

This assertion, made nearly four hundred years before Dr. Sol Snyder at Johns Hopkins discovered the body's own opiate— endorphin (see Preface)—might have placed Dr. Jones in the foremost ranks of scientific genius had he not become so absolutely obsessed with the drug as an aphrodisiac. He compared the sensual ovation, magnanimity and boldness arising from a dose of opium to nothing less than the vitality of wild beasts in rut, and swore that it increased seed and promoted a "great promptitude to Venery, Erections etc" in men, and breast development in women; and that it did so in imitation of the oily stimulating salt which Jones finally concluded opium most closely resembled—*semen Humanum*. The true mystery of opium he revealed was that it tickled the venereal membranes.

While Jones knew that opium "stimulated" something like endorphins, Dr. John Brown of Edinburgh, reading his book and not having the endorphin intuition, gathered that it "stimulated" the whole body. He spread the word via numerous books and papers that health depended on the ability of the individual to experience stimulation and maintain bodily excitability, and touted regular doses of laudanum as an effective, dependable tonic.

A two hundred-year-long scientific debate ensued as a result of Jones's and Brown's works over whether opium was a stimulant or a depressant. Never resolved to anyone's real satisfaction (though opium is officially classified as a narcotic which dulls the senses), the controversy still generated an unprecedented amount of clinical research on the effects of opium and other drugs on humans.

In 1799 one such researcher was sixteen-year-old Friedrich Sertuerner, a pharmacist's apprentice in Paderborn, Germany. Having observed wide variations in the potency of crude opium, he was convinced that it contained a simple active ingredient, varying in proportion to those troublesome refinous parts which blighted the wonderful drug. His aim: to isolate the pure stuff of poppy juice.

Just four years later, working in the Royal Pharmacy at Einbeck, he discovered that if opium was first dissolved in acid which was then neutralized with ammonia, tiny gray crystals precipitated out. But tests of these crystals on animals produced none of opium's usual effects. It took several more months of work before Sertuerner found his error—that a further washing with ammonia and alcohol was required to precipitate even tinier white crystals out of the gray powder. Much to his amazement these white crystals were alkaloids. (According to all the textbooks of the day, plants didn't contain alkaloids.) Of greater significance, tests on dogs of this opium alkaloid (dissolved in alcohol), in tiny amounts, or so he thought, of 2.5–5 grains, were absolutely conclusive: the animals almost immediately became comatose and died. By reducing doses to what seemed like miniscule levels, however, excellent non-lethal results were produced both on dogs and people. Just prior to leaving Einbeck, in the shadow of a scandal that erupted over his tests of the powder on three local teenagers, Sertuerner excitedly wrote up his conclusions.

> I have been fortunate enough to find in opium, still another substance which has been unknown until now...It is neither earth, gluten nor resin nor the compound I found last year, but an entirely individual one. This substance is the specific narcotic element of opium...the *Principium somniferum*.

He named his brainchild morphine.

The isolation of morphine excited little attention until 1817, when important scientific journals in France and Germany simultaneously featured articles on it. Sertuerner's process was easily duplicated and in a few short decades pharmaceutical manufacturers were distilling morphine "salts" by the bin: the giant multinational Merck, Sharpe and Dohme is the most prominent of many still-prospering pharmaceutical supply houses which owe their early success entirely to the manufacture of morphine.

Morphine-based proprietaries—readily available in European pharmacies cheaply and without prescription until the end of the nineteenth century—however, were never as plentiful or popular among the masses as crude opium preparations like laudanum. Generally people were introduced to morphine by doctors, among whom the pure alkaloid, with its magical technological aura, won a wide and devoted following. They were convinced that here, finally, was the blessed offspring of the scientific quest to perfect and tame opium begun by Galen and extended by Paracelsus and Sydenham. Clearly the best, most reliable, fastest-acting, longest-lasting and, surely, the safest form of opium had to be this morphine. The high regard for Sertuerner's invention among physicians was most aptly expressed by the emminent English practitioner Sir William Osler. "Morphine," he declared, "is God's own medicine."

Physicians also enthusiastically seized on a new and attractively technological way of administering morphine: injecting it under the skin, using a syringe. The discovery of this new technique was claimed by Dr. Alexander Wood of Edinburgh in 1843. (Christopher Wren had been forgotten.) Using an Anel's syringe—a clumsy, innaccurate gizmo with a blunt, unwieldy nozzle—he had managed to inject the drug into an incision in the skin of his patients with outstanding results. Not only were morphine's effects nearly instantaneous, when administered this way, its potency was fully tripled as well.

The most ardent advocate of the new technique was the inventor Charles Hunter of London. By substituting a thin, pointed needle with a lateral opening for the nozzle of Wood's syringe, Hunter created the hypodermic needle pretty much as we know it today. His vigorous salesmanship on behalf of his invention is generally credited with spreading the practice of hypodermic injection throughout England, France, and Germany. He wrote numerous papers on the subject, and demonstrated his device across the Continent, winning the favorable attention of the day's preeminent physicians.

By the 1870s the medical community was abuzz with opinions and theories on when, where, and how to inject morphine (see Chapter 11). Injected morphine was prized mostly as a fast-acting anodyne for physical pain, but it was also tested as an agent against pain that was decidedly non-physical. A German doctor named O. J. B. Wolff, writing in the *Archiv fur Psychiatrie* (1871), claimed moderate success in treating serious mental disorders by injecting patients with morphine in the "anterior and lateral portions of the neck," aiming for a direct hit on the vasomotor center of the brain. Though patients grew no less mad, Wolff announced, they did become wonderfully calm.

Opium, in its disparate forms, was used extensively in the treatment of insanity at this time. Since the beginning of the nineteenth century its use in the care of the mentally ill—in contrast to straightjackets, beatings, and terror—had been viewed as a progressive, humane step forward. The irony, of course, is pointed out by historian Virginia Berridge: "By the end of the century, its use was increasingly viewed as both a cause of mental illness and as a form of insanity itself."

The changing attitudes toward opiates and their use are detailed in the following chapters. Suffice it to say for now, that after nearly three centuries of steadily rising imports and, at times, enchanted acclaim, the use of opium in all its various shapes and forms was now prodigious in Europe. England alone in the 1860s was importing some 1,000 tons annually. It was not until the 60s, when the first measures to restrict the sale and use of opiates were enacted, that anyone really paid attention to the phenomenon of addiction. Prior to that, with opiates so readily available, such troublesome side-effects as junk-sickness appeared only on those extremely rare occasions when supplies of the drug were cut off, or when people were too poor to buy it.

The habit-forming properties of injected morphine were first noted (reluctantly) by Dr. Clifford Allbutt in England in 1870, after prolonged self-experimentation:

> Injected morphia seemed so different to swallowed morphia, no one had any experience of ill effects from it, and we all had the daily experience of it as a means of peace and comfort, while pain on the other hand was certainly the forerunner of wretchedness and exhaustion. Gradually, however, the conviction began to force itself upon my notice, that injections of morphia, though free from the ordinary evils of opium-eating, might, nevertheless, create the same artificial want and gain credit for assuaging a restlessness and depression of which it was itself the cause.

Similar warnings were issued later in the decade in Berlin by Eduard Levenstein, the most prominent cure specialist of the day. Medical intervention in cases of opiate addiction was not new. As early as 1816 Coleridge had put himself in the able hands of Dr. James Gilman, who had succeeded in stabilizing if not curing his laudanum habit (see Chapter 5). Since then a handful of specialists had promoted addiction cures of one kind or another, but in reality they offered little but the hard choice between sudden and gradual withdrawal, neither of which was very pleasant, or, for that matter, effective. In the end, most cure specialists ended up, like Dr. Gilman, simply maintaining their patients on opiates.

Levenstein favored cold turkey—sudden and complete withdrawal of all opiates—comparing gradual reduction to cutting off a dog's tail a piece at a time. If patients agreed to total seclusion and management by the clinic staff, Levenstein could guarantee to have them opiate-free in about a week. Whether they'd stay that way was another matter. He conducted the earliest follow-up study on detoxed addicts in 1875, and found that fully 75 percent of them relapsed. And no cure developed in the hundred years that have elapsed since then has done any better.

By Levenstein's time, though, with public attention beginning to focus on opiates as a health hazard, there was more interest than ever before in addiction cures, more people seeking them, and more pressure on the medical and scientific communities to undo the damage caused by the problematical wonder they'd created: to find what amounted to a container for the universal solvent. In the three hundred years since Paracelsus first concocted his Stone of Immortality out of opium thebaicum, citrus juice, and quintessence of gold, science had come full circle. The search was now on for the *anodyne specific specific*, a drug which would instantly, painlessly, and completely end physical dependence on opiates.

FOUR
THE
BRITISH EXPERIENCE

The exhilirating effects of her last dose had passed off and given place to that wretched lowness of spirit in which the life of an opium taker alternates. As the repulsive-looking hag sat upright in her filthy bed by the chimney corner, her uncouth and cavernous features streaked by the various courses her tears had taken in her intervals of despondency. With her tangled grey hair hanging over her shoulders, her shrunken neck, and withered arms which were exposed to view as she rolled up another pill of the filthy-looking drug, and raising it trembling to her discouloured lips, presented a spectacle more loathsome than any could imagine.

The correspondent for the London *Morning Chronicle* may have been no master at fashioning individual sentences, but his flair for description leaves no question about what he thought of opium addicts in the Fenlands around Saint Ives. This particular addict, he noted in passing, had broken her hip six years before, and just as the bones had refused to knit, so the wretch stubbornly refused to leave off her revolting indulgence in narcotics. Another grotesque example of the notorious Fenland opium-eaters: the correspondent manfully fought down his righteous gorge, and got back on the new Norwich–to–London line to file his improving story on the desolate human relics of the northern moors.

The scandal of the North Country opium epidemic broke with

the penetration of the railroads into the district in the very early 1800s. Before this, the soggy, depressing, and wholly unhealthy Fenlands bordering on the Wash tidal basin had been about as remote from the rest of England as Turkey itself. When the railroads brought the Fens into the world, it was discovered that the people there were given to drugging themselves with opiates of every description, even as so many Constantinopolitans. The travels of Baron Alphonse du Tott, entitled *Memoirs of the Turks and Tartars*, had only recently been translated from the French; it was all the rage, and the Baron's description of Turkish opium addicts most certainly influenced the *Morning Chronicle*'s account: "These devotees, their faces pale and sad, can only inspire pity, with their long necks, heads lolling to the left or right, crooked spines, shoulders twisted up toward their ears, and other bizarre postures that result from their malady..."*

Rickets, in du Tott's estimation, were the sure result of opiate addiction among the Turks; just as the Fenland woman's refractory broken hip, in the estimation of the *Morning Chronicle* hack, was only a natural complement to the variety of afflictions which must certainly beset anyone who dabbled with this repulsive drug.

The esteemed Dr. Jonathan Pereira, author of the standard British text on therapeutics, however, was quick to point out that such symptoms were confined exclusively to the poor and starving. Rich, well-fed opium addicts didn't get rickets, though they were sorely afflicted when deprived of their drug. Yet until the examples of De Quincey and Coleridge shifted the public's attention to the opium torments of *real* people, inane scandal stories about the uncanny folk of Saint Ives were a dependable, improving journalistic feature once the opium epidemic there came to light. The exotic lifestyle and unintelligible dialect of the Fenlanders punctuated the thrill of spicy voyeurism. From *Alton Locke*, by Charles Kingsley, an improving novel of 1850:

> "Yow goo into druggists' shop o' market day, into Cambridge, and you'll see the little boxes, doozens and doozens, a'ready on the

---

*The Baron, however, did not share the *Morning Chronicle*'s wholehearted condemnation of opium addicts. An hour after swallowing their pills, he continues, "Each returns to his lodging in a state of total unreason, but also simple and total joy which reason cannot procure. Deaf to the hoots of passersby, who amuse themselves by tormenting them, each believes he possesses happiness itself: reality offers so much less."

counter; and never a venman's wife goo by, but what calls in for a ha pennord o' elevation, to last her out the week. Oh! Ho! ho! Well, it keeps womenfolk quiet, it do; and it's mortal good agin ago pains."

"Elevation" was their colorful rustic slang-term for the opium that figured so largely in their soggy, clammy, misty, faraway lives. "Ago" meant "ague," the chronic, skincrawling feverless shivers that inevitably characterize people who live in places like the northern swamps of England; ague is a spasmodic nervous affliction, exquisitely uncomfortable and often incapacitating, but it does respond most excellently to opiates. Due to their wretched diet and environment, the Fenlanders were also prey to rheumatism, rickets, recurrent fevers, earaches, toothaches, lung ailments of all sorts, malaria, black melancholy, and ulcers—opium is specific for every one of these afflictions.

So the dank bog-plains of Cambridgeshire, Lincolnshire, Huntingdonshire, and Norfolk seemed scandalously polluted with opiates when they were discovered by the rest of the world. In "the opium-eating city of Ely," recorded the papers, "the sale of laudanum... was as common as butter and cheese." A physician of Doddingham, deep in the Fens, corroborated: "Opium, laudanum and other narcotics seem here to supply the place of dram-drinking in other towns."

On market day, the chemists, groceries, general stores, and market stalls of Fen towns would be amply stocked with opium preparations: bottles of ruby-red laudanum tincture, black chickpea pills, inch-square "pennorth sticks," and even pound bricks. "In the small town of Thorpe," Samuel Taylor Coleridge recorded with interest, "the Druggist informed me that he commonly sold on market days two or three Pounds of Opium, and a Gallon of Laudanum."

Due to the fluency of demand, opium in the Fens was extraordinarily cheap—threepence an ounce for laudanum in Ely, and at least thirty grains to every pennorth stick. And it was good opium too, the best Turkey import,* or the juice of the most

---

*Although the British East India Company and independent traders were moving tons of Indian opium into China, the Turkish product continued to dominate the domestic British market throughout the nineteenth century: fully 80 percent of the opium consumed in England was from Turkey.

tenderly-cultivated, white-petaled, homegrown "medical" poppy, which sprouted proudly among the Fenlanders' turnips and rhubarb. They had, from every indication, been growing opium ages before the world discovered them, long before commercial opiates were available there.

Farmsteaders also set off special stands of hemp from the industrial rope crop, grooming the female plants especially for their buds, and these buds, harvested and dried, were commonly smoked or brewed into tea.* In every respect they were past masters at taking the edge off an extremely uncongenial climate. And this is precisely how they were viewed in time; by the mid-nineteenth century, prodigious self-medication with opiates, so shocking and exotic when it first surfaced in the Fens, had become commonplace everywhere in England. As this happened, the focus of improving horror stories shifted to the urban working class, and to gentleman-addicts like De Quincey and Coleridge. As for the Fenlanders, they were eventually held up, by apologists for the Indo-China opium trade, in debates before Parliament as examples of how whole communities could use opiates sensibly, with moderation and control.

In hospitals of the nineteenth century, opium was administered abundantly for all manner of conditions, since whether or not it alleviated any patient's afflictions, it marvelously conduced quietness and order in the wards. Dr. Pereira's *Elements of Materia Medica and Therapeutics* (1839) recommended the drug "to mitigate pain, to allay spasm, to promote sleep, to reduce nervous restlessness, to produce perspiration and to check mucuous discharges from the bronchial tubes and gastro-intestinal canal." He also listed it as a treatment for cholera, and dysentery, and "a most effective palliative" for gout, sciatica and neuralgia.

As an anesthetic, opium was useful for minor surgery, tooth extraction, wound cauterization and such, though it was of in-

*Hashish, cannabis resin, became known in Britain gradually over this period, as an extravagant Oriental hallucinogen. But not until the late 1800s did word get around about ganja and bhang, Indian preparations of cannabis buds prepared especially for smoking and for tea. By that time the Fens had been drained, and the Fenlanders solidly acculturated; so the abuse of marijuana by a sizable portion of the English population is an historical scandal that has so far gone unexploited.

different value in more extensive surgical procedures. Opiates do not block the transmission of pain impulses, they only alter the perception of them, and then only to a finite degree, unless enough is administered to bring on a profound coma. Surgery patients were only sedated with it; knowledgeable surgeons mixed hyoscyamine with the opium to promote amnesia afterward, which was the best patients could hope for.

Opium and henbane were helpful to the surgeon, but the job was still one of the most nervewracking, dehumanizing professions short of slaverunning. The most sublimely opiated patient would come directly to full shrieking consciousness once the scalpel went in; and later, however vague and cloudy the hyoscyamine may have rendered the event in the patient's memory, the mere appearance of the surgeon tended to prompt hysteria. It was precisely this vague abhorrence which inspired this doggerel poem about an eighteenth century practitioner:

> *I do not love thee, Dr. Fell.*
> *The reason why I cannot tell;*
> *But this alone I know full well,*
> *I do not love thee, Dr. Fell.*

If the prevalence of opium in Britain back then looks a bit shocking to us today—22,000 pounds of it were imported from Turkey and India in 1830 alone—we ought to keep in mind what a visit to a doctor commonly entailed. Not only did these officially licensed quacks kill many people with their Heroic therapies, but their fees were very nearly as ruinous to the average household budget as doctors' fees are today. No wonder opiates, good for nearly anything that ailed you and eminently safe when used with plain common sense, were ubiquitous all through the United Kingdom.

Besides its medicinal application, naturally, opium was used to get high. Even more than Fenland opium-eating, the use of opiates as intoxicants by the working-class prompted grand alarm in the press, in the government, and in the best circles of enlightened charitable gentry. Middleclass people always have a special horror of inebriety among the poor, who are collectively perceived as a homogenous mob seething with some apopleptic, all-consuming anger which is certain to detonate any time they become intoxicated. Gin was horrible enough for the poor, being reasonably cheap—"Drunk for a penny," the grogshop posters guaranteed, "and dead drunk for tuppence"—and immensely toxic, promoting dyspepsia and delirium tremens. Opium, being even cheaper, was even more dreadful, and its use by the poor was bewailed with special piteousness by benevolent Christain liberals. Jeremiads against opium, like the *Morning Chronicle*'s Fenland reports, proliferated. Of course, speaking realistically, it was difficult to precisely identify any particular *harm* opium might wreak on any individual factory hand, who after all had only the means and opportunity to take it once a week, on the blessed Sabbath; it takes at least three months of daily high doses to get even mildly addicted to plain opium, and unlike gin it tends to be *good* for your body in moderate quantities.

The benevolent middleclass ombudsmen of the poor resolved this paradox, as they always have, by simply lying about the drug, and suppressing the truth. If the truth were to be openly told, an apothecary candidly predicted in 1763,

> many people then might indiscriminately use it, [and] it would take from them that necessary fear and caution, which should prevent their experiencing the extensive power of the drug; for there are many properties in it, if universally known, that would habituate the use, and make it more in request with us than the Turks themselves; the result of which knowledge must prove a general misfortune.

The medical profession went early on record as supporting the benevolent restriction of opiates from access by the striving masses. "To make the people exert themselves to improve their conditions," prescribed Dr. Thomas Wakely in the *Lancet* in 1830, "pain, destitution and wretchedness must be their stimulants."

Spearheaded by the developing guilds of pharmacists and physicians, legal restrictions on opiates began tightening in the last half of the 1800s; discussions of the gradual consolidation of the opiate industry into the hands of professional healers and policemen are offered copiously elsewhere in this book. In the present context, the striking fact is that no very broad or vocal public outcry ever arose against opium use during this period when it was commonest everywhere; in contrast to the anti-alcohol temperance controversy, the phenomenon of opiate inebriety just never inspired the sort of evangelical hyper-moralism that promotes mass meetings, professional lecture circuits, sermons, pamphlets, hymns and restrictve legislation.

The *idea* that the poor, in the faceless scores of thousands every Saturday night, were eating opium to get high, was sufficiently reprehensible to provoke the formal dismay and concern of their betters, but what did it really amount to? A person dreaming on opium, after all, presents only the remotest threat to the status quo. Opium eaters didn't hang out in laudanum taverns, sing antiestablishment ballads, argue politics, and hoot rudenesses at passing gentlefolk; there were no opium-smoking dens for the purpose, until legislative bans on opiates made them necessary. It is not a convivial drug; you imbibe the entire high in just a couple of perfunctory gestures, wander about awhile thoughtfully to see what the rest of the world's up to on Saturday night, and then you go home to admire the back of your hand awhile, and so to bed.

> . . . nobody will laugh long, who deals much with opium: its pleasures are of a grave and solemn complexion; and in his happiest state the opium-eater cannot present himself in the character of *l'Allegro*; even then, he speaks and thinks as becomes *Il Penseroso*.

It was the drug of last resort, Thomas De Quincey acknowledged, taken only when liquor was too expensive. "Whereas wine disorders the mental faculties, opium, on the contrary . . . introduces amongst them the most exquisite order, legislation and harmony. For poets and the like this may amount to something special, but it's hardly what a hardworking diecutter looks to in a Saturday night rip-tear.

Addiction was not commonly stigmatized as a problem, nor does it appear to have been a widespread phenomenon, even with unlimited access to the drug. Everyone knew the proper and improper ways to use it, so unintentional overdoses were rare. A physician from Whittlesea in the Fens told a Royal Commission looking into the question that he'd concluded "beyond all doubt: 1) that the habit is extremely prevalent; 2) that the quantity consumed is very great; 3) that, after all, it does very little harm." Dr. Thomas Stiles, who practiced in the Fens from 1813 to the 1880s, deposed: "During my professional career extending over

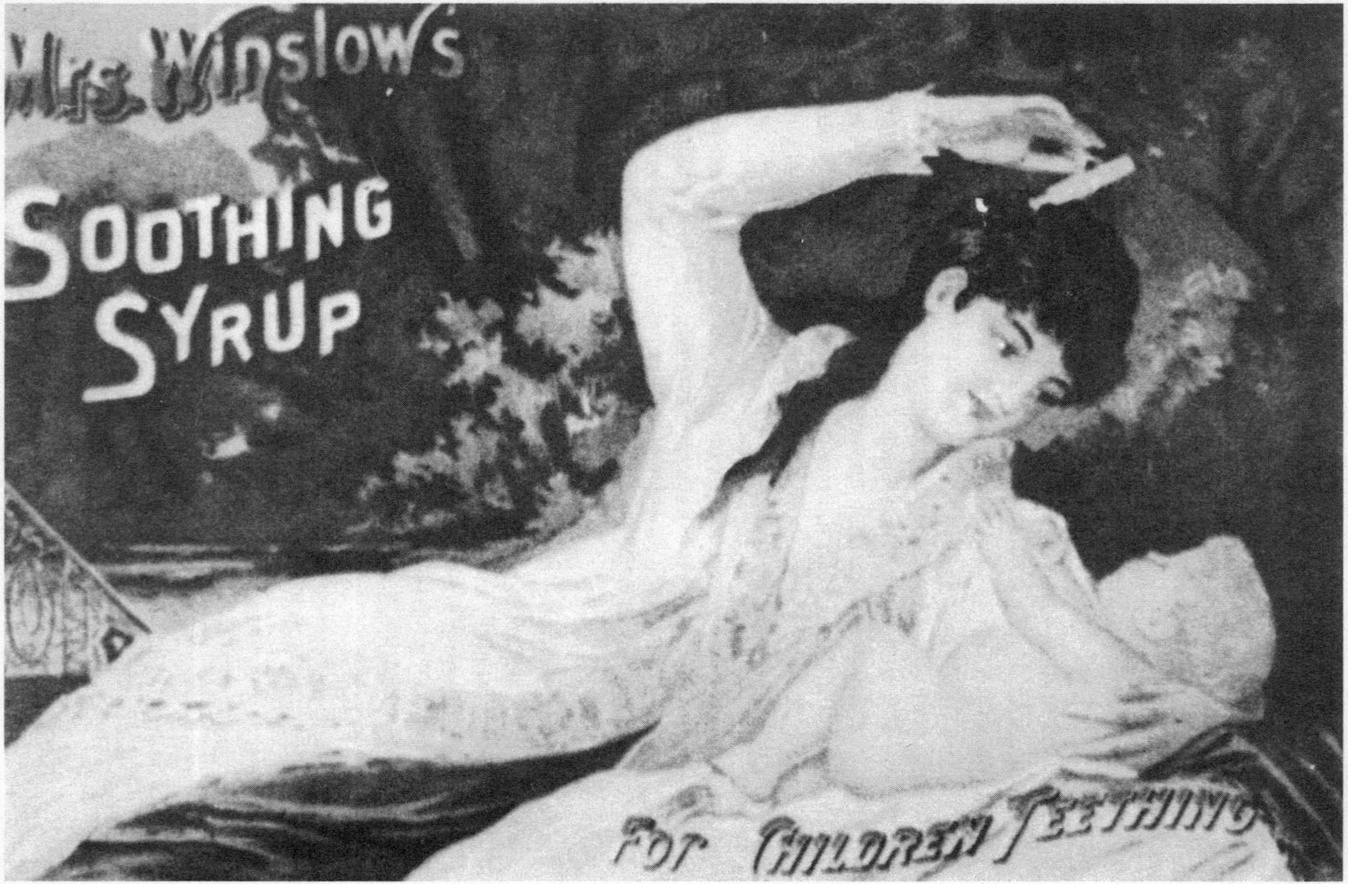
Mrs. Winslow's
SOOTHING
SYRUP
FOR CHILDREN TEETHING

a period of sixty-two years I cannot call to my remembrance that life has been shortened by the use of opiates or its being the cause of disease."

All very well for the yokels of the Fens, and the faceless multitude that inhabited England's tenements and shacktowns, but what about the better sort of people? There was an abiding conviction that people who labored in trade were a physical species apart from those who had better things with which to occupy themselves. As the Industrial Revolution progressed, and more people graduated out of the slums into the better circles, the differences between them and the faceless horde grew significant and fine. In *The Three Brides*, an 1850 improving novel by Charlotte Yonge, Lady Rosamond Charnok's infant is overdosed on Godfrey's Cordial by a slatternly nursemaid. After resuscitating the poor thing, the physician allows,

> It only remains to be proved whether an aristocratic baby can bear popular treatment. I dare say some hundred unlucky infants have been lugged out to the race-course today, and come back squalling their hearts out with hunger and fatigue, and I'll be bound that nine-tenths are lulled with this very sedative, and will be none the worse.

Well-off people took opiates, just as the mob took opiates, any time they got sick. Fewer of them probably took opium for the high, since they could afford spirits; but more of those who took them probably became addicted to opiates because they could afford them regularly. If they became addicted it usually resulted from their taking laudanum for the alleviation of physical maladies, generally abdominal complaints. Some became addicted on just a little opium, some took enormous quantities and never became addicted; some became "addicts" and made the drug the fulcrum of their daily existence, others took it as casually as they

Dosing babies with nostrums such as Mrs. Winslow's Soothing Syrup— a 10 percent morphine solution— scandalized the small British opium reform movement, but few others, in the mid-nineteenth century.

brushed their teeth in the morning; some got the crawly horrors, some got happy. A lot never noticed anything special at all.

> The King had this night a spasmodic bilious attack, though much slighter than in the month of June. He therefore wishes to see Sir George Baker as soon as convenient, and desires he will bring one of the opium pills in case the pain should not have entirely subsided.

Yes, King George III took opium and went crazy, in that order, but it wasn't junk-sickness that put him over the edge. His particular affliction was *porphyria*, a supremely fascinating hereditary nervous disease. In his proper person, the King was a supreme twitch, a perpetual self-caricature of tics and shakes and stutters and phantom anxieties, seemingly on the edge of catastrophic personality disintegration. Between that and the concomitant bellyaches, he was a fairly copious consumer of opium—until the grand fit of 1789, when his personality *did* disintegrate. That is to say, all of a sudden the tics and shakes and stutters disappeared, leaving him clear as a silver bell inside his head—and a million miles high. He couldn't eat, he couldn't sleep, he couldn't stop talking, and he couldn't remember from one half-hour to the next exactly who he was or what he was about. A new physician was brought in, Dr. George Willis, who suspended all medication and treated him with orthodox Heroic therapies—bleeding, blistering, leeching, sweating—and supportive psychotherapy. Gradually George pulled out of it, resumed the twitchy antics and the throne, and stayed more or less "sane" until 1810, when his mind fell apart for good and all. Toward the end, which was horribly delayed for ten more years, physical ailment ordained a resumption of the opium.

Though in limbo for longer than a decade, George remained officially the regent, which was one of the factors that sent the Prince of Wales to the bottle. His nerves never picked up even after he was finally anointed George IV, and the shakes periodically got so bad that opium was brought in as a detoxicant. Gossiped the Duke of Wellington:

> He drinks morning, noon and night, and is obliged to take Laudanum to calm the Irritation which the use of Spirits occasions . . . The Accoucheur and Halford don't agree about the use of Laudanum by the King. The former says it will drive him *mad*. Halford says

spirits will drive him mad, if Laudanum is not given, and that he will take it in larger doses if it is not administered in smaller. "At all events," he says to the Accoucher, "if you will get rid of the Spirits, I will of the Laudanum." So much for the King of England.

With everyone from kings to chimneysweeps so plentifully exposed to opiates, the British Empire would surely have crumbled into a land of craven drug addicts if there were any truth to the currently accepted thesis that the availability of narcotics precisely determines the number of addicts in the population. But the Empire was never in stouter shape than during this extremely extended opium epidemic. The vast majority of people who took opiates simply did not get addicted, and few who did stayed that way.

"It is not beyond conjecture," pathologist Dr. William Ober has concluded, "that addiction and drug-induced hallucinations may be culturally determined." The opium that was available freely to everyone in the English-speaking world before 1870 was fully as powerful as the miserably-diluted heroin that is blamed for calamitous addiction epidemics today; but the cultural mind set that obtained with opium in Britain was entirely different. It was mainly viewed as a medicine, taken on the occasion of illness, and taken regularly, in high doses, primarily in the face of death. Above all it was a death drug, associated in poetry with the waters of Lethe, the river of oblivion from which the dead drink to sever themselves from all living things. People whose lives could benefit positively from episodes of oblivion, like the working poor, took opiates for what a middle-class observer might misinterpret as "stimulation." Just about everyone else took it to ease illnesses that were otherwise intractable.

Dying on opium presented a moral quandary for the religious. Should one go to God insensible on a cloud of poppy dust, or with all faculties intact? Dr. Samuel Johnson opted for the stoical route, and discontinued all medication when the dropsy got impossibly out of hand: "I will take no more physick, not even my opiates; for I have prayed that I may render up my soul to God unclouded." The mother of Robert Southy was troubled by no such delicate considerations in her final moments. "She saw the colour of the water," the poet laureate recorded, "and cried, with a stronger voice than I had heard during her illness, 'That's nothing, Robert! thirty drops—six and thirty!'"

FIVE
THE DREAMERS

They were neighbors in the Lake Country of Westmoreland, and, very appropriately, they shared the services of Dr. Thomas Beddoes, the venerable apothecary of Bristol. Thomas De Quincey was thirteen years younger than Samuel Taylor Coleridge, and somewhat less disposed to infirmities, which may explain why he never became quite so addicted to laudanum. Coleridge was the ultimate addict: he had absolutely no control over his habit. He guzzled nearly two pints of laudanum per day for most of his life, and led a seesaw existence between pits of self-loathing and peaks of exalted creativity.

De Quincey's handle on the social graces was solid by comparison, though still quite unsteady: he was a confirmed eccentric, shabby, erratic, working all night and sleeping days, living on laudanum, tea, a few grains of rice and scraps of meat, in dusty rooms piled high with soiled, wrinkled, perpetually unfinished manuscripts. However, he kept appearances up to a level acceptable to the rather casual standards of the pre-Victorian nineteenth century, and anytime he saw himself getting close to a pint a day of the ruby-red elixir, he assiduously stepped down his dose.

De Quincey began taking laudanum at age twenty-eight, to medicate a chronic gastric ulcer dating from an episode of near-starvation ten years earlier, when young Tom spent a desolate winter in London without money or friends, save for a fifteen-year-old prostitute—Anne of Oxford Street—who in later years was a frequent apparition in his opium dreams. De Quincey had heard of opium as something exotic and mysterious, "as I had of manna or of ambrosia," when he tried his first-ever dose. The effects were fully up to his fanciful expectations.

"That my pains had vanished, was now a trifle in my eyes," he expounded some twenty years later. "This negative effect was swallowed up in the immensity of those positive effects which had opened before me—in the abyss of divine enjoyment thus suddenly revealed...Happiness might now be bought for a penny, and carried in the waistcoat pocket: portable ecstasies might be corked up in a pint bottle."

Since the time of ibn Sina, opium has worked wonders for ulcers, and the elixir quickly settled De Quincey's stomach; but he continued using it for its high, fascinated by the time-expanding, luminous, poetical hyperaesthesia it invoked. He'd set aside an "opium evening" every month, when he would quaff a hapenny's worth of laudanum and go out walking through the crowded London streets and marketplaces, awash in amplified color and sound. He kept up this practice until 1813. He was living in the Lake Country of Westmoreland then, a close friend of the Wordsworths, when he suffered a crippling ulcer attack and began taking laudanum daily. Within a few years he was up to a pint a day, which is where he tried to draw the line. He kept trying for the rest of his life.

The relations between De Quincey and the Wordsworth family, characterized by closeness and warmth since his move to Westmoreland in 1809, now became strained. Mrs. Wordsworth—having just nursed poor Coleridge through a prodigious bout of abstinence and relapse—was particularly horrified at Tom's decline. It helped not at all when instead of marrying, as had been expected, the Wordsworth's own Dorothy, he took up instead with a local farmer's daughter—Margaret Simpson—by whom he had a son in 1816, and married the following spring.

Though this casual marriage permanently chilled his relations with the Wordsworths, Margaret was good for Tom. He duly detoxified, gradually stepping down his dose to a half-pint per diem over a four-month period, and by 1821 to a mere jiggerful, but he never freed himself from the bonds of a daily dose, and was not really inclined to try. De Quincey's relation to his opium was at most times amicable, and sometimes exultant.

> Oh! just, subtle, and mighty opium! that to the hearts of poor and rich alike, for the wounds that will never heal, and for "the pangs that tempt the spirit to rebel," bringest an assuaging balm, eloquent opium! that with thy potent rhetoric stealest away the purposes of wrath; . . . that summonest the chancery of dreams, for the triumphs of suffering innocence . . . thou hast the keys of Paradise, oh, just, subtle, and mighty opium!

So he wrote in the *Confessions of an English Opium-Eater*, published anonymously in 1821 in *London* magazine. The book was an immense hit with the public, and rightfully so. The *Confessions* is one of the most succinct and insightful books on the subject of opium ever written; describing, in turn, the honeymoon pleasures of early use, the lethargy and nightmares of over-indulgence, and the "writhing, throbbing, palpitating" agitation of withdrawal, all in a thoroughly charming style. Readers and critics alike were delighted with De Quincey's "impassioned prose," his balmy collection of pseudo-Oriental drug fantasies, and with the phenomenon of recreational opium use itself.* Everyone in literary London wanted to meet the opium-eater. Coleridge, on the other hand, wanted to throttle him.

De Quincey was still experimenting with "opium evenings" in 1807 when the two men first met by chance in Bridgewater.** Coleridge by then was habituated to huge daily doses of laudanum, was no longer writing poetry and though producing some

---

*On the Continent, too, De Quincey's *Confessions* excited keen interest. Charles Baudelaire—who experimented with opium (as well as hashish) himself—included his translation of the *Confessions* in his book *Artificial Paradise*. Baudelaire was part of a circle of artists and writers calling themselves Le Club des Hashashchins. They toyed briefly with the idea that opium was a *machine à penser* (a thinking machine), and met regularly at the Hotel Lauzun to test the effects of opium and hashish on automatic writing.

**De Quincey exquisitely recorded the incident for posterity: "In height he might seem to be about five feet eight . . . his person was broad and full, and tended even to corpulence; his complexion was fair, but not what painters technically style fair, because it was associated with black hair; his eyes were large and soft in their expression, and it was by the peculiar appearance of haze or dreaminess which was mixed with their light that I recognized my object. This was Coleridge; I examined him steadfastly for a minute or

icily lucid literary criticism, was convinced that his genius had been irredeemably poisoned by opium. To make matters worse, between binges on the drug and repeated attempts to give it up at the hands of expensive quacks, he was continually short of money. De Quincey, recognizing in Coleridge a Brahmin of addiction, began tiding him over the worst of his debts.

When De Quincey settled in the Lake District the following year, they saw each other frequently, but their encounters were generally characterized not—as one might expect—by subterranean chatter about their strange mutual obsession, but by veiled allusions and suspicion. De Quincey was perfectly open about his opium-eating, but poor Coleridge was woefully embarrassed by his.

So he was understandably shaken when in the *Confessions* De Quincey, after noting that he himself had taken opium "to an excess not yet *recorded* of any other man," pointedly alluded to the *unrecorded* excesses of "one celebrated man of the present day." Coleridge, of course. The resulting scandal reverberated even after Coleridge died. In 1834 his editor, Joseph Cottle published a posthumous letter in which the poet accused De Quincey of taking opiates for pleasure, while defending his own use of the drug as *strictly* medicinal, "nor had I at any time taken the flattering poison as a stimulus." This, naturally, inspired De Quincey to launch acerbic broadsides at Coleridge in *Reminiscences of the Lake Poets* and the revised *Confessions*, attesting certain knowledge that Coleridge had on occasion enjoyed a surfeit of laudanum, and satirizing his uptight defensiveness.

To the end of his life, irascibly unredeemed, De Quincey would have none of the stigma of shame improving moralists and newspaper hacks attached to opium-taking. It would appear that the

---

more, and it struck me he neither saw myself, nor any other object in the street. He was in a deep reverie . . . The sound of my voice, announcing my own name, first awoke him; he started and for a moment seemed at a loss to understand my purpose or his own situation, for he repeated rapidly a number of words which had no relation to either of us. There was no *mauvais honte* in his manner, but simple perplexity, and an apparent difficulty in recovering his position amongst daily realities. This little scene over, he received me with a kindness of manner so marked it might be called gracious . . ."

majority of his countrymen shared this opinion (if they had one at all). Though his immoral stimulant use of the drug was soundly condemned in *John Bull*, and one moralist accused him of seducing others into "this withering vice through wantonness,"* public reaction to *Confessions* remained calm and even amused (several parodies of the book appeared in the popular press).

Though never able to repeat the success of the *Confessions*, the opium-eater took his laudanum and wrote prodigiously until he died, at 74, in 1859.

SAMUEL TAYLOR COLERIDGE

Samuel Taylor Coleridge was quite another story. Owing to the nature of the ailments for which he took it, and the extreme severity of his symptoms upon its withdrawal, opium was a mass of contradictions for him: it represented a terror and a blessing, solace and desolation, moral slavery and freedom from pain, exultation and "incurable depression." His compulsive use of laudanum in the early years of his career is all but universally blamed for throttling his creative capacities; throughout his life Coleridge himself encouraged this analysis. Yet, he assuredly couldn't deny that the drug was an inspiring force behind his most formidable poems—"Kubla Khan," "The Rime of the Ancient Mariner," and "The Pains of Sleep"—or that it literally kept him alive for many more years than might reasonably have been expected, given the state of the medical arts in the nineteenth century and the preposterous range of physical and emotional afflictions with which Coleridge was continually beset.

Although there is no doubt that he thoroughly appreciated the physical euphoria and emotional centeredness which opium conveyed—"struck with the deepest calm of Joy," he called it—all evidence indicates that, although he took it in prodigious quantities, he never took opium for the euphoria itself. Always he used it for the alleviation of pain and anxiety which, in the case of poor Coleridge, provided reasons enough.

---

*To which De Quincey replied: "Teach opium-eating! Did I reveal the mystery of sleeping?"

When Coleridge died and the predictable swarm of tabloid pundits and literary ghouls set out to lay the cause of his demise to opium, Dr. James Gilman of Highgate, London—who tended Coleridge from age forty-four to his death at sixty-three, doling out minimal daily maintenance doses of laudanum—promptly defused the rumors by discreetly circulating the postmortem results among the editors of literary journals. A monstrously enlarged heart had been discovered, along with a gross exuberance of lung fluid, the characteristic signs of acute bronchopneumonia occurring as a complication of long-standing chronic rheumatism, not opium poisoning.

Rheumatic fever so rarely crops up in industrialized countries that its etiology is now treated vaguely and perfunctorily in medical texts. It appears to be a "stress" disease, a periodic imbalance of adrenocorticotrophic functions involved not with bacteria or viruses, but with the individual's fundamental reactivity with the environment. It's in that class of diseases where the terms "psychosomatic" and "organic" are ineluctably mixed. It can be touched off arbitrarily by changes in the weather, by emotional stress, and maybe even by regular fluxes in the circadian or lunar cycle. Its acute advent is manifested by a sore throat and coughing—a nonviral cold—progressing to congested lungs, inflammation of the heart and stomach, goutlike swelling in the hands and feet, dizziness, fainting, shooting pains, insomnia, and migraine. With age, swelling of the heart and cardiac irregularities dependably develop, and the victim succumbs either to cardiac arrest or, like Coleridge, to pneumonia. The symptoms were gruesomely complicated and the attacks woefully frequent in Coleridge's case, but they could be miraculously quieted with laudanum.

On the slightest action of an uncongenial Air, from without, on the skin, or distressing disquieting Thoughts on the Digestive Organs from within, the *Secretories* of the skin commence a diseased Action/ if the *Absorbents* become languid, I have swellings, with moveable Fluid, in my knees and ancles/ & am bed-ridden/ if by means of opiates I revivify the actions of the Absorbents, I have no swellings nor eruptions—no bad knees, no Boils in my neck, & Thighs, no little agony-giving ulcers in my mouth, et

super Scrotum/ and *then* the diseased Action of the Secretories of
the Skin seems to be propagated into the Stomach, unless I so far
increase the Dose, as to enable the Stomach to repel it—in which
case the whole System obtains a *Temporary* Peace by the Equipose
of hostile Forces.

Coleridge was not sickly by nature. On good days he enjoyed
rock-cliff climbing, and immediately after any immobilizing illness, he made a point of hiking publicly at least sixty miles
nonstop. But this didn't keep him from getting truly sick on
occasion, with symptoms that would undoubtedly be treated with
powerful anabolic steroids today, but that were always treated
with opiates in the nineteenth century.

Coleridge had attacks of rheumatic fever from the age of nine,
when, in a fit of spite after his mother sided with a brother in an
argument, he ran away from home one evening and spent the
whole night on a clammy fen. As day broke he could hear men
dragging the Ottery River for his body, and giving up on it, while
he lay in the weeds immobilized with his throat swollen so thick
he could barely croak for help.

He was finally located that afternoon and rescued, sick half
to death. "I was put to bed and recovered in a day or so, but I
was certainly injured. For I was weakly and subject to the ague
for many years thereafter." The first flare-up of rheumatic ague
coincided with his father's death not much later.

Rheumatic agues were a familiar malady among people who
lived around clammy fens, as the exceptional prevalence of opium
in the soggy northern shires of England in this period indicates
(see Chapter 4). Opium was administered in heroic doses, of
course. When Coleridge's rheumatism blew up grandly during
orals at Jesus College, Cambridge, when he was nineteen, he
spent weeks in the infirmary. By every indication he became
thoroughly addicted there in 1791, and was never afterward very
far from a laudanum bottle.

For some reason, his most sympathetic biographers always try
to date his "onset of addiction" after 1800 though, probably so
that his "great" poetry, like "The Rime of the Ancient Mariner,"
would be uncontaminated by opium—as though anything created
by an "addict" ceases to be great as soon as the addiction is

disclosed.* Dating it after 1800 may also help pass the buck to "bad acquaintances" like Dr. Thomas Beddoes, who encouraged Coleridge's laudanum consumption for "stimulation," and Thomas Wedgewood, the inventor of silver-salt photography, who, together with the poet, experimented with hashish, chloryl hydrate, and henbane, as well as opium. Before 1800 he was presumably influenced by good acquaintances like Southey and Wordsworth. But it is apparent that, even as he and Wordsworth midwifed the Romantic movement in the 1790s with *Lyrical Ballads*, edition II, Coleridge was regularly dosing himself with opium and struggling to convey in words the ineffable mysteries of the drug.

That goal remained elusive. He could adequately convey the subjective sensations of opium, but it was hardly the proper stuff of romantic sonnets:

> What a beautiful thing Urine is, in a Pot, brown yellow, transpicuous, the Image, diamond shaped of the Candle in it, especially, as it now appeared, I have emptied the Snuffer into it, and the Snuff floating about, and painting all-shaped Shadows on the Bottom.

Besides, this is mere hyperasthesia, the acute stirring of the neophyte's entire sensorium on introduction to any agent that stirs it so very intimately. It happens with marijuana, but with opium it quickly ceases to occur with regular use because the body so readily gets cozy with the drug. After he'd gotten solidly readdicted in 1803, Coleridge rarely again sought to dwell so vividly on the immediate changes in perception induced by opium.

He was by then, anyway, much more concerned with the more distressing realities of opium use. Nightmares invaded his sleep as his dose wore off. Coleridge distinguished two sorts of "screamers" as he called them, "dreams of sorrow and pain" that left him "worsted but not conquered," and a special sort of imageless, limitless perception of haunted existential havoc that kept him afraid to go back to sleep for nights on end. There was also the bane of every addict's existence, constipation:

---

*Precisely this *did* happen. John Mackinnon Robinson attacked "The Ancient Mariner," "Christabel," and "Kubla Khan," after Coleridge's laudanum habit had been fully disclosed, as "*an abnormal product of an abnormal nature under abnormal conditions,*" all having been "*conceived and composed under the influence of opium.*"

> The dull quasi-finger on the Liver, the endless Flatulence, the frightful constipation when the dead Filth *impales* the lower Gut— to weep & sweat & moan & scream for the parturience of an excrement . . . O this is hard, hard, hard!

And, of course, there were the "allovers"—the withdrawal symptoms that set in whenever, with an excess of feeling healthy, he might suspend use. These appear to have been none too severe early on, consisting mainly of lively intestinal phenomena: "The wind & the hiccups," he called them, "as if the Demon of Hurricane were laying waste to my trillibub-plantation." But as time went on, any abrupt cessation of laudanum brought on far more catastrophic results:

> Distortion of the Body from agony, profuse and streaming sweats & fainting—at other times loosness with driping—frightful dreams with screaming—*breezes* of Terror blowing from the Stomach up thro' the Brain . . . frequent paralytic Feelings . . .

If these manifestations of junk-sickness seem preposterously colorful for mere laudanum, it helps to consider the particular brand which Coleridge favored—the Lancashire Genuine Black Drop, heartily commended by the renowned Quaker physician who produced it, Dr. John Airey Braithwaite. The unique virtue of Braithwaite's Black Drop, priced at the connoisseur rate of eleven shillings per four-ounce bottle, was its strength. To the Braithwaites, as devout Quakers, alcohol was a pernicious and unmanning poison. They accordingly bought only the "best Turkey Opium dried," and steeped it for days in saffron, cloves, and powerful *acetic acid*. The resulting nonalcoholic suspension was advertised as four times the strength of ordinary laudanum, and that was probably a modest claim. As in the case of Paracelsus' Anodyne Specific (see Chapter 3), prolonged acetylation of the morphine content of Lancashire Genuine Black Drop must have converted a good fraction of it into straight heroin.

Despite the pangs of rheumatism, Coleridge was constantly trying to leave off his "Old Blacky," never with more than transient success. In 1804 he attempted to detox on an ocean voyage to Malta. On Gilbraltar, however, during a few days' stopover, he appears to have sustained his first heart attack. "Heart . . . gnawing, palpitating—strange sense of stopping." Back on board, with the rheumatism oozing back into his lungs, Coleridge broke out the laudanum—just in time for the boat to be becalmed for nearly two weeks in the torpid Mediterranean. Perversely, a great handsome seabird materialized on the foresheets to be sniped at by the crew—a special thrill of gothic horror for Coleridge who was then in a horrendous phase of acute relapse. On Malta he manfully abstained for a week, but the ultimate "falling-abroad"—"My whole body & heart panting & shivering like an ague fit"—was sufficiently alarming that a local physician specifically prescribed laudanum for it. Soon after that experience, he stopped writing poetry and lapsed into chronic addiction.

From this point forward it appears that any attempt by Coleridge to detox brought on a prompt recurrence of full-blown rheumatism, filling his lungs with fluid and sparking dangerous fibrillations of his enlarged heart. This isn't to say he didn't try though. His last *"serious"* effort to rid himself of his laudanum habit occurred shortly after his chance meeting with De Quincey, described earlier in this chapter. On that occasion, Coleridge moved in with the Wordsworths at bucolic Allan Bank. For ten months in 1810 he stayed remarkably drug free, but in the early spring the rheumatism came back, and perforce came back Old Blacky, to the scandal of all. Dorothy Wordsworth, writing in her diary, lamented:

> We have no hope of him—none that he will ever do anything more than he has already done. If he were not under our Roof, he would be just as much the slave of stimulants as ever; and his whole time and thoughts (except when he is reading and he reads a good deal), are employed in deceiving himself, and seeking to deceive others.... This habit pervades all his words and actions, and you feel perpetually new hollowness and emptiness.

At length it was necessary for the Wordsworths to nag him out of the house. He moved to London, where he lived in a lamentable state of self-depredation, opium-intoxication, and squalor until 1816 when he had the good fortune to be introduced to Dr. James Gilman. That same year, at the age of forty-four—"in *all* but the Brain," he was aware, "an *old* man!"—Coleridge yielded himself up to the Gilman family in Highgate. He anticipated a month's stay but abode there for thirteen years. Having gone through no less than seven detox attempts in the six years since the Wordsworths had evicted him from Allan Bank, Coleridge was none too sanguine about the prospects of success. His various wardens before Dr. Gilman had scrupulously endeavored to keep him away from Old Blacky altogether, which was not only quixotic, but inimical to his health.

However, kept by Dr. Gilman on a low drug dosage, Coleridge thrived and even found his ultimate *metier* as a transcendentalist philosopher, deliverer of grand monologues in the style of Dr. Samuel Johnson, to a perpetually enthralled audience of young bluestocking ladies and brooding incipient poets. His "table talks" in the Gilman dining hall evolved into a veritable tourist attraction, especially for visitors from America, where a full-blown Coleridge cult had developed.

In this enlightened day and age, Dr. Gilman would be properly jailed for giving laudanum to any addicted patient, however renowned. As the physician on the spot, Gilman's conviction that Coleridge's complicated and agonizing rheumatic maladies required opium a great deal more than the conventions of propriety required him to abstain from it, would be insignificant nowadays.

Gilman even appears to have brilliantly incorporated Coleridge's notorious sneakiness into his maintenance schedule; once every five days, a local chemist's apprentice later revealed, Coleridge would skulk furtively into their shop and buy a four-ounce bottle of laudanum. After Coleridge was safely dead—struck down by the "gout", preceded by considerable suffering, at Highgate in 1834—Thomas De Quincey published a few choice anecdotes along this wise.

> He went so far as to hire men—porters, hackney-coachmen and others—to oppose by force his entrance into any druggists' shop. But, as the authority for stopping him was derived simply from himself, naturally these poor men found themselves in a metaphysical fix, not provided for even by Thomas Aquinas or the prince of Jesuitical casuists. And in this excruciating dilemma would occur such scenes as the following:—
>
> "Oh, sir," would plead the suppliant porter—suppliant, yet semi-imperative (for equally if he *did* and if he did *not*, show fight, the poor man's daily 5s. seemed endangered)—"really you must not; consider, sir, your wife and—"
>
> *Transcendental Philsopher.*—"Wife! What wife? I have no wife."

Porter.—"But, really now, you must not, sir. Didn't you say, no longer ago than yesterday—"

Transcendental Philosopher.—"Pooh, pooh! yesterday is a long time ago. Are you aware, my man, that people are known to have dropped down dead for timely want of opium?"

It went on like that as long as Coleridge stayed under Dr. Gilman's care—thirteen years. And though it plagued him and shamed him this was, thanks to his laudanum, a good deal longer than he had any reasonable prospect of living at all.

Though at first associated with only the careers of De Quincey and Coleridge, in time opium surfaced in the lives of Elizabeth Barrett Browning, John Keats, Wilkie Collins, and so many other literary lights of the nineteenth century that it became the subject of scholarly inquiry and fierce critical debate. "Is drug mentality to set a standard for English poetry and prose? Is drug imagination to be the matrix in which we shape the imaginative powers?" lamented Jeanette Marks in *Genius and Disaster.* "It means a clear-eyed acceptance of the abnormal, of the diseased, of the morbid, as pacemaker in what we call our best literary achievements." Other critics have taken a psychoanalytic tack, groping for a consistent pathological thread of morbid imagery in the work of the writers who have taken opium.

The attempt to define "drug imagination," or to find consistency in the opium experience, however, flies in the face of biological fact; for no two people are affected by opium in exactly the same way, and in the highly individual world of writers and poets this is especially the case.

De Quincey would spend time in his florid Chinese chambers (things Oriental were all the rage then), with all manner of chinoiserie bric-a-brac about him. Here, understandably, he was "hooted at, grinned at, chattered at by monkeys, by perroquets, cocatoos . . . ran into pagodas . . . was fixed for centuries in secret rooms . . .was worshiped . . . was sacrificed . . . fled from the wrath of Brahma through the forests of Asia . . . was buried for a thousand years in stone coffins with mummies and sphinxes . . . was kissed with cancerous kisses by crocodiles and laid, confounded with unutterable slimy things, amongst reeds and Nilotic mud." Coleridge studied his urine in the chamber pot. A century later, the French filmmaker and poet Jean Cocteau nodded out in Pablo Picasso's elevator after a dose of opium and saw an angel. Graham Greene, after a night in a Saigon opium den, met the Devil "wearing a tweed motoring coat and a deer-stalker cap."

Surely, it's not the drug, but the dreamer. This is nowhere more clearly illustrated than among the other literary opium-eaters of England.

WALTER SCOTT

Sir Walter was the victim of recurrent gastric troubles which several times led him to work up a high opium tolerance, but he never failed to kick it as soon as his digestion was back in trim. Scott viewed opium as a necessary but unpleasant medication; the high for him was just an annoying clouding of consciousness, the lethargy was an obnoxious interference with his social life, and the sniffles and runs after it was discontinued were just another predictable annoyance of this miserable nostrum.

Afflicted with periodic abdominal complaints as severe in every way as acute appendicitis, Scott *had* to take opium, as nothing else would work. "Roaring like a bull-calf" with the agonies, he would dictate his fiction to an appalled bedside stenographer, literally writhing around in the sheets with cramps, taking just enough laudanum to keep himself articulate through the pain. In this way he composed an entire historical romance, *The Bride of Lammermoor* (soon to be a major Verdi opera), in 1819. On this occasion, though, the pain was so bad, that Scott actually dosed himself into a state of ultimate abstraction. After he'd detoxified, and they gave him the proofs to correct, "he did not recollect one single incident, character or conversation it contained." Scott gingerly proofread *The Bride*: "For a long time I felt myself very uneasy in the course of my reading, lest I should be startled by meeting something altogether glaring and fantastic." Though to a casual reader *The Bride* fits in pretty well with the rest of Sir Walter Scott's historical fables, he himself termed it "monstrous, gross and grotesque." Sir Walter simply did not *like* opium; it was a strictly medical necessity, and he shed it with minimal trouble as soon as the bellyache went away.

JOHN KEATS

This morning I am in a state of temper indolent and supremely
careless... my passions are all asleep from my having slumbered
till nearly eleven and weakened the animal fibre all over me to
a delightful sensation about three degrees this side of faintness—
if I had teeth of pearl and the breath of lilies I should call it
languor—but as I am* I must call it laziness—in this state of
effeminacy the fibres of the brain are relaxed in common with the
rest of the body, and to such a happy degree that pleasure has no
show of enticement and pain no unbearable frown.

*Especially as I have a black eye.

The afternoon before John Keats put this in his private journal,
in mid-March of 1819, he had been clouted on the eye with a
cricketball during a lively match in the yard of his chum Charles
Armitage Brown. A nasty mouse appeared on the twenty-four-
year-old poet's sublime peaches-and-cream countenance, smart-
ing and upsetting him. Brown had a little opium and gave Keats
some of it that evening as a palliative, recalled a friend later, and
the euphoric afterglow of the following morning, as described
above, remains perhaps the choicest description of the state of
mind sought by all occasional users of opiates.

Keats was—in contemporary street argot—a chipper, the first
case on record of anyone primarily using opiates for the sake of
the high, in sub-therapeutic doses, at extended, nonaddictive intervals. The occasion of his black eye at Armitage Brown's was
obviously the first time he'd done it himself—the flavorsome
sense of novelty conveyed in his private journal next morning
leaves no question about that, though he'd certainly observed the
same thing in others before then. A certified apothecary, former
intern at Saint Thomas's hospital in London, Keats was thoroughly familiar with the effects of laudanum. All through the
previous year, for instance, Keats had nursed his older brother
Tom through a long drawn-out case of terminal tuberculosis.
Laudanum was a specific treatment for consumption, since it
quelled coughing and reduced phlegm, and Tom must have
needed plenty of it. But ultimately he died, after weeks of repeated
crises during which John stayed alone with him in one stuffy
room. By the following March, John himself knew that the cough
he'd developed afterward was going to kill him.

More than the pain of the cricketball shiner, then, Armitage Brown's opium clearly defused that physically-felt premonition of fulminating doom in the poet's mind and lower thorax; and it arrested the rush of time, centering Keats in a luscious English springtide, maybe his last. A couple of weeks later, "Ode To Indolence":

> *Ripe was the drowsy hour;*
> *The blissful cloud of summer-indolence*
> *Benumb'd my eyes; my pulse grew less and less;*
> *Pain had no sting, and pleasure's wreath no flower.*

Over the next year, Keats did his best work: "The Eve of St. Agnes," "Lamia," "Ode To A Nightingale," a concentrated corpus of the finest English verse of the Romantic movement. Of it all, only "Ode To A Nightingale" has paid off for later analysts looking for evidence of "drug influence" on Keats's work. In the sense that "Nightingale" conveys typical drug-induced perceptions, like the blending of space into time and the transmutation of colors to tastes and odors, it unquestionably shows that Keats had closely observed his own subjective experiences on opium. Ecstatic poets like John Donne, in whom such sensory events were prompted by plain premorbid insanity, never could have blended them into Keats's sublime unitive apperception of Romantic wholeness within the living world. Withal, this conception of ecstatic wholeness was preexistent in Keats and capable of attainment by ordinary reflection and meditation. "Nightingale" was not an advertisement for laudanum as an agent of transcendental consciousness; it was a very successful experiment in conveying the whole experience in conventions of opiate imagery.

Speaking broadly, Keats's work in the period when he was chipping seems mainly informed by a monumental desire to have it all said, as much as he could possibly say, as perfectly as possible in the Romantic idiom. The cough kept coming back, with headaches and lassitude, all the signs of consumption so unmistakably manifested that even his friends became aware of it. The outpouring of brilliance over these last two years of Keats's life was prompted most by his inward conviction of responsibility to have it all said before it was too late.

If anything, opium may have interfered a little with this frantic project, by introducing young John to concepts that were rather outside the classic range of romantic imagery. Since he never became addicted, he never recorded the spectacular nightmares or grotesque intestinal claustrophobia of Coleridge and the others. But there were definitely things shown him by opium which stirred him profoundly, while staying a tantalizing trace beyond his repertoire of expression.

He was in love, impossibly in love, with Fanny Brawne, a young lady his friends and family openly considered beneath him. So he kept his love a secret, fearful lest a candid revelation of his feelings might upset those closest to him. For this same reason, presumably, Keats secretly masked his tubercular symptoms with laudanum. The progress of the disease must have shocked him since, as a trained physician, he could tell from the signs, even masked by opium, how desperately little time he had left. But to tell his friends that he was self-medicating with laudanum would have horrified them just as deeply as to learn that he was critically ill. Four years before, Samuel Taylor Coleridge had been the scandal of the literary world, sunk into the uttermost craven depths of laudanum addiction, alternately scrabbling for help from his friends, brutally humiliating them, and reverting to hopeless squalor. Coleridge was now sequestered respectably away from temptation—at least he was no longer public—and laudanum had become the very *bête noir* of all Keats's well-meaning friends and guardians.

So when he was finally found out, there was hell to pay. With his creative outpouring that year had come national celebrity, and the inevitable clutch of old creditors demanding payment. John's upward-striving brother George had involved the whole family in a series of improbable financial speculations, most notably an American investment scheme which had featured some expensive transatlantic junketing, and ruinous bills. In January of 1820, financial obligations mounted to the point where John was fain to drop all works in progress to attend to them. In the subsequent depression—he never did, after that, have time to finish anything as perfect as "St. Agnes"—someone caught him taking opium, and tattled to his grand friend and guardian, George Armitage Brown, who later congratulated himself:

It was discovered by accident, and, without delay, revealed to me. He needed not be warned of the danger of such a habit; but I rejoiced at his promise never to take another drop without my knowledge; for nothing could induce him to break his word, when once given.

Keats assuredly knew at this point that his consumption had proceeded beyond the point where laudanum could mask it.

At this point Keats was no longer looking at laudanum as a medication anyway, or even as an interesting high, but as a possible alternative way to go.

His months at Tom's bedside, just over a year before, were understandably vivid for John. "Ode to Melancholy" written in 1819 is pervaded with veiled suicidal imagery, in which the oblivion-inducing waters of the River Lethe unmistakably refer to his laudanum bottle: "No, no, go not to Lethe," there's time yet. A year later, in September of 1820, his benevolent friends agreed that a change of air would be just the thing for the wasting youngster, and they put him on a ship to Italy. From there his artistic companion, Joseph Severn, wrote, just weeks before Keats finally died in a spectacular access of coughing:

> The hardest point between us is that cursed bottle of opium . . . he had determined on taking this the instant his recovery should stop . . . he says to save him the extended misery of a long illness . . . in his own mind he saw this fatal prospect . . . the dismal night . . . the impossibility of receiving any sort of comfort . . . and above all the wasting of his body and helplessness . . . these he had determined on escaping . . . and but for me . . . he would have swallowed this draught 3 months since . . . in the ship . . . he says 3 wretched months I have kept him alive.

ELIZABETH BARRETT BROWNING

There were as many diagnoses for Mrs. Browning's troubles as there were physicians to attend her; whatever may have been wrong with her, modern palaeodiagnosticians pretty much agree that the reknowned invalid of Wimpole Street was basically afflicted with agoraphobia, a morbid fear of leaving the house. And why indeed *should* she leave the house? From 1837 on she was taking pure isolated morphine for her "neurasthenia," the status affliction of cultivated Victorian ladies. As she explained to Robert, when he asked if she mightn't think of dropping her dose:

Elizabeth Barrett Browning (1806–61).
"So the medical people gave me opium—a preparation of
it, called morphine, and ether—and ever since I have
been calling it my amreeta draught, my elixer—because
the tranquillizing power has been wonderful."

It might strike you as strange that I who have no pain—no acute suffering to keep down from its angles—should need opium in any shape. But I have had restlessness until it made me almost mad: at one time I lost the power of sleeping quite—and even in the day, the continual aching sense of weakness has been intolerable—besides palpitation—as if one's life, instead of giving movement to the body, were imprisoned undiminished within it, and beating and fluttering impotently to get out, at all the doors and windows. So the medical people gave me opium—a preparation of it, called morphine, and ether—and ever since I have been calling it my amreeta draught, my elixer—because the tranquillizing power has been wonderful.

"I do not suffer from it in any way, as people usually do who take opium," she related reassuringly. "I am not even subject to an opium headache." Any time she felt a headache coming on, without doubt, she promptly consulted her amreeta draught. Her idea of heaven was to sit forever in a whispering grove of cedars with tablet and quill, "in an hourly succession of poetical paragraphs and morphine draughts." She supposedly detoxed briefly after marrying Robert, long enough to have their baby (though the idea of Elizabeth Barrett Browning getting through full-blown morphine withdrawals challenges the imagination), but she stayed on her elixer the rest of her life, with no recorded troubles. Since no one told her there was anything wrong with taking morphine—it had none of the stigma attached to opium—then there *was* nothing wrong with it. From every evidence, it was very good for her indeed.*

WILKIE COLLINS

When Charles Dickens died in 1870, leaving behind the half-finished manuscript of *The Mystery of Edwin Drood*, with only the mutterings of an old opium-eating hag hinting at a solution to the mystery, Dickens' publishers started ferreting around for someone to finish the tale. Their first choice was Dickens' close friend Wilkie Collins. Though he declined, Collins was an apt

---

*Today "the medical people" most commonly put neurasthenic women on Valium.

choice to decipher such opiated ramblings. His own book *The Moonstone*, published two years before, revolved intimately around opium: the hero Franklin Blake, under the influence of a surreptitious dose of laudanum, snatches the valuable Moonstone diamond, and despite the unswerving attentions of Scotland Yard's famous Sergeant Cuff, the mystery is only unraveled when a retiring doctor's assistant, Ezra Jennings—who is himself an opium addict—prompts Blake to recreate the crime by giving him another draught. This plot device was hardly an accident. Collins, it was well known, swallowed daily doses of laudanum and morphine.

He began taking opiates in 1862 to relieve the spasms of a rheumatic gout, which wracked his face and attacked his eyes with special vengeance. "His eyes were literally enormous bags of blood," wrote his friend Charles Kent, describing one of Wilkie's famous attacks. Collins suffered a particularly agonizing spasm during the writing of *The Moonstone*. Years later—borrowing to what degree we will never know from the life of Walter Scott—he was fond of describing how his writhing and moaning drove away two secretaries, and how his laudanum put him in such a daze that he did not recognize the finale of the book as his own.

Yet, Collins shared none of Scott's antipathy for opium, which was, as he thought, a tonic "to stimulate the brain and steady the nerves," as well as a remedy for eye-gout. And over his lifetime he consumed a prodigious amount of it to make him better when he was well, as well as when he was sick.

He spoke about all this openly, and without the slightest guilt, to family, friends and—to their dismay—even to strangers, relishing the stunned reaction of dinner guests at the revelation that his daily dose was more than enough to kill a normal man. To illustrate, he would jovially relate the sad tale of his manservant, George Hello, who out of curiosity one day drank only half of Collins' normal dose, and promptly died.

But neither Wilkie Collins's writing style nor his output seems to have been influenced at all by opium. He churned out his long intricately-plotted thrillers in crisp clear prose with a machine-like efficiency that still confounds those who would argue that the continued use of opiates freezes the creative juices. In fact hardworking, jolly, and extremely sociable Collins was an exception to almost every addict stereotype. He was so self-possessed that he was able to maintain—apparently without emotional havoc or scandal—a "morganic" family, consisting of two mistresses and two sets of children living within blocks of each other in London.

Laudanum did, however, present a few inconveniences. There was the persisting idea that someone was standing behind him, and that "reptile of the pre-Adamite period" that sometimes sat in his study staring at him, and those phantoms that followed him to bed when he worked late, and that green woman at the top of the stairs, the one with the tusk teeth who bid him goodnight, every night, by biting a piece out of his shoulder. Collins, however, approached his hallucinations as he approached everything else in life, with jocular equanimity: he continued to carry his silver hip flask of laudanum with him wherever he went, and scrivened away until his death, after a stroke in 1889.

There were others, of course. All the Romantic poets—with the exception of Wordsworth—are on record as having experimented with opiates, mostly to alleviate their ailments, sometimes for the high, and in at least one case, to medicate a broken heart.

Byron kept a vial of laudanum with him constantly during the breakup of his marriage. Lady Byron, going through a trunk he'd left behind after they'd parted, found a bottle of Kendal Black Drop and—still more horrifying—a copy of deSade's *Justine*. Though Byron found laudanum a superb therapeutic to deaden the pangs of love-sickness and grief, as soon as he was back on his feet, he stopped taking it. "I don't like laudanum as I used to do," he noted in 1821, adding that he found spirits quite more stimulating and pleasurable.

Shelley took opiates for nervous headaches, Robert Southey for hay fever, and George Crabbe for a cranky stomach. Crabbe— the venerable Anglican parson—began taking laudanum in 1790 at the age of thirty-eight, and was still taking it daily when he died at the age of eighty. Crabbe's use of opium was strictly medicinal, and there is no shred of evidence that it affected either his dulcet, realistic verse—always precisely rendered in heroic couplets—nor his impeccable morals.* His loved ones in fact encouraged his practice of taking opium. "To a constant but slightly increasing dose of it," wrote his son, "may be attributed his long and generally healthy life."

Though critics may rave amain about the effects of opium on the creative imagination, one thing is abundantly clear: there was nothing abnormal, morbid, or diseased about the way opium relieved the physical ailments of these writers. When illness struck, opium was as much a boon to them as it was to everyone else in the eighteenth and nineteenth centuries.

Well, almost everyone else.

Charlotte Bronte, though she wrote a long evocative opium dream into her last novel *Villette*, swore she never took so much as a grain of opium during her whole chronically-ill lifetime. Charlotte and her sister authors, Emily and Anne, lived most of their lives with their father, the Rev. Patrick Bronte in Haworth, Yorkshire—a district far north of, and every bit as clammy and pestilant as the Fens. The citizens of Yorkshire, like the Fenlanders, were noted mainly for their loutish ways and loathsome ailments. The health of the two younger sisters was broken in short order, and first Emily (at twenty-nine), then Anne (at twenty-seven) went coughing daintily to melancholy graves. Charlotte lingered to thirty-nine, wrote three novels, and suffered constantly from "indigestion, nausea, headache, sleeplessness, all combined to produce miserable depression of the spirits." But she stoically renounced opiates.

Her attitude was surely influenced to a degree by her father, the pious Rev. Patrick, who'd dedicated his life to turning away

---

*Crabbe was about as far removed from the stereotypic image of a craven drug fiend as one can get. In fact he is most often portrayed as an ultra-amiable square. A case in point occurred in 1817, when Crabbe—then sixty-five and a widower—journeyed to London to receive the accolades of the literati there. At a party he was set upon by Lady Caroline Lamb—a notorious woman, who had penned a naughty book, *Glenarvon*, and had broken up Byron's marriage. Crabbe was dumbfounded by her chatter—"The woman absolutely holds for the doctrine of irresistible passion," he wrote later. He was even less prepared for the breathless letter he received the next morning from Lady Caroline, declaring that the previous evening had been "like a corkscrew in my heart . . . pray forgive all this do not write an answer I need none and burn this letter." (She affixed an addendum advising him to use leeches, not opium for a toothache, "for all opiates inflame the gum.")

the Haworth yokels from such loutish vices as cursing, drinking, and opium-eating. But in the case of the Brontes of Haworth, shame as well as piety and pride shaped their attitude toward opiates. In the household, there was a pariah-child, a drug-abuser—brilliant, unhappy brother Branwell.

Thomas De Quincey's wicked *Confessions* were sometimes blamed for Branwell's downfall, but the real precipitating cause seems to have been the young man's entanglement with a married woman, a certain Mrs. Robinson. Branwell was twenty-one years old when he met her, and twenty-seven when the affair ended disastrously, and the heartbroken wretch—much to his family's dismay—began dosing himself with opium.

The last three years of his life (he died in 1848, age thirty) were a continuing horror for the Bronte family. There were con-frontations, tears, promises to renounce the drug, inevitable re-lapses, screaming tantrums and lies to put up with. "In procuring it he showed all the cunning of the opium-eater," wrote Charlotte Bronte's biographer Elizabeth Gaskell. "He would steal out while the family were at church—to which he professed himself too ill to go—and manage to cajole the village druggist out of a lump." All of which made poor Charlotte and her sisters fright-fully upset. There were nights, Miss Bronte confessed, when they lay awake trembling and sick with fear, waiting for a pistol shot from the bedroom shared by Branwell and the senior Bronte; in the morning, double-bind recriminations, resentment, guilt. Stunned by the spectacle, Charlotte allowed, "No sufferings are so awful as those of dissipation."

After Branwell died, life returned to normal in the dank Bronte cottage. The week of the funeral Charlotte complained: "Head-ache and sickness came on . . . I could not regain my appetite. Then internal pains attacked me. I became at once much reduced. It was impossible to touch a morsel. At last bilious fever declared itself . . ." But opium was never again seen in the Bronte house-hold.

SIX
CHINA:
THE OPIUM WARS

By hugging close to the long sandy spit south out of Singapore harbor, and then standing far out into the Karimata Straight, an opium clipper could catch the dependable northeasterly winds most times of year, and bear straight up past Siam through the South China Sea to Hong Kong Harbor. Handsome vessels these clippers, testament to American ingenuity: in full bloom before the wind, white and fat to the top t'gallants, skysails and moon-rakers sweeping wide to either side of the lowslung hull, a clipper could scud through the tropical swell at twenty-some knots, proud and white and felicitous as a pregnant hen. The only impediment to an opium clipper's handsome pace was the two or three tons of cast-iron ordnance aboard, big-bellied cannon and squat black sea mortars, for the benefit of the Borneo pirates. By the 1830s, when Jardine-Matheson and Company of London began putting Baltimore clippers on the opium line, the pirates already knew better than to take out after any ship running the Union Jack and the Jardine-Matheson corporate colors.

Pilotage became delicate and important whenever the ship finally approached the island-dotted outermost lighting of Hong Kong Harbor, three weeks out of Calcutta, five from Bombay. The pilot, generally a native familiar with the outer islands, would be hoisted aloft to the mainmast lookout with mirror-signaling semaphore gear, and cry out whenever he sighted Jardine's

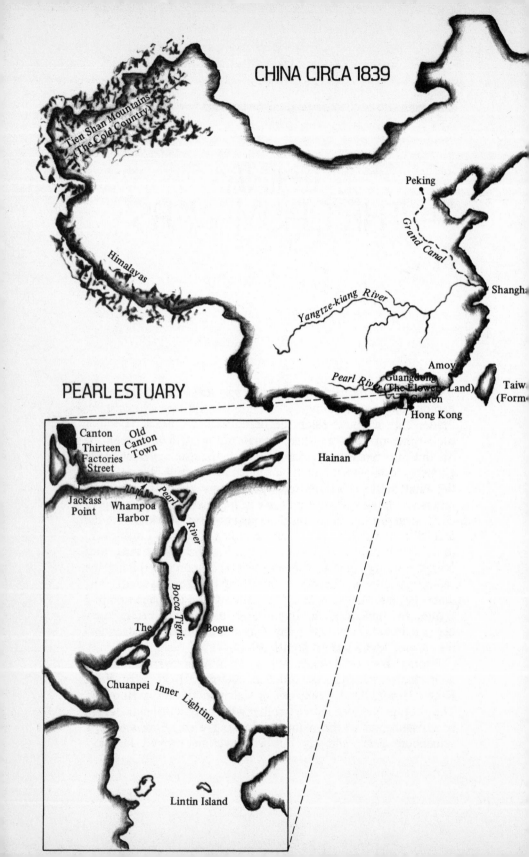

CHINA CIRCA 1839

Tien Shan Mountains
(The Cold Country)

Himalayas

Peking

Grand Canal

Shangh

Yangtze-kiang River

Pearl River

Amoy

Guangdong
(The Flowery Land)
Canton

Taiw
(Form

Hong Kong

Hainan

PEARL ESTUARY

Canton
Thirteen
Factories
Street

Old
Canton
Town

Jackass
Point

Whampoa
Harbor

Pearl

River

Bocca Tigris

The

Bogue

Chuanpei Inner Lighting

Lintin Island

Point—the very tip of the first misty blue mountain to poke up over the horizon (now Victoria Point). The pilot would signal the Jardine-Matheson Company crew permanently stationed on the point, as the ship reefed in sail to the navigational foreshrouds, and began circling patiently in the water, well out of sight of land. Daily, the Jardine's Point shoreline crew would mirror back a holding pattern to the opium ship, down over the horizon, day after day as she circled invisibly, until the time was ripe for her to proceed ahead to Chuanpei Bay and the Pearl River.

With this arrangement, none of the opium buyers at the smuggler's market on Lintin Island in Chuanpei would know that an opium clipper was standing off Hong Kong, packed with drug. Sometimes, when the Lintin buying price was quite low, the Jardine's Point signalers would stack up three or five opium cutters at once below the horizon, until an opium drought set in at Canton and prices went back up.

Jardine-Matheson and Company weren't the only opium traders in Hong Kong, unfortunately. The Portuguese in the thirties still ran a brisk trade through Macao, the romantic colonial city they leased from the Celestial Empire at the western end of vast Chuanpei Bay, and the Portuguese could still upset the market considerably with huge unexpected shipments of Malwa opium from West India, though the Honourable Company back there was efficiently pushing out the last of them. Much more annoying were the independent traders, American interlopers running in regular consignments of Turkey opium, and small India-based firms like David Sasoon & Sons delivering the stray cargo of Malwa now and then.

Whenever one of these scabby entrepreneurs turned up, Jardine-Matheson and Company would have to quickly reverse policy and instigate a ruinous smuggling glut at Lintin. When their agents sighted a Yank or Sasoon opium ship tying up at Lintin, they would summon up the fastest clipper they had on hand off Hong Kong, moor her right next to the interlopers, and methodically undersell the cargo. This would be a great day for the CoHong opium buyers at Canton, who now could pick up untold catty chests of drug for a song, and the poor Jardine-Matheson corporate clerks in Hong Kong would fret for weeks about skimpy prices and lack of buyers; but if the underbidding put Jardine-

British opium inspector in India, circa 1908.
Though British traders were shipping far less opium
to China, cultivation of the poppy in Patna and Malwa,
which had expanded enormously as a result of British-
instituted management techniques, continued unabated.

Matheson a little in the red for a bit, it would hopefully *ruin* whoever had invested in that independent load of opium. "Competition has ruined the opium trade for a time," Joseph Jardine would reflect philosophically, "and now we must wait for the trade to ruin our competitors."

The wonderful thing was that opium was technically illegal in China. Jardine-Matheson could pull even less savory stunts than underbidding on their European competition, and never worry about lawsuits, writs of distraint, or outright arson-and-battery charges being pressed by the victims. "If the trade is ever legalized, it will cease to be profitable from that time," Jardine-Matheson's directors were forever warning their shoreline connections. "The more difficulties that attend it, the better for you and us."

> The Bengal Opium is made into balls about the size of two fists, and covered over with a hard skin, made of the petals of the poppy, each ball having a separate apartment in the chest when sent off to market. The chest is made of mango-wood, and consists of two stories, each story containing 20 balls.

By official record, about 18,000 such double-decker catty chests were run from India to China in 1833, mostly by Jardine-Matheson and Company, and more were moved every year thereafter. All through this encouraging expansion, true to Jardine-Matheson theory, the legal difficulties which beset the trade intensified; commerce in "this article" manifestly throve on the succession of ferocious prohibitions which the Imperial authorities officially imposed on it.

One basic advantage of prohibition to the trade was that it very effectively tightened up the buying end of the connection. The Canton CoHong merchants—ten family guilds licensed by the emperor in Peking, over his better judgment to trade with foreigners—became smugglers by legal definition in this matter of trading opium. The offloading crews they sent down from Canton to Lintin to pick up the drug—professional pirates from Borneo, the Andamans, Molucca, the Phillipines—were sufficient by themselves to scare off neophyte interlopers, as they came swarming out in veritable war-praus, called "scuttling crabs," to cluster nightly around the opium ships.

> These boats are in general manned by 30 or 40 persons of a very active class, armed with pikes, stones, and other missile weapons,

which they are very dexterous in throwing. On receiving the opium it is usually taken out of the chests and put into bags, as a more ready package to remove it in, and one that exposes them less to discovery; for although the Mandarins, under the influence of extensive bribery, which their cupidity seldom prevents them from accepting, are generally blind to the operations passing within their district, yet they are obliged, frequently from policy as well as from other causes, to shew great vigilance, which sometimes ends in capture.

Why the official Chinese would periodically raise such a righteous fuss over opium was quite beyond the understanding of Jardine-Matheson and their ilk. But then, that whole end of the India-China trade was in general a characteristically Oriental conundrum, obscure and infinitely complex, the source of continual annoyance for the trade. Mandarin import-export officials would blithely go along for years with the traditional Cantonese bribery rituals—the Squeeze—and then temporarily become ferocious proponents of law and order, and then lapse just as abruptly back into the Squeeze. They were liable to be cashiered by Peking, with terrible humiliations and mayhem, whether they went along with the Squeeze or fought zealously against it. There was no telling, from day to day, which Hong corporation of the extensive Canton Interest might be in official favor, and thus trustworthy to deal with on credit; for a particular Hong guild might be flush as the King of Siam one month, place an enormous opium order with Jardine-Matheson, and be not just broke when the clipper presently hauled in from Calcutta, but be most inconveniently dispersed—some investors beheaded, others strangled or mutilated, a few exiled to the faraway Cold Country, and the rest parading daily down Chaoyin Street, shorn of their queues, wearing great oaken punishment yokes called "cangues" and placards advertising their wickedness as traffickers in the foreign mud for smoking. This sort of nonsense kept the trade in continual disorder, prices forever in a muddle, buyers either scrabbling for more drug, or too fat and smug to buy at any price. Or dead.

If the Chinese would only have confided in the European commodity movers, the trade could have been prosecuted with much more expedience. But no, a perfect veil of obscurity confounded the entire China market: no one knew whither the Canton Interest moved the drug once bought, or whom exactly its consumers were, how many of them there might be, how much money they might have from month to month, whether they were enfamished or prosperous, earthquake-smitten or cyclone-struck—damned unsatisfactory way to do business, this, by rumor and hint. But the Mandarins and CoHong guilds of Canton—the only trade port in the whole Heavenly Empire of 300,000,000 souls—kept their lips religiously sealed about everything pertaining to the Inner Land. All that Jardine-Matheson could tell of China, with any assurance, was that its people harbored a bottomless appetite for opium, and that official opposition to the trade was snowballing ferociously as time went on, to the magically augmented profit of Jardine-Matheson and Company of London and Calcutta.

To understand the official Chinese antipathy to opium in the early 1800s, you have to understand that it was a relatively—but not wholly—new thing there, in its powerful new form for smoking. Edible opium, as a medicament, had been known for ages. Herbal manuals since the invention of printing had offered *ying-tzu-su*— an infusion of crushed poppyheads and seeds in water—as an antidote to mercury poisoning, geriatric impotence and general indigestion. Taken in this form it provided a mild high, a pleasant access of centered benevolence, the sort of thing favored by thoughtful and orderly persons, such as this poet of the Sung Dynasty, circa A.D. 1000:

> *I see here the Hermit of the Shade,*
> *And the long-robed Buddhist priest.*
> *When they sit opposite I forget to speak.*
> *Then I have but to drink a cup of this poppy-seed brew.*
> *I laugh,*
> *I am happy,*
> *I have come to Ying-Chuan,*
> *And am wandering on the banks of its river.*
> *I seem to be climbing the slopes of the Lu Mountain,*
> *In the far West.*

Choice medical opium from the Egyptian gardens at Thebes— *opium thebaicum*, which went everywhere the Arabs traded, and far beyond—was moving into China well before A.D. 400. Poppyhead preparations were peddled by apothecaries in confections "made up into cakes shaped like fish"—to be used, that is, as aphrodisiacs. "The desideratum of no less than 3,000 phallic strokes" resided in each fish-cake, sang the poets. "It is also for diarrhea and dysentery accompanied by inflammation," a twelfth-century herbal declares; then warning, "great care must be taken in using it, because it kills like a knife."

"The poppy is found everywhere," a Sung herbal commissioned by the emperor Jen T'sung noted: "Many persons cultivate it as an ornamental sunflower.... When their capsules have become dry and yellow, they may be plucked." The point was clearly to prepare low-yield poppyhead tea, hardly a plausible drug of abuse. Opium itself—*af-u-yung*, after the Arabian *af-yon*—was strictly a Western import. "*Af-u-yung* is produced in Arabia from a poppy with a red flower," a fourteenth-century merchant's survey observed: "The capsule, while still fresh, is pricked for its juice." There is no indication that the opium-yielding incision process, which is viciously laborious and requires large-scale, irrigated poppy cultivation, was picked up in China at any time before the last hundred years.

When it appeared around 1500, therefore, real smoking opium was an exceedingly exotic thing in China, and hence patently subversive. The Portuguese started it all, from the little trade-factories they had established on Formosa and Amoy in the East China Sea. They were a generally distressful lot, those Portuguese, the first *Huang-Maou* ("redheaded barbarians") to ever directly trouble the Celestial Empire with importunities to engage in foreign commerce. Before this, girt about securely by the Himalayas and Siberia, China's experience with barbarians had been mainly restricted to Mongols and Turks, leaving them with a decided animus toward barbarians in general. These new Huang-Maou of Formosa and Amoy may have been few in number, but they had the monstrous habit of going about like dragons, spouting plumes of horrid gray *smoke* from their mouths and nostrils.

To do them credit, the Portuguese of the East China Sea showed considerable invention when they took to smoking their opium; it was the first time since prehistoric Mycenae (see Chapter 2) that anyone had ever thought of doing this. Smoking itself, as a way of consuming tobacco, had been picked up only in the last generation from the North American aborigines; it still looked as shockingly bizarre to most Europeans as it did to the Celestials, but the world-ranging Portuguese sea-dogs were ready to try anything. When they came down with malaria and dysentery on the pestiferous East China sea-coast, they resorted to opium for relief, and it served wonderfully. And the effects were instantaneous when it was smoked, so smoke it they did.

If you really *work* at it, puffing whole ounces of opium, day in and day out for months, you can cultivate a noticeable tolerance for it, with the concomitant compulsion to smoke more and more. It's not known if the Portuguese in this period consciously thought to exploit the special commercial property of opium, but it would hardly signify anyway. Once they'd set up their "trade factories" and found that they really could offer the self-sufficient Chinese blessed little that was worth their buying, they went straight into commercial piracy. The Portuguese notion of "trade" in China was to plunder offshore merchant junks at random, haul the booty to the nearest port, and sell it for whatever they could make: a wholly inefficient mode of imperialism.

When the Dutch chased the *Portygees* out of Formosa in 1663, they ordered things rather better. With their North Atlantic commercial contacts, the Dutch were able to move in a considerable quantity of fancy factory-made stuff, quilted cottons and woolen fabrics mainly, to respectably exchange for Chinese tea, silks and Ching Dynasty ceramics. Chinese coastal traders commenced to partake of the new European goodies so enthusiastically—some of them even began paying good Chinese gold and silver for them—that in 1683 the Emperor Kanghai stepped in and chased these Huang-Maou out. The Chinese were *not* interested in trading with the barbarians on any scale that might pose a potential drain on the Imperial treasury of the Inner Land.

China was resolutely and pridefully the self-designated Inner Land. Early Huang-Maou voyagers marveled to find the ocean coast of many-peopled China virtually deserted. Only in the deltas of the great rivers, at Canton on the Pearl, and Shanghai on the Yangtze-kiang, did very many people live close to the sea, and these cities were regarded by Peking with grave suspicion as likely spots for barbarian contamination. The Ching Empire was so ill-disposed toward seaborne commerce that it never even developed deep-sea naval ships of its own, for fear of encouraging merchants to do likewise.

The Peking dynasts were certainly correct in their suspicions of the Cantonese. A full four thousand miles from Peking—as far away as it was possible to be within the Celestial Empire—the canny Guangdong Province traders took to dealing with the Huang-Maou just like so many Phoenicians. Even after the Dutch were banished by proclamation, the Canton Interest perversely went on dealing with British, French, Americans, Swedes, Portuguese—as though there were any meaningful distinction to be drawn between one species of Huang-Maou and any other.

As long as this distasteful business could be restricted to the Canton Interest, some considerable good could be wrung out of it. Barbarians of all sorts were crazy for *tea* once they discovered it and tasted it. Something in tea possessed them with an insatiable desire for more—they became, in a word, addicted to the caffeine in it—and since China seemed the only place in the world where it grew, the Huang-Maou would brawl each other bloody over the privilege of paying for it, and so it was in Peking's material interest to suffer the Guangdong traders to keep the Pearl River harbor open. The licensed Hongs, limited always to ten families, were allowed to operate in Canton under stringent Mandarin supervision; but Shanghai was kept off-limits to foreigners under any circumstances.

The clumsy woolies and cottons of the barbarians presented no real threat to the balance of payments. Among the ten thousand kingdoms of the Celestial Empire were produced every conceivable commodity necessary to life and pleasure, and as long as the magnificent Imperial apparatus of canals, dikes, aqueducts, roads, and mails remained in trim, China could make do with domestic felt, hides, down, and silk without recourse to foreign textiles. And the foreign tea-bullion made a most welcome increment to the Pekinese Exchequer.

Opium was the one thing that did not exist in China for which there was any significant and steady Chinese demand, and so it was duly outlawed as early as 1729 by Imperial edict. From the sound of it, it was already too late: besides banning trade in opium and the consumption thereof, the edict went on to describe and forbid public opium parlors and private opium-smoking paraphernalia in detail. Already, therefore, there existed a full-blown opium-smoking industry within the Inner Land, complete with trade routes, retail outlets, and customers galore; in fact, in that very year, the Portuguese moved in two hundred catties of Malwa opium from Goa to the Canton Interest, which was the occasion for the total ban of the drug.

The ban did not work because conflict arose between the Canton Interest and the Black Tea Men. The latter, the established tea factors of the Inner Land, regarded the Canton CoHong guilds as a mere facility for moving their tea across the docks at Whampoa to the Huang-Maou, and to dish the European bullion back to the interior. The Black Tea Men saw no reason for splitting hard-cash profits with these Guangdong dockworkers—which motivated the CoHong guilds to strike up some hard-cash flow of their own between the Europeans and the folk of the Inner Land. The one European commodity for which the Chinese always would pay hard cash was opium, and so the Canton Interest commenced moving the drug to the Inner Land all by themselves along their own secret trade routes, cutting out the Black Tea Men entirely; they would collect the hard specie for it by themselves and give it to the Huang-Maou for more opium, abstracting a respectable skimoff for the Hong proprietors.

Three hundred years of dealing with the Portuguese on Macao had developed in the Canton CoHong a shrewd appreciation for the value of a dollar; the Spanish dollar being the most dependable medium of international exchange just then, handsome palm-sized eight-*réal* pieces minted with Fernando VII's coat of arms in Mexico, Potosi, Madrid, Santiago, Seville and Guatemala: Pieces of Eight, the original issue. One reason the Hongs took so enthusiastically to buying Indian opium from the British was that the British were happy to be paid for their drug in Indian sycee, the silver coin of the Moguls, which was worth significantly less by weight than Spanish silver. It amounted to a highly felicitous enterprise, selling tea and silk for vast quantities of Indian sycee, and then buying even vaster quantities of opium with the devalued coin, cutting the Black Tea Men in on only a fraction of the net. The anti-opium decrees that issued from Peking ever more frequently as the trade prospered—ordaining progressively fiercer penalties for sale and possession—reflected the progressively more indignant lobbying in Peking of the Black Tea Men against the pirate Hongs of Canton.

But once opium was technically illegal, that made it just so much better for the pirate Hongs. Now they would never have to pay import duties on this article, and they were relieved from having to account for their profits to the Imperial tax collectors.

By 1800, illegal or not, the opium trade was putting a palpable drain on the Imperial Exchequer: in that year the British East India Company alone ran six thousand catties of opium into Canton, inspiring the emperor Kia King to mount a comprehensive crackdown. "First foreign coin, now Chinese specie is lost!" Increasing the 1729 opium penalties from flogging to execution or transportation to the Cold Country, Kia went further and gave it a *moral* twist:

> The use of opium originally prevailed only among vagrants and disreputable persons...but has since extended itself among the members and descendants of respectable families, students, and officers of the Government. When this habit becomes established by frequent repetition, it gains an entire ascendance, and the consumer of opium is not only unable to forebear from its daily use, but, on passing the accustomed hour, cannot refrain from tears or command himself in any degree. The extraordinary expense of this article is likewise to be noticed...which the fortunes of the bulk of the community are unable to satisfy, and are therefore wholly dilapidated and wasted away.

This edict was the equivalent of a green light for the Canton CoHong, which went *wholly* underground in the matter of opium. From this point on, the guild merchants dealt with the Huang-Maou opium traders strictly through intermediaries, pirate dock and transport crews composed of homicidal felons from all around the Pacific. These gangs developed secret societies all their own, complete with esoteric code words, gestures and handshakes, and mythological signets, cult tattoos, elaborate initiation rituals, and quasi-religious ceremonies—the colorful Tong gangs who still, to this day, move heroin out of Hong Kong and Singapore all over the world.

With the tightening penalties, the squeeze system became ever more elaborate and expensive. It was now worth a Mandarin port official's job, and maybe his head, to get stuck with the responsibility for all that drug moving up into the hinterland. A hint of displeasure in a communique from Peking was now sufficient to motivate the Mandarins to a full-fledged drug crackdown, com-

*Ceremonial burning of opium pipes accompanied Chinese
antiopium crusades throughout the nineteenth century.
After 150 years of frustration, the movement to abolish
opium smoking in the Celestial Empire had succeeded
by 1910, when this photo was taken, in convincing the
British to dismantle the India-China opium trade.*

plete with public torture and execution of scores of people at a time. This worked to bring the formerly-squabbling Hongs much closer together, in order to ransom one another's members from the law whenever necessary; by and by, the British opium-factors were complaining that the CoHong was actually working as a unit to set prices.

Once across the docks in the hands of the Hongs, the opium disappeared totally from human ken. No multi-million-dollar enterprise in history, flourishing over whole generations, was ever conducted under such a perfect blanket of oblivion as the inland Chinese opium trade. Presumably the Hong wholesalers were the first to break up the brittle, treacly balls of opium, boil them down to a smooth smokable licorice consistency, and cut the mess with molasses or dung. It's reasonable to assume that the drug was further diluted each time it changed hands, and became logarithmically more expensive as it graduated through the Inner Land. Considering the immense number of people among whom opium moved in China, and the pathetic potency of the diluted drug at the end of the line, the horror stories of epidemic addiction offered by Mandarin opium decrees have to be viewed with a measure of skepticism.

William Hunter of New York City ran opium through Canton for over a dozen years on behalf of the American firm of Russell and Company. In contrast to most Huang-Maou in the trade, who were typically obsessed with making a mint of money and hauling it home as soon as possible, Hunter cultivated a species of affection for the Cantonese among whom he lived. When he retired he wrote in his biography:

> While the opium trade was going on, discussions often occurred as to the morality of it, as well as to the effect of smoking on the Chinese. None of the Hong merchants ever had anything to do with it, and several of the foreign houses refrained from dealing with it on conscientious grounds. As to the influence on the inhabitants of the City and suburbs at large, they were a healthy, active, hard-working and industrious people, withal cheerful and frugal. They were intelligent in business, skillful in manufacture. . . .
>
> These traits are inconsistent with habitual smoking, while the costliness of the prepared drug was such as to render a dilution

of it (to bring it within the means of the masses) utterly harmless. Amongst the wealthier classes, no doubt, it was more or less common, this we knew; but I myself, and I think I may fairly say the entire foreign community, rarely, if ever, saw anyone physically or mentally injured by it . . . In fact, smoking was a habit, as the use of wine was with us, in moderation. As compared with the use of spirituous liquors in the United States and in England, and the evil consequences of it, that of opium was inconsequential.*

Even Christian missionaries uniformly observed that Chinese opium casualties were not nearly as pathetic as European alcoholics (before the missionaries introduced morphine to China, anyway), which supports the general impression of minimal opium use by Chinese consumers. Chances are likely that most people really *did* buy it for medicine. Only very well-to-do individuals, enjoying high-society connections with the importers, could have had the means or opportunity to buy pure enough opium to get addicted to it. But it's people like this who most dependably provoke the wrathful authorities of any nation into comprehensive drug crackdowns.

"Furthermore," an 1821 Imperial edict fulminated, after further strengthening opium penalties, "it is the practice of foreigners to sit in sedan chairs, and hire Chinese to carry them, to live licentious lives, to indulge in acts of violence, and to break the laws in every way." The occasion for this 1821 crackdown was the slaying, evidently by accident, of a Chinese woman by a Sicilian sailor—the *Emily* incident, to be covered in Chapter 8. This new edict virtually made it a capital offense to deal with the abominated Huang-Maou in any way whatsoever. The new opium penalties were wallpostered all over Canton:

---

*This view was shared by one Dr. Eatwell, the English surgeon general and the Honourable Company's chief medical apologist. "It has been too much the practice with those who have treated the subject to content themselves with drawing the sad picture of the confirmed debauchee, plunged in the last stage of moral and physical exhaustion," Eatwell argued. "Having passed 3 years in China I can affirm thus far, that the effects of the abuse of the drug do not come very frequently under observation, and that when cases do occur, the habit is frequently found to have been induced by the presence of some painful chronic disease (or) the same morbid influences which induce men to become drunkards in even the most civilized lands."

For selling:
The Cangue one month,
transportation to the Cold Country.

*For selling to "the sons
of respectable families":*
Strangulation.

For smuggling:
100 blows of the rattan,
transportation to the Cold Country.

For receiving bribes:
100 blows of the rattan,
two months of Cangue.

For personal use:
100 blows of the rattan,
one month of Cangue.

Opium "tends to excite the animal spirits and remove obstruction," railed the emperor. "Involved in the deepest depravity is a race of vagabonds, men and women alike, who use it as an excitement to sensual appetite, and seduce the simple and unwary. It is a great detriment to the lives of individuals and the welfare of families."

> If the opium smoker be deprived of his pipe a single day, mucus from the nose, tears from the eyes, begin to flow, and meet the saliva at the corners of the mouth. At last the moisture of the body is dried up, the back and shoulders rise, and the head sinks between them, till the human figure presents the appearance of a decayed and rotten tree, as if life would become extinct at every breath; and yet the victim seems insensible of the cause.

On this occasion, two CoHong junks full of opium were seized on the Pearl River by the Customs Hoppo, and the guild merchant who had contracted for them was publicly divested of his queue, flogged, and cangued down Chaoyin Street. Lesser culprits were strangled, drafted into the army, or carted off to the Cold Country. Sitting in his company headquarters out on Hong Kong, James Matheson noted hopefully, "War seems inevitable, the result of which it is hoped will be a settlement of our own, on which to establish ourselves under the British flag, besides safe and un-restricted liberty of trade at the principal marts of the Empire." But the inevitable war was still twenty years off.

To understand the relish with which James Matheson contem-plated the prospect of an Opium War—with himself flush in the middle of it, a prime *causu belli*—you have to understand what was involved in being an opium factor during the heyday of the China trade. Jardine-Matheson and the rest had fallen heir to a most peculiar and unpredictable part of the world, on which only the solemn logic of economics could be imposed. If they were soulless and impossibly calculating, it might be because they were only part, after all, of something enormous and unprece-dented.

They had the Imperial burden of India to take care of, both for the sake of the Crown and for India herself; and India had become something supremely strange and vulnerable by the time they latched onto her. They inherited India (and her opium) in the 1830s, when the Honourable East India Company was divested of its mandate to rule and dictate the trade policies of British India.

The East India Company, contrary to popular belief, did not start out with the objective of being an opium monopoly; in fact, no sooner did the monopoly begin to function properly than the Honourable Company was divested of it. Silk and spices and raw cotton for Europe, and a monstrously huge human potential for consuming European factory goods are what brought the Com-pany to India, nothing less noble than that. Had it not been the Honourable Company, it would assuredly have been someone else. And whereas the Company did only move into opium very late on, with every evidence of reluctance, chances are good that few *other* European monopolies would have exhibited half so many qualms. One of the first Portuguese adventurers to light in India, the admiral Alphonse de Albuquerque, was struck straight off with the obvious possibilities of an opium monopoly. Mincing no terms, he wrote to King Manuel II from Cananor in 1513:

> I also send you a man of Aden, who knows how to work *afyam* and the manner of collecting it. If Your Highness would believe

me, I would order poppies of the Azores to be sown in all the fields of Portugal, and command *afyam* to be made, which is the best merchandise that obtains in these places, and by which much money is made; owing to the thrashing we gave Aden, no *afyam* has come to India, and where it was once worth 12 pardoes a faracolla, there is none to be had at 80. *Afyam* is nothing else, Senhor, but the milk of the poppy; from Cayro, whence it used to come, none comes now through Aden; therefore, Senhor, I would have you order them to be sown and cultivated, because a shipload would be used yearly in India, and the labourers would gain much also, and the people of India are lost without it, if they do not eat it; and set this fact in order, for I do not write to Your Highness an insignificant thing.

King Manuel evidently opted for the more practical course, which was to grow the *afyam* in India itself, while making sure the Crown got its due. The Portuguese, rigorously secretive about all their Imperial affairs, left infuriatingly few written records detailing their commercial activities from Angola to Burma throughout the 1500s; though early on, explorer Duarte Barbosa remarked that a sizeable opium traffic was conducted by Arabs from Aden down the Malabar coast of India to the Sunda Straights of Malacca, where it was picked up by Chinese traders based at Singapore, who moved it at least as far as east Siam. Presumably the Portuguese, over their 120 years of ferocious dominion, squeezed the Arabs out by encouraging poppy husbandry in India, moving it themselves between the Mogul kingdoms and Singapore.

When Purchas made his famous pilgrimage to India in 1617, opium was well known to the natives. It "makes them goe as if they were halfe asleep," he noted. And, when the British East India Company "appropriated" most of India in the 1760s, they found a flourishing domestic trade in *post*—Hindi for opium— and considerable acreage under relatively scientific cultivation. This was entirely agreeable to Robert Clive, the Company chief, since he was a lifelong opium addict himself.

At what point Clive became addicted is unclear, but it seems that opiate addiction was an occupational hazard for anyone who socialized with the nawabs, pashas, begums, beguins, sheikhs, maharajas, nizams and nabobs of Mogul India. Since this was how Clive went about his appropriations—taking these petty dynastic warlords into the Company's jolly confidence, then setting their armies against each other—he may have become addicted to plain *majoon*, the opium-laced confections which served as aperitifs on fancy social occasions, which there were plenty of for a company satrap. On religious occasions one drank *amalpani* and *kusumba*, traditional low-proof beverages made from crushed poppyheads. Smoking was another ceremonial necessity, and the preferred blend included tobacco, rose leaves and opium. For devoted connoisseurs, *madak* and *chandu* were available, and these were brands of hightest Malwa opium that had been stewed in various preparations of green aspergillus extract—a highly acetic solution which magically converted a good part of the morphine in the opium to what we now call heroin.

Clive may have become addicted for medical or psychological reasons—he had bad stomach troubles before he visited India, and melancholic suicidal spells—but chances are he did it for the good of the Honourable Company. To cozy up to the Moguls, it was mandatory to do as the Moguls did. And everybody, rich and poor, was using opium in civilized India: out of eleven million people in Hyderabad alone, one million were confirmed addicts, suggesting that *post* use was universal. Along the Ganges in northwest India, where a Bengali confederation of Maharatta chiefs presided, a loosely organized opium council existed around Patna, supervising poppy agriculture from the November sowing through the March culling. "It produces so much opium," admired an early British visitor, "that it serves all the countries of India in that commodity." The Patna Council did its best to standardize opium quality and set the prices for the annual auction at the Company docks in Calcutta, where ships from the world over collected each April to bid on the crop. A well-established colony of Armenian exporters, with names like Saukeis and Bagram, had been middlemaning between the Indians and the Portuguese for centuries at Calcutta; they were quite content to carry on business with the British.

The Honourable East India Company appropriated the native Patna Opium Council when it took over the rest of Bengal, after the Maharatta War of 1757, which Clive prosecuted to become Baron Clive of Plassey. The Company inherited a sizeable opium business on that occasion, so afterward it was incumbent on the

Company to keep that business in trim, for the sake of the Company and for the Bengali farmers themselves. So efficiently did it take to this responsibility that by 1767, the Company was running two thousand chests of opium per year into China: "A chest of Opium, bearing the Company's marks, passed among the Chinese and Malays like a bank note," it was proudly recorded, "unexamined and unquestioned."

This pleasing state of affairs did not come about all by itself. Left to their own devices, the Indians were shockingly inefficient and short-sighted about the enterprise. "From the ingenuity of the natives of this region, and from their imperfect notion of fair trade," a scandalized Company man reported to the Court of Directors, they would very commonly *adulterate* their drug, "either by the frequent addition of water, or the burying of it in a damp piece of ground." When the harvest had been poor, or the early Calcutta auction prices were temptingly high, these scoundrelly *post-wallahs* (opium-vendors) had various means for stretching their drug, and a trained eye was needed to avert this.

Pounded poppyseeds might be added to the opium, so sample balls should be cored at random before purchase. Thornapple pulp might be mixed in the drug—providing a nasty *dhatura* trip for the unwary consumer—or plain mud, but the texture would be distinctive. One should carefully check the smell of a consignment, to guard against molasses or cow dung, and plain sand could always be "at once detected by its grittiness when rubbed between a plate and a spatula."

The presence of such adulterants, so prejudicial to the quality of the article and to the Honourable Company's very reputation, would be quite unnecessary, if only the *gomasta* overseers would take adequate care of the crop in the fields. By Company estimate, up to a third of any season's crop was commonly lost out of sheer negligence, beyond the depredations of weather and insects. If the *gomastas* could only be taught to go down among the *koeri* opium-cullers at harvest, and show them precisely how to do it: make the bulb incisions late on a moderately humid evening, promising for the coming morning an ideal dew, which "allows the milk to thicken by evaporation, and to collect in irregular tiers" of white-red and rose-red milk along the sides of the capsules.

But you couldn't get the *gomastas* to go mingle civilly among the lower caste *koeris* for money or threats of thrashing. The *gomasta* troubled himself only so far as to see that the crop came in on schedule, by taking a rattan to the *koeris*'s backsides when he saw them shirking; the quality of the drug, or even quantity, was none of his concern. It was the *ryot* plantation-owner who worried about the end-product, and was likeliest to "sophisticate"—cut—the drug to make up for the *koeris*'s negligence. If the *koeris* were too Untouchable for the *gomastas*, how much more so for the *ryot*? Thus the Patna opium trade passed through three impermeable layers of caste (to mention only these three), and the work, such as it was, got done mainly by brute force.

Under the benevolent guidance of Clive's successor, Warren Hastings, opium-growing was restricted to the states of Patna and Behar so that the surrounding states could furnish the opium cultivators with rice and fruit, allowing them to devote *all* their land to poppy. Hastings sent in well-trained opium inspectors to look at each season's crop, plantation by plantation, before it was loaded on the godown skiffs for the Calcutta auction docks. It was a painful educational process, but eventually word trickled down from the *ryots*, through the *gomastas* to the *koeris*, that real care had to be taken with the crop at each culling, or the *ryot* would be ruined and the *koeris* and *gomastas* would starve. And thus the Honourable Company arrived, at length, at what was best for all concerned: a uniform, dependable, trustworthy, and altogether desirable article of merchandise.

> The great object of the Bengal Opium Agencies is to furnish an article suitable to the peculiar tastes of the population of China, who value any sample of opium in direct proportion to the quantity of hotdrawn watery extract obtainable from it, and to the purity and strength of the flavour of that extract when dried and smoked through a pipe.

The object was not necessarily to furnish the most potent possible *dope* to China's millions, the Honourable Company repeatedly assured its home critics, who were legion. Uniformity of quality was the only goal, so that the price of opium at Canton would not be forever rising and falling erratically. Uniformity ought to mean mediocrity, it was hoped. Warren Hastings himself piously allowed that:

It was undesirable to increase the production of any article not necessary to life, and that opium was "not a necessary of life," but a pernicious article of luxury that ought not be permitted, but for the purpose of commerce only, and which the wisdom of the Government should carefully restrain from internal consumption.

There was a moral point to be made for selling it as dearly as possible at Canton, too: "When the price was moderate, many had recourse to the drug who never used it before; when it was extravagantly high, many who had before used it moderately, desisted altogether," stated a Patna broker. The Company seems truly to have cut down Indian consumption considerably, under Hastings's program, by charging more for opium than most people there could afford. This had the added benefit, for the Company, of releasing much more drug onto the China market, where it was needed desperately—to put the Portuguese out of business.

The sole and exclusive object of it is to preserve to ourselves the whole supply by preventing Foreigners from participating in a trade of which at present they enjoy no inconsiderable share—for it is evident that the Chinese, as well as the Malays, cannot exist without the use of opium, and if we do not supply their necessary wants, Foreigners will.

This was the bottom line of it all: if foreigners *would* persist in trying to undercut the profits of the East India Company, then they were effectively threatening not just India's starving millions, but the revenue of the Crown itself. For it was Hastings's avowed aim to get the Company and all its monopolies in shape, and turn the whole complex over to the Crown. There were many in England who despised this idea—he was savagely impeached for it later—but to Hastings it was a matter of moral necessity.*

---

*No sooner had Hastings retired, at 53, from the Governor-Generalship of India (now a Crown Colony in everything but name), than the Whig opposition attacked "the prodigal and corrupt system which Mr. Hastings has introduced into the finances of India." He was denounced in Parliament by the liberal coalition of Edmund Burke and Charles Fox, who were hell-bent on wiping out slavery, Crown-run monopolies, and all other excrescences of paternalistic imperialism. In a precedent-setting impeachment trial (it was subsequently cited as a model of procedure by the United States Watergate prosecutors), Hastings was charged with subcontracting the Honourable Company's opium monopoly to an unqualified party, in exchange for a kickback. Though it took years, Hastings

The Honourable Company had changed India so drastically by then that it would be cruel to pack up and leave: all those poor people growing poppies in Patna and Behar would *starve* if England wouldn't move their opium to China every April.

Taking responsibility for India meant taking a considerable bit of lean along with the fat. The Subcontinent just wasn't producing enough spices to compete with the Andamanese or Moluccan monopolies, which were run by the Dutch and Portuguese. Silk? The Chinese no longer moved it through India, one bought it at Canton now. Worst of all, the entire cotton market fell apart after the American Revolution; with no production quotas on Georgia and Alabama cotton, the price of Madras went way down on the London 'Change. For the time being at least, India had blessed little besides opium that anyone else, anywhere in the world, wanted. And opium in India, testified a Company pamphlet, . . .

> enriched the value of the land fourfold, enriched the *Zemindars*, maintained thousands of people employed in collecting and preparing the drug, and benefited the commerce and shipping of Calcutta.

This was undoubtedly a wonderful thing for the opium monopoly, but it hardly solved the host of afflictions that beset the Honourable Company in nearly every other area of its trade. The European demand for tea had become so vast that the Company's ships could hardly move enough of it away from Canton. As a result, the amount of European gold and silver entering China to pay for tea was *six times* the amount passing back the other way, making for a highly unsuitable balance of accounts. The

---

ultimately absolved himself of all charges. The lucrative contract for collecting Patna opium and moving it down the Ganges to the Company docks at Calcutta had been sold to one of the top bidders, Steven Sullivan, who was the son of a Company executive; this Hastings admitted freely. But, he argued, "opium was of that nature, and so liable to frauds and adulteration that it was detrimental to the interests of the Company to give a contract upon such low terms as to drive the contractor to the necessity of debasing its quality, to preserve himself from loss." That is, Mr. Sullivan had paid so much for the Patna collection license that he was sure to contract it out to responsible parties vigorously dedicated to making a steady profit over the long run. A lesser bidder might have been merely interested in recouping a quick profit in one heavily-sophisticated crop, and then abandoning the project—to the ruination of the Indian producers and the disgrace of the Honourable Company.

Honourable Company felt particularly guilty about the endless crates of Indian sycee it was shipping to Canton. The only way to drag even some of that cash back out of China was to boost opium production, and try to edge all competitors out of the market. The series of desperate measures undertaken in this line—the total appropriation of the Patna Opium Council, armed incursions into Western India to grab the Malwa trade away from the Goa-based Portuguese, and restriction of opium carriage even from British vessels unregistered with the Company—were bluntly justified by Hastings's successor, Lord Cornwallis.

> The opium now serves as remittance to China to answer for the bills drawn upon Canton for the provision of the investment [in Chinese tea and silk]. Were the trade to be laid open, it is probable that this reserve might in some measure fail and occasion the exportation of silver from this country [India], already too much drained of its circulating specie.

This was brutal language, recognized as such in its own time, and loudly deplored by the Whigs. It was everywhere known, by 1810, how the Honourable Company was conducting this business. They had established a sizeable complex of warehouses—"factories"—at Black Butter Bay, just south of Macao, to which they were moving some 4,500 catties of opium every year, along with odds and ends of cotton, gum, wheat, and European-manufactured knicknacks, all under the Company's guaranteed-quality stamp. It prompted no end of controversy back home, especially from liberal free-trade advocates, who were sure that the whole inefficient setup would be wholesomely reversed if only the Company's monopoly were dissolved and opened to independent shippers. Thus was born the fiery Opium Controversy, which flared up in regular cycles throughout the nineteenth century, with every new development in the China trade.

In the 1820s, the Company was obliged for form's sake to give up moving the drug on its own ships, which conciliated the free-traders somewhat. Independent shippers would pick up Company-stamped opium at Calcutta and move it to the Company factory at Black Butter Bay, where Company agents would arrange to have it transferred to smuggler scuttling crabs for transportation over reefs and up backwater creeks to the Hong's buyers. For a while this conduced to a distressing inferiority in opium quality, as the independent "country ships" took to moving in, alongside the Company opium, lots of low-quality, sophisticated Persian produce—"Isfahan juice," it was called. The Hong buyers, deeply insulted, complained to the Company, who demanded an explanation from the top independent shipper James Matheson. "I would in almost every case attribute it to disintegrity on the part of the agent," admitted Matheson, "the article having for some time been attended with such large profits as to hold out more than common temptation to the weak passions of our nature." The debasement of "the article" would, he confidently predicted, be reversed once the smaller opportunists—"men of little capital"—were squeezed out of the competition.

Eventually the Honourable Company insisted on licensing every ship that contracted to haul its drug, the license stipulating that no unstamped, non-Patna opium could be moved alongside the Company catties. This was in comic contradiction to the voyage-by-voyage shipping orders issued from the Company, which stipulated that no opium at *all* should be carried aboard the vessel in question, "Lest the Company be implicated." Despite this sop to home anti-opium sentiment, the controversy mounted in Great Britain.

"We are drugging to death the man whom we should like to see enter our shop, purse in hand," people were squawking. The abolition of both the opium and slave trades became linked as progressive political clauses, along with the abolition of restrictive government trade monopolies. When the Whigs finally succeeded in wrecking the slave trade, the opium traffic was accorded merciless, and often absurd, vituperation:

Why, the slave trade was merciful compared with the opium trade. We did not destroy the bodies of the Africans, for it was our immediate interest to keep them alive; we did not debase their natures, corrupt their minds, nor destroy their souls. But the opium seller slays the body after he has corrupted, degraded and annihilated the moral being of unhappy sinners, while every hour is bringing new victims to a Moloch which knows no satiety, and where the English murderer and the Chinese suicide vie with each other in offerings at his shrine.

Various societies for the suppression of opium sprang up in England, bewailing the soulless mercantile policy of furnishing drugs to addicts in faraway lands (but not, curiously, in England itself, see Chapter 4). They were never nearly so popular or well-supported as societies for the suppression of other vices, such as teenage prostitution and gin-swilling among the industrial poor, which were more conspicuous and immediate. And also there was this about opium: Most of the same free-trade advocates who were out to bust the Company's drug trust were in no way averse to the prospect of moving this article themselves some day, if only they could get their hands on it.

It was Jardine-Matheson and Company who ultimately cornered the opium trade, when the Whigs finally divested the Honourable Company of their monopoly in the 1830s. Many other private outfits initially took a bite out of the trade—old Asia hands like Reid Beal, W. S. Davidson, and "Holly" Magniac—but Jardine-Matheson pretty much succeeded in driving them out of the market eventually, by means both fair and foul. Joseph Jardine and James Matheson, two North Britons who fit the caricature of carnivorous Victorian industrialists as neatly as Scrooge and Marley, had been operating throughout Southeast Asia for years in bitter scrambling competition with the Honourable Company. Accomplished smugglers, they had, in the twenties, set up their own factory complex on Hong Kong, to move independent shipments of Malwa opium to Chinese traders *north* of Canton. It was the twenty-year-old Matheson who pioneered this audacious ploy in the great Jardine-Matheson man-of-war *Hercules*, making new arrangements with independent Chinese smugglers along the coast, bribing new Mandarin port officials, and intimidating the captains of Celestial war-junks through occasional loud and smoky displays of brute force. They discovered that the coastal Chinese warmly remembered opium—"water tobacco" they called it—which years before had been traded from Formosa and Amoy by the Portuguese and Dutch.

Jardine-Matheson and Company enjoyed several advantages over the East India Company. Unlike Company officials who had never felt entirely comfortable dealing with the CoHong outlaws of the Canton Interest, with their unseemly mobster nicknames and secret society smuggler gangs, James Matheson felt entirely at home in the South Asian *demi-monde*. Better yet, Jardine-Matheson was a long-term investor in Malwa opium, which was much preferred over the Company's Patna drug by the Chinese; Malwa tended to taste abrasive and bitter because it yielded a more concentrated morphine content after boiling, but precisely because of that, it got you nearly twice as high. With the Company easing out of the picture, Jardine-Matheson-borne Malwa from Bombay surged unimpeded into Canton: 8,099 catties in 1830, 12,856 in 1831, 9,333 in 1832 and so on.

Prime among Jardine-Matheson's 150-odd Indian contacts was the esteemed Jamjetsee Jeejeebhoy and Company of Bombay. A venerable parsee mercantile clan, the Jeejeebhoys had started out as cotton brokers for various London companies, until the bottom fell out of Madras cotton after the American Revolution. They then deftly diverted into opium wholesaling, forming the joint-account Malwa Opium Syndicate with Jardine-Matheson on the London Exchange.

To court the Chinese end of the connection, Jardine-Matheson coaxed one Rev. Dr. Charles Gutzlaff into the firm as company interpreter. A High-Church medical missionary with a rare facility for picking up Chinese dialects, Gutzlaff at first had his reservations, but Joseph Jardine was cooly persuasive. Beyond salary, the corporation would be glad to run off Dr. Gutzlaff's evangelical magazine on its Mandarin press, giving him a unique advantage over other missionaries. The important thing was for Gutzlaff to get out in the field and convert the heathen under any aegis at all, Jardine reminded him, before the slavering Jesuits should get to them.

> Tho' it is our earnest wish that you should not in any way injure the grand object you have in view by appearing interested in what by many is considered an immoral traffic, yet such a traffic is absolutely necessary to give any vessel a reasonable chance. Gain sweetens labour and, we may add, lessens very materially the risk incurred in the eyes of those who partake therein. . . . and the more profitable the expedition the better we shall be able to place at your disposal a sum that may hereafter be usefully employed in furthering the grand object you have in view, and your success in which we feel deeply interested. . . . We have only to add that

we consider you as surgeon and interpreter to the expedition, and shall remunerate you for your services in that capacity.

Off went the Reverend Dr. Gutzlaff to the pagan millions of China, then, aboard the Jardine-Matheson cutter *Sylph*. He turned out to be a capital negotiator, throwing the fear of God into his Celestial contacts, larding them down with Bibles and evangelistic tracts, teaching them hymns and drenching them with baptisms, and in the end making some extremely advantageous bargains for Jardine-Matheson. Even before the 1840 Opium War, while the mounting Imperial drug crackdowns prompted Jardine-Matheson to open up ever more ports northeastward along the China coast, Gutzlaff led the way in the *Sylph* with Bible and drug. Prohibition of opium, he came to realize, only encouraged the authorities to be unjust, immorally searching and jailing innocent people under drug pretexts; and the informant system promoted gross lying among the people, for, "whoever had a grudge against his neighbour, denounced him as a transgressor of the laws against the drug." The Reverend Dr. Gutzlaff became a stalwart company man, and the company prospered amain.

All these increments to the firm's prosperity were abetted considerably by mounting official opposition against the trade in China. The Emperor Tao Kwang, having himself been an opium smoker in his wastrel youth (according to Jardine-Matheson published rumor, at least*) was cracking down on opium with all the hysterical passion of a converted addict, with results generally beneficial to the drug barons. He threw a mild scare into them in 1821 when he superseded the Whampoa Customs Hoppo—an established Squeeze recipient—with military inspectors who went over incoming vessels from keelsons to crow's nests, rooting out caches of foreign drug.

Analyzing the developments in the *Canton Register*, Jardine allowed that the viceroy of Guangdong Province, Teng T.ingchen, was under fierce pressure from Peking to clean up Canton. To tone down the presence of opium-dealing around Whampoa Harbor and the Bocca Tigris narrows, which were crowded with

---

*Another Jardine-Matheson rumor about Tao Kwang had all three of his sons dying from opium overdoses.

public shipping, it was decided to pick a more sequestered smuggling *entrepôt*. Lintin Island, a sizeable location in the inner lighting of Chuanpei Bay, was selected for the site of operations, at least until the Canton authorities might be rehabilitated in the emperor's esteem.

Once the new opium factories had been set up at a seemly remove, with storeships moored invisibly across the mole in greater Chuanpei Harbor, the British movers established a snug stranglehold on drug availability, using the Jardine's Point semaphore system described at the beginning of this chapter. "The trade has . . . recovered its usual serenity," rejoiced a hack for the *Asiatic Journal*, a Jardine-Matheson mouthpiece; "and although a prohibited commodity, opium may be obtained in China without any other inconvenience, probably, than enhancement of price."

In the privacy of his corporate letters, Matheson was hell-bent on a China war of any sort. For a while he entertained the possibility of a rebellion of the Hongs and Guangdong opium smokers against Peking: "An insurrection is the only chance we see of any great relaxation." But after the viceroy Teng, on a crackdown binge, jailed two thousand unhappy opium smokers in one week in 1838 without a single complaint from any of them, Matheson realistically abandoned this notion: "Not an opium pipe to be seen, not a retail vendor of the drug. . . . They are timid fellows here, and stand a great deal from their oppressive rulers." Open rebellion was therefore obviously a highly remote prospect.

Matheson also warmly forecast an uprising of the British public every time the English tea tax went up, and infringed on Jardine-Matheson's imports of *that* article. The tax reached really phenomenal rates in the early thirties, as King William's ministers anxiously sought to cut down on the specie drain to China by discouraging tea consumption. But this was patently unsatisfactory, because the British were so irremediably hooked on tea by now that all such discouragements only invigorated the smuggling of the stuff along the unpatrollable Cornish coast. If things went on in this way, Great Britain would be in the same fix as China in respect to smuggled opium, but without the sweetening gain of a profitable overall trade balance.

So in 1834, Foreign Minister Lord Palmerston resolved to set up an official British trade representative in China. An 1817 endeavor to plant a Crown consul in Peking had come awkwardly to naught, when the envoy Lord Amherst flatly refused to "kow-tow" to the Celestial Emperor, and was sent packing. In the interim, the Swedes and Americans had been allowed to establish consulates in Canton, so in '34 Palmerston sent Lord William John Napier there from India.

This was not the Lord Charles Napier who cut a bloody swath through much of India for the Company in the following decade. But Lord William was a Napier through and through, warmly endorsing his cousin Charles's famous theory on how best to subdue any refractory population of wogs, niggers, abos, or whatever: "first a lot of thrashing, and then a lot of kindness." So he came on like gangbusters as British Trade Superintendent, moving in his staff and their families, and inviting the likes of Matheson to return to Canton from Lintin, before the Emperor, four thousand miles away, could forbid it. Then Napier went further and plastered the town with wallposters denouncing the "ignorance and obstinancy of the Viceroy." Viceroy Teng responded with posters calling Napier a "lawless foreign devil," and threatened to burn down the newly-reopened British trade factories. This fired up Napier considerably, and he rashly took two armed warships up the Pearl River to threaten the viceroy's palace—to find no one around the place to shoot at, and his way back blocked by stakes and booms planted in the water behind him. Worse yet, the Chinese took to setting empty junks on fire and heading them downstream toward Napier's very inflammable ships. And he came down with malaria! At length he had to humbly borrow a fast junk from the Chinese to row him back to Whampoa, where he promptly died.

Coincidentally, in the Forbidden City of Peking, one Tsu Naitsi, vice president of the Sacrificial Court in the Forbidden City, was actually moved to recommend the legalization of opium in China. The way things now stood, Tsu insightfully declared, illegal opium was only fattening foreigners at the Exchequer's expense, and even worse, contributing to the wholesale corruption of the Imperial civil service.

The laws and enactments are the means by which extortionate minor officials and worthless scoundrels use to benefit themselves; and the greater the serverity of the laws, the larger and more numerous are the bribes paid to extortionate underlings, and the more subtle are the schemes of such worthless scoundrels.

Tsu proposed the legalization of the drug to all but scholars, soldiers, and state officials; foreign movers would have to pay a stiff import duty on every catty of drug moved through Canton, in cold cash, and the CoHong would be forbidden to pay for the drug in anything but barter merchandise. If ever there was a plan to yank the bottom out of a smuggling racket, this was it. Matheson sounded a rare note of real panic in a memo to Jardine in Calcutta when he heard that Tsu's proposal might be enacted.

> The order of the Government prohibiting the payment of cash for opium will never answer in practice. . . . *Without sycee or gold as remittance to India we should never be able to get on*; and I am of the opinion that the opium will never be brought in if the regulations laid down are strictly enforced.

The faithless Canton Interest naturally fully endorsed Tsu's proposition, providing the legal trade could be restricted to Whampoa. Viceroy Teng backed Tsu heartily, adding that the legalization of poppy-growing within his district would absolutely and forever ruin all the Huang-Maou. One magistrate, Judge Yao, "dived in secrecy into all societies, for the purpose of detecting misery and vice," and recorded of opium-smokers that "all whom he has met in the indulgence have appeared to him an orderly sort of person." For a while, prospects were bleak indeed for Jardine-Matheson and Company.

But the Mandarins acted true to form after all, once Tsu's proposal had sat around long enough for a properly moralistic backlash to set in. Chu T'sun, sub-chancellor of the grand secretariat and Tsu's superior on the Board of Rites, led off with a grand alarm: too many stout Chinese soldiers, scholars, and statesmen had already fallen prey to this corruptive and enfeebling substance, and more youth every day were being seduced by it.

The very suggestion of legalization had *already* wrought immeasurable evil, Chancellor Chu asseverated: "The instant effect has been, that crafty thieves and villians have on all sides begun to raise their heads and open their eyes, gazing about and pointing the finger, under the notion that when once these prohibitions are repealed, thenceforth and forever they may regard themselves as free from every restraint." Having so injudiciously entertained this obscene possibility of opium legalization, the grand secretariat concluded, the Emperor Tao was obliged to make up for it by cracking down more ferociously than ever on the opium-trading barbarians and their running-dog Guangdong lackeys.

At length such a pitch of righteous indignation was achieved that the emperor countenanced a dreadful secret plan—the Hsu-kiu Memorial—to arrest all together the Huang-Maou drug dealers and their diplomatic mouthpieces, hold them hostage at Canton until the drug trade died forever, and force them to publish remorseful confessions of their complicity in the detestable traffic. The official resolution, slyly omitting any reference to the foreigners, called for the instant apprehension of

> ... the willful natives who sell the drug, the Hong merchants who are responsible for dealings with the foreigners, the agents who purchase wholesale, the boat-people who convey the drug, and the naval officers who receive bribes; and having with the utmost strictness discovered and arrested the offenders, we must inflict the severest punishments upon them.

Joseph Jardine in India, hearing of the unhoped-for new Pekinese crackdown, told the Jeejeebhoys to disregard the melancholy noises Matheson had been making from Canton. The legalization issue was a dead letter, he assured them. A ferocious new crackdown was surely at hand: "In the interim it should reduce prices with you. Therefore please invest all our funds in Malwa."

> Let it be asked, though the foreign soldiers be numerous, can they amount to one ten-thousandth part of ours? Though the foreign guns be allowed to be powerful and effective, can their ammunition be employed for any long period without being expended? If they venture to enter the port, there will be a moment's blaze, and they will be turned to cinders. If they dare to go on shore, it is permitted to all the people to seize and kill them. How can the said foreigners remain unawed?

Whenever a genuinely dire crisis arose in the great Ching Empire, which was not more often than once in a generation, the emperor might appoint a unique and terrible official, the *Kinchae*. In the

Kinchae were invested all the powers of the emperor himself, which is to say, the power of life and death over everyone in the realm, power to cast down and plough under everything that stands, to mobilize armies and militias to exterminate whole populations. Only four Kinchae were appointed in three hundred years after the Chings gained power in 1644, and the last of these was Lin Tse-hsu, whose admonitory wallposters went up all over Canton weeks before he arrived there in the spring of 1839.

Previous Kinchae had been summoned to quell large-scale rebellions in the far backwaters of the Empire, or to repel nomad Muslim incursions across the distant frontiers. Only when drastic, massive military action had to be undertaken in places at weeks' remove from Peking did the emperor ever delegate the dangerous powers of a Kinchae to anyone. But what was going on in Guangdong province was neither an invasion nor a rebellion; it was unlike anything previously known to history. Guangdong was in a perpetual condition of malaise and mounting discontent, pullulating with weird cults and paramilitary gangs, rotten with Mandarin officials impotent and corrupt and universally despised by the commonfolk. Incendiary inflation prevailed there, corroding everything. Silver bullion was cascading out of Guangdong to the West, squandered by crooked local officials on the purchase of opium: ten million dollars' worth of silver lost in the last year alone. True to form, the commoners were stuck with the tab; copper currency, with which rents and taxes were paid to the drug-dealing authorities, was now effectively without value there, so that the cost of living was spiralling out of control. There was *trouble* in Guangdong, drastic, critical, and it involved opium, which always made the emperor see red.

"Now the thundering wrath of the Celestial Majesty has been aroused, the axe of the executioner is whetted, and the existing laws must be enforced to their extremity, awarding death to all the guilty," announced the wallposters. "I, the Great Minister," averred Lin, "having with trembling obedience received the stern Imperial decree, have now only to point to the heavens, and swear by the sun, that with unabated energy I shall exterminate the evil." Special posters went up all over Thirteen Factories Street, the cloistered enclave on the left bank of the Pearl River in Old Canton Town, where the Huang-Maou were suffered to abide in their warehouse-offices along the quay. They demanded, in solemn crimson ideographs, an explanation from the three hundred-odd Europeans quartered there:

> Why do you bring to our land the opium which in your land is not made use of, by its defrauding men of their property and causing injury to their lives? I find that with this thing you have seduced and deluded the people of China for tens of years past; and countless are the unjust hordes you have thus acquired. Such arouses indignation in every human heart, and it is utterly inexcusable in the eye of Celestial reason.

The Huang-Maou deliberated the significance of it all, pretty sure that this time it was more than just another cosmetic drug crackdown. Teng T'ing Chen, the weathercock viceroy of Guangdong, had abruptly reversed his pro-legalization posture as soon as he heard that a Kinchae was being hauled in over his head: "Foreign countries would not endure such contraventions of their laws," Teng was fuming patriotically now; "how much more must the government of this Empire punish the contumacious disobedience of barbarians!" It really did look as though the long-awaited fireworks were finally set to blow.

James Matheson may have prudently wished to get out of Canton before the Kinchae's fearsome advent, or to at least move his young son Alexander away, but it was too late. Weeks before Lin officially took up residence, the Canton immigration police began gently obstructing the exit of selected Huang-Maou from the district. Nothing moved in or out of Whampoa, drug or dignitary, without these gentlemen's knowledge and sufferance, and in late March they commenced holding up the exit permits required by Matheson, his clerks and factors, and their families. It was all done pleasantly enough — mere delays in the paperwork, respectful apologies to all concerned — but it was accompanied by a visible escalation in the level of general hostility. In the winter of 1839, on several occasions, Chinese military junks had opened fire on opium-clippers, and new cannon and artillery were moving into the forts flanking the Bogue, the thirty-mile stretch of narrows between Whampoa Harbor and Chuanpei Bay. Whoever controlled the Bocca Tigris, as this stretch of the Pearl was called, could effectively mandate the entire commerce of the Flowery Land.

Then, one bright morning the Canton Huang-Maou awoke to the racket of scaffold-building and the rumor of fascinated voices. At the edge of the square near the Swedish Hong factory rented by the American firm of Russell and Company, in a vegetable garden right under the Stars and Stripes, a crowd of hundreds had gathered to watch the municipal executioners setting up a garrote-pillory—a tall stake with a hole bored through it at the victim's neck level, through which a leather loop was passed, to effect his slow strangulation once he'd been lashed upright to it. The morning's candidate was one Hu Lao-kin, convicted of buying opium wholesale from the Huang-Maou. The purpose of the exemplary execution, explained the Imperial herald, was...

> to challenge attention, to arouse careful reflection, and cause all to admonish and warn one another; in the hope that a trembling obedience to the laws of the Celestial Empire might be produced.... Those foreigners, though born and brought up beyond the pale of civilization, yet have human hearts, and ought surely to be impressed with awe and dread, and self-conviction.

It was an affront that the Huang-Maou were not about to tolerate, though. The diplomatic square was a residential area, they huffed indignantly, white women and children present; a public torture-murder, howsoever salutary in intent, was out of the question. The marine legation guard from the American consulate waded into the crowd brandishing quarterstaves and formed a phalanx around the pillory, physically lodging "a protest against turning the factory garden into an execution ground." The crowd swelled to nearly ten thousand, and was working up a fine hostile froth when Viceroy Teng underwent another change of heart. He sent forth a magistrate with a squad of troops, "and, by a free use of the rattan, the crowd, in its thousands, was soon cleared from the factory grounds." Hu was duly strangled in Chaoyin Street, traditional site of such improving spectacles.

Lin's ultimate arrival coincided with the appearance on the scene of the newly appointed British superintendent of trade, Captain Charles Elliot, who was anxious at this point to forestall hostilities. After Lord Napier's demise amid the unpleasantries of '36, the British administration under Foreign Minister Henry Temple, Lord Palmerston, had pursued a policy of cautious conciliation on the opium question. Elliot himself was prone to contempt for the likes of Jardine-Matheson, entrepreneurs "pursuing those guilty and sordid practices"; he considered the opium trade a squalid, pennyante racket, prosecuted by commercial upstarts whose venal profiteering only complicated the whole Asian trade, and brought contumely upon Her Majesty's proper representatives. And it was plain wicked: "No man entertains a deeper detestation of the disgrace and sin of this forced traffic than the humble individual who signs this dispatch," he wrote Lord Palmerston. "I see little to choose between it and piracy." When Elliot caught wind of Lin's impending tantrum, he cut short a holiday in Macao and lit for Canton, prepared to sink the whole drug trade if necessary.

Captain Elliot had a good long time—once he got to Canton, in very close quarters with Matheson—to have his opinions turned around. He got there just in time to attend a formal reception at the viceroy's palace where the Kinchae Lin Tse-hsu, terrible in black-and-scarlet military dragon-gown, laid down the law:

> When this order reaches the foreign merchants, let them deliver up to the Government every particle of the opium on board their store-ships. Let the Hong merchants make lists of the opium delivered by each firm, in order that all surrendered opium may be burnt and destroyed and that thus the evil may be entirely extirpated. There must not be the smallest atom concealed or withheld. At the same time let those foreigners give a bond, written jointly in the foreign and Chinese languages, making a declaration to this effect: "That their vessels, which shall hereafter resort hither, will never dare to bring opium with them and that, as soon as discovery shall be made of it, the opium shall be forfeited to the Government, and the parties shall suffer the extreme penalties of the law; and that such punishment will be willingly submitted to."

A rude jolt, this. Captain Elliot, Her Majesty's superintendent of trade, was being *ordered* to gather up the private property of British citizens in the Queen's name. Would the Queen feel quite right about buying all that opium? Worse yet, if Elliot acceded to this proposal, he'd be exposing British subjects to "the extreme penalties of the law" in China, torture and garroting and exile to the Cold Country. He told Lin he would have to talk all this over with the British Chamber of Commerce, and went back to Thirteen Factories Street by the docks.

The Chamber of Commerce, of which James Matheson was the foremost voice, amicably offered to give up their opium to the Kinchae prompt and proper: one thousand catties of drug. When Lin scornfully retorted that he wanted the whole 20,291 chests—$6,000,000 worth—he knew to be on hand in Whampoa, they were startled at the obvious accuracy of his intelligence service. This was too much to ask—it was the whole Malwa harvest, half the year's India crop—and they advised Elliot against handing it over.

Receiving the expected refusal, the Kinchae Lin proceeded to enact the secret Hsukiu memorial, which he and the Mandarin conservative faction in Peking had worked out in the course of the previous year's legalization debate. A detachment of troops was marched into Responditia Walk, the broad piazza facing the factory square, where public criers demanded the instant appearance of all Chinese subjects employed in Huang-Maou households. Forth they came, valets and cooks, ayahs and boot-wallahs, in trembling obedience. Then a special squad of Manchu Tatars, selected for their imposing presence, was detailed to stand guard before the foreigners' doorsteps, allowing no one in or out. The Huang-Maou would either surrender the opium and sign good-behavior bonds for the future, or they could starve to death.

Not that anyone went hungry during the six-week Canton quarantine. Quarantine or no quarantine, the American, Spanish, Austrian and Parsee firms stayed open for business, and Thirteen Factories Street was still the site of a continuous Cantonese carnival: "peddlers, hawkers, peep-show men and loungers, cobblers, sailors and sellers of tea and nuts, not to speak of men who just stared and begged loudly." When demonstrations were held, thousands of coolies would clog Responditia Walk shrieking bloody havoc, but the Mandarin cheerleaders kept them orderly enough. The ornate three-story English factory which housed Captain Elliot, James and Alexander Matheson, John Dent, the Reverend Dr. Charles Gutzlaff, and various other opium celebrities was the one spot on which Lin's men kept their eye. But however close the surveillance, Matheson kept up a regular coded correspondence with his company heads in Hongkong, and Elliot promptly advised Lord Pam of this embarrassing turn of events; victuals passed in even as letters passed out, so that the opium hostages really sustained according to one Yankee there, "no greater inconvenience than the loss of their servants."

While he waited for the drug surrender, Lin formally explained himself in a series of remarkable letters to Queen Victoria, about whom he appears to have had some unlikely notions. Alexandrina Victoria was barely twenty years old—still "Drina" to her friends—raised to eminence mainly through the connivance of the liberal Whig coalition under William Lamb, Lord Melbourne. At this point she was mainly a puppet of Melbourne and Palmerston (she grew out of this in due course), but it's doubtful if Lin Tse-hsu could have conceived of such a thing. A throne, to Lin, was a *throne*:

The Great Emperor Tao Kwang, intoned Lin to Victoria,

> . . . who alike supports and cherishes those from the Inner Land, and those from beyond the seas—who, if a source of profit exists anywhere, diffuses it over the whole world—who, if the tree of evil takes root anywhere, plucks it up for the benefit of all nations—

and challenged Her Britannic Majesty, though born of barbarians, to rise to His level. "Our Celestial Empire rules over ten thousand kingdoms! Most surely do we possess a measure of godlike majesty which ye cannot fathom." Still, even the relatively benighted Huang-Maou of Great Britain were obviously aware of the evils of opium, Lin reasoned, since "We have heard that in your honourable nation the people are not permitted to inhale the drug." (Europeans, that is, drank it as laudanum, presumably for medicinal purposes only.) Therefore, Lin proposed, the Queen should enter "conjointly" with the Emperor on a global drug crackdown. To this end, Tao Kwang had already forbidden opium-smoking in China on pain of death, but

> what is the prohibition of its use, in comparison with the prohibition of its sale and manufacture, as a means of purifying the source? . . . We would now then concert with your Honourable Sovereignty, means to bring to a perpetual end this opium, so hurtful to mankind, we in this land forbidding the use of it, and you in the nations under your dominion forbidding its manufacture. Will not the result of this be the enjoyment by each of a felicitous condition of peace?

So much for the pleasantries. Now, whether Victoria was aware of it or not, "There is a tribe of depraved and barbarous people who, having manufactured opium for smoking, bring it hither for sale, and seduce and lead astray the simple folk, to the destruction of their persons and the draining of their resources." The injustice of it cried up to heaven: "The Great Emperor hearing of it actually quivered with indignation." Some of these said barbarians had lately been detained in Canton, where, it was confidently assumed, Her Majesty would countenance their punishment by the Chinese, though they be British subjects—"as these pass but little of their time in your country, and the greater part of their time in ours."

This fellow was actually hinting at *blackmail*!

"I suppose war with China will be the next step," Matheson confidently predicted when he heard what Lin was telling Queen Victoria.

Lin's manifesto got to London just in time for maximum impact. It happened that Melbourne and Palmerston were in dire straits just then, under fire from all directions, and especially vulnerable in the area of foreign trade policy. The conservative Tory faction, led by Sir Robert Peel, was forcefully advertising all the ills that the Whigs had brought upon the nation by taking over India. Anything to do with that great white elephant was portrayed as a sorrowful mistake, and the opium scandal was particularly fruitful for the Tories. Evangelist W. H. Medhurst had just come home after several years in China, charging loudly that the opium movers were killing people. Withdrawals from opium were invariably fatal, Reverend Medhurst swore, but the drug was so irresistable that the coolies would spend every cent they had on it, until they couldn't afford any more, and death supervened:

> Thus they may be seen, hanging their heads by the doors of the opium shops, which the hard-hearted keepers, having fleeced them of their all, will not permit them to enter; and shut out from their own dwellings, either by angry relatives or ruthless creditors, they die in the streets unpitied and despised.

Such affecting portraits and Lin's fiery communique got a sympathetic ear in Tory quarters, and led in part to the passage of a no-confidence vote against the Melbourne cabinet. Even when rumors of the Canton quarantine reached England, and patriotic hotheads began indignantly talking of war, Dr. Thomas Arnold of Rugby (Tom Brown's schoolmaster) moralized earnestly against any such idea.

> Ordinary wars of conquest are to me far less wicked than to go to war in order to maintain smuggling consisting in the introduction of a demoralizing drug which the Government of China wishes to keep out, and which we, for the lucre of gain, want to introduce by force.

Meanwhile at Thirteen Factories Street in Canton, six rather jumpy weeks of quarantine passed for the sequestered Huang-Maou, with mobs of coolies out front chanting night and day for their scalps. Lin kept up a steady pressure on Elliot to order a surrender of the opium, a proposal increasingly onerous to Her Majesty's superintendent of trade. James Matheson was undoubtedly pressuring Elliot too; the drug was already doomed, but if Elliot would buy it so Lin could destroy it, that would not only cut Jardine-Matheson's losses but probably start a *war*! Every time one of Lin's incendiary wallposters went up outside the English Hong, Matheson would translate it for Elliot with open relish.

Things came to a head in late May, when Lin again demanded a set of signed good-behavior bonds from Elliot on behalf of all British merchants, with the penalties clearly delineated: if any traders should break the bonds by smuggling opium, "the parties shall be left to suffer death at the hands of the Celestial court— a punishment to which they agree to submit."

Hearing this, the British Chamber of Commerce gratefully disbanded, "as the whole situation had now assumed a political rather than a commercial aspect." Elliot, pushed beyond patience, fatefully superseded his powers as trade superintendent and ordered all British merchants in the area to "surrender to the service of Her Majesty's Government" all stores of opium, in exchange for paper scrip redeemable at the pleasure of the Royal Exchequer. In justification, he told Lord Pam that the only alternative would have been to sign the good-behavior bonds dictated by the Kinchae Lin, and he was entirely "without confidence in the justice and moderation of the said Imperial Commissioner."

There had been men with naked swords before our doors, day and night, for more than four weeks, and, as it was presumed they had orders to kill us if we attempted to escape...there could be no need for our bonds of consent to the killings of other people at some future period.*

Rife with anticipation, Matheson had mustered every Jardine-Matheson ship in the area to the Bogue, where they were already waiting for Lin's war-junks to take off the opium. Curiously, while the Jardine-Matheson ships lined up along with the Dent vessels to disgorge their mango-wood catties on the Jackass Point quay, it was observed that the American Russell and Company vessels, loaded with bottoms of Turkey opium, sat at one side unmolested. The British were advised to quit Canton with the next tide, of course, and they most readily complied.

The Kinchae Lin had resolved against burning so much opium all at once, since the fumes would pose an obvious hazard to public morals. Instead, three deep flagstone-paved trenches were dug at right angles to the creek which flowed through the Huang-Maou factory compound into the Pearl. The trenches were furnished with walkover planks and stop-sluice gates, and filled with water. They were in continual operation for no less than twenty days, dawn to dusk:

> The opium in baskets was delivered into the hands of coolies, who going on the planks carried it to every part of the trench. The balls were then taken out one by one, and thrown down on the planks, stamped on with the heel until broken in pieces, and then kicked

---

*There were plenty of independent British traders perfectly willing to sign goodbonds at risk of their necks and cargoes. The masters of two Calcutta-based cotton brigs, the *Thomas Coutts* and the *Royal Saxon*, had their shipboard interpreters work up English copies of the bonds so they could sign them:

A TRUE AND WILLING BOND

The foreigner_____commander of ship belonging to_____under_____consignment, present this to His Excellency the Great Government of Heavenly Dynasty, and certificate that the said ship shall carry_____goods come and trade in Canton; I, with my officer, and the whole crew are all dreadfully obey the new laws of the Chinese Majesty, that they dare not bring in any opium; if one little bit of opium was found out in any part of my ship by examination, I am willingly deliver up the transgressor, and he shall be punish to death according to the correctness law of the Government of Heavenly Dynasty; both

into the water. At the same time, other coolies were employed in
the trenches, with hoes and broad spatulas, busily engaged in
beating and turning up the opium from the bottom of the vat.
Other coolies were employed in bringing salt and lime, and spreading them over the whole surface of the trench. . . . The sluice was
two feet wide, and somewhat deeper than the floor of the trench.
It was furnished with a screen, made fine like a sieve, so as to
prevent any large masses of the drug from finding their way into
the creek.

There went the first half of the Indian opium harvest for 1839.
When they heard about it back in Bengal and Bombay, desolation
swept the land. It turned out that Her Majesty's Exchequer was
not about to redeem that opium scrip after all, not right away at
least; it left a lot of very respectable commodity brokers, like the
Jeejeebhoys, impossibly over-extended, the only honorable
course being suicide. And when men of that rank committed
suicide, their wives were morally obliged to *suttee* themselves
on the funeral pyre. "Only the forebearance of the creditors prevented an epidemic of selfdestruction"—i.e., Jardine-Matheson
and Company bailed the brokers out, and got them ever more
tightly under their corporate thumb.

Some Indians, though, took the obvious advantage offered by
the recent two-month drug drought at Canton. "It is said that
some Parsees even retail it from their factories," Matheson snorted
disgustedly while describing the influx of fly-by-night drug movers that descended on the Pearl River to replenish the supplies
depleted by Lin. Captain James Innes, one of the more notorious
privateers operating out of Macao, was hauling opium right up
into the Bocca Tigris even before the quarantine officially ended,
and Jardine-Mathesone got back into action. Along with this glut,
the price of opium went way down, which irritated Matheson,
to say the least.

---

my ship and goods are to be confiscate to the Chinese Officer; but if there found no opium
on my ship by examination then I beg Your Excellency's favour permit my ship enter
to Whampoa and trade as usual; so if there are distinguish between good and bad, then
I am willingly submit to Your Excellency: and I now give this bond as a true certificate
of the same. Heavenly Dynasty, Taou-Kwang, year moon day.

Name of Captain_____

If Matheson was dissatisfied, imagine poor Lin Tse-hsu's state of mind. "Although opium exists among the outside barbarians," he was pleading on his wallposters, "there is not a man of them who is willing to smoke it himself; but the natives of the Flowery Land are with willing hearts led astray by them."

> Opium may be likened to the stupefying medicines of kidnappers and the poisonous drugs of sorcerers, all used by them to seize upon and destroy the property of innocent individuals. Now your property is the means by which you support your life, and your specie, which is by no means to be easily obtained, you exchange for dirt and poison. It is ridiculous as well as lamentable.

But the specie was flooding out of the Flowery Land now, and the opium flooding in, like never before, in spite of, and very largely because of, Lin's seizure of the British opium. The Pekinese bureaucracy—many of whom lost no love on Lin Tse-hsu—began raising serious questions about the Kinchae's competence.

Captain Charles Elliot was spending most of his time off Macao, aboard HMS warships *Volage* and *Hyacinth*. Macao was Sin City of Southeast Asia, a wide-open pirate port with resort trappings. The Portuguese had amply stocked the lovely colonial settlement with 2,500 women of all nations—rather more than the male population, usually—and British officers of the Indian Army were rotated there by the shipload for rest and relaxation. Established Company officials even took along their wives and families to enjoy "gay and inspiriting amusements"—horseraces on the Racing Green, amateur theatricals at the Bishop's Head, concerts and masques in the English Garden—during "the season" each spring.

Elliot all this summer was waiting for some sort of signal from London, and as time went on he was more and more convinced the only proper signal would be a fleet of warships bearing invasion troops. The legitimate China trade was at an all-time ebb for British merchants, the emperor having put a ban on the sale to them of "our tea and rhubarb, which they are never more to have." To add insult to injury, the Chinese greatly relaxed trade restrictions on the American companies of Olyphant and Russell, who were factoring Chinese goods to the British at usurious rates—*while* freely moving in their abominable Turkish opium.

Then in midsummer, a gang of British tars out whoring in Macao reportedly murdered a Celestial citizen, one Lin Wei-hi. The incident, real or only alleged, was never properly investigated, because overnight it became a *causus belli*. As soon as he heard of it, the Kinchae Lin Tse-hsu—no relation, presumably—made Lin Wei-hi into a household word. From this point on, the Kinchae's non-negotiable demands to the British ritually included the surrender of "the murderer of Lin Wei-hi," for summary beheading. On Elliot's predictable refusal—from Macao—to contemplate any such thing, Lin formally declared war, Chinese-style. Wallposters went up throughout the Flowery Land:

> Assemble yourselves together for consultation; purchase arms and weapons; join together the stoutest of your villagers, and thus be prepared to defend yourselves. If any of the said foreigners be found going on shore to cause trouble, all and every one of the people are permitted to fire upon them, or to make prisoners of them. They assuredly never will be able, few in number, to oppose the many. Even when they land to take water from the springs, stop their progress.

This blood-curdling proclamation was backed up with a food embargo, which Lin tried to enforce by stationing a corps of rocket-firing war-junks near the *Volage* and *Hyacinth*, both anchored now off Kowloon. Considering himself effectively at war, Captain Elliot opened fire on the junks with his terrible seamortars, handily dispersing those that weren't burnt to the waterline. Because of this, the Portuguese chucked all the holiday British out of Macao, in fear of Lin's retribution, and denied Elliot entrance when he next came in for water. So the *Volage* and *Hyacinth*, crammed with their officers' families and servants, had to put in at the Jardine-Matheson smuggling enclave at Hong Kong, and await London's signal.

Lin Tse-hsu was properly scandalized, and fired off another series of letters to the Queen of England. What self-respecting monarch, after all, would bivouac her official emissaries in a den of drug pushers? How could she hold it against Lin if he went in and strangled the whole dastardly pack? It was no less than the murderers of Lin Wei-hi deserved

> Suppose that individuals of other nations were to sell opium in your kingdom and to seduce your people to smoke it, you would

be greatly incensed and would by all means stamp it out. We therefore expect you not to do to us what you would not like others to do to you.

...Pause and reflect for a moment: if you foreigners did not bring the opium hither, wherefore should our Chinese people get it to re-sell? It is you foreigners who involve our simple natives in the pit of death, and are they alone to be permitted to escape alive? If so much as one of these deprives our people of his life, he must forfeit his life in requital for that which he has taken:— how much more does this apply to him, who by means of opium destroys his fellow-man? Does the havoc which he commits stop with a single life? Therefore it is that those foreigners who now import the opium into the Central Land are condemned to be beheaded and strangled.

Lin, knowing that India was only six weeks distant by clipper, may not have been acutely aware that England was four *months* away. "Please let your reply be speedy," he concluded snappishly. "Do not on any account make excuses or procrastinate. A most important communication."

Lord Pam, four months later, exploded triumphantly in Parliament:

An insolent barbarian wielding authority at Canton has violated the British flag, broken the engagement of treaties, offered rewards for the heads of British subjects in that part of China, and planned their destruction by murder, assassinations, and poison!

That was the *sine qua non* of the first great opium debate in Parliament, as far as the Whigs were concerned anyway. A cheeky Chinaman was threatening to inflict revolting tortures on stout British lads because of a little opium and the unproven murder of *another* Chinaman. Lin's rather unpolitic communique took a weight of uneasiness off everyone's shoulders in London, because by the time it arrived, the whole business had long been settled anyway. About the same time as the Kinchae learned of Lin Wei-hi's infamous murder, Parliament learned of the Canton embargo, the humiliating opium surrender, the resulting panic in India, suicides, suttees, and the drop in sycee when the Malwa crop was liquidated. The great opium debate was effectively settled when free-trade promoter Stephen Warren published a pamphlet titled, simply and sensibly, *Opium*:

From the opium trade the Honourable Company have derived for years an immense revenue and through it the British Government and nation have also reaped an incalculable amount of political and financial advantage. The turn of the balance of trade between Great Britain and China in favour of the former has enabled India to increase tenfold her consumption of British manufacture; contributed directly to support the vast fabric of British dominion in the East, to defray the expenses of Her Majesty's establishment in India, and by the operation of exchanges and remittances in teas, to pour an abundant revenue into the British Exchequer and benefit the nation to an extent of a million yearly without impoverishing India.

A free-trade policy would be pursued with China in this matter of opium, even if the merchandise had to be moved in on warships.

No one said "war" out loud, mind you. "Satisfaction and reparation" were to be sought by the whole India fleet, with plenty of sepoy marines and lascar infantry for the "injurious proceedings" of the Chinese warmongers. Captain Charles Elliot was to be joined by his cousin, Admiral George Elliot of the India fleet; both of them to enjoy co-plenipotentiary rank in dealing with the Chinese, and to enact retribution, "irrespective of innocence or guilt," for the illegal detention of Crown subjects at Canton. They were to blockade Canton until the Chinese paid for all that wasted opium and agreed to engage sensibly in trade. And while they were about it, the Elliots were instructed to open up the great Yangtze-kiang near Shanghai to British merchants and appropriate the island of Chusan in its delta.

After the monsoon, Admiral Elliot arrived at last, and that was a spectacle worth waiting for. Sixteen men-of-arms with 540 guns, 4,000 India troops on 26 transport vessels, and a giant frigate—and best of all, four steam-driven destroyers. It was only necessary for Commodore Sir James Bremer to take up a blockade station in Chuanpei Bay, and Lin Tse-hsu was stymied.

About all he could do now was try to discourage the Huang-Maou from coming ashore. Bounty lists went up everywhere:

For the capture of an English officer $30,000
For his head $10,000

For the capture of an English soldier or sailor	$ 5,000
For his head	$ 300
For the capture of a sepoy or lascar	$ 100
For his head	$ 50

"China lay," at this point, as one capitalist historian graphically put it, "prostrate and available, like a beached whale." Leaving four blockade boats in Chuanpei, the Elliot cousins headed straight up the coast for gorgeous and prosperous Shanghai, prize of the Yangtze-kiang. They carried a chop for the emperor detailing their various requests for "reparations," and at Amoy they tried to have it delivered. Captain Bucher aboard HMS *Blonde* headed into the harbor there, flying a great white parley flag—and was nearly blown out of the water by the shore batteries. These cheeky Orientals wouldn't recognize a white flag! After that, wherever Her Majesty's navy went, they simply fired first.

Lamentably, the Chinese really *couldn't* recognize a white flag, having never heard of this custom before. Even more lamentably, they'd never heard of the flank attack. Whenever the sepoys came ashore the Imperial troops met them head-on, toe-to-toe in valorous medieval fashion; when they were subsequently hit from one side, they died scandalized. Chusan City was taken the day it was sighted, with a liberal use of grapeshot cannon down "long narrow streets thronged with men, women and children. . . . They were mowed like grass, and gutters flowed with their innocent blood." The *Indian Gazette*:

> A more complete pillage could not be conceived than took place. Every house was broken open, every drawer and box ransacked, the streets strewn with fragments of furniture, pictures, tables, chairs, grain of all sorts. . . . The plunder ceased only when there was nothing left to destroy.

Tinghai, on Chusan Island, was taken by four cruisers and ten gun-brigs after nine minutes of concentrated fire. "When the smoke cleared away a mass of ruin presented itself to the eye," reported an officer, "and on the place lately alive with men none but a few wounded were to be seen." The expeditionary force subsequently burned the town to the ground, quite by accident.

All this unnecessary bloodshed and destruction later brought re-proof from thoughtful people in England, who insisted that the Indian sepoys really ought to be taught how to properly conduct themselves on campaign.

By midsummer 1840, Tao Kwang in Peking was in a state of supreme perplexity. He had tried to quell the disorders in the faroff Flowery Land by the extraordinary policy of sending thither a Kinchae: and far from being quelled, the disorders had progressed with blood and fire right up the coast to Shanghai. The Huang-Maou were lodged at Peiho, Tinghai and Chusan, with their terrible war-engines, and were consolidating all the coast ports behind them with ease. It was hard for the emperor to get a solid grasp of events, because nobody ever wanted to be the messenger who brought him bad news. Wherever the Huang-Maou went ashore, the Ting magistrate would most commonly commit suicide after hearing their demands rather than convey those humiliating orders to Peking and face the wrath of the emperor.

Finally, in August 1840 the third secretary of the Imperial cabinet, a Manchu Tatar named Kishen, volunteered to meet with the Huang-Maou. The Tatars, generally speaking, were temperamentally more flexible in such affairs than Mandarins like Lin Tse-hsu. Late in the month, therefore, Secretary Kishen set off with his diplomatic entourage down the thousand-mile Grand Canal that stretched from Peking clear to Shanghai. The Huang-Maou's campaign secretary, Lord Jocelyn, was impressed.

> His queue...was remarkable from its length and the care that was evidently bestowed on it. He was dressed in a blue silk robe, with a worked girdle; on his legs were the white satin boots common to all the higher orders; his head was covered with a mandarin summer cap, made of fine straw; in it was placed the deep red coral button denoting the rank of the wearer, and the peacock's feather drooping between the shoulders.

This was a gentleman one could parley with properly. The Reverend Dr. Charles Gutzlaff, who was on loan to the British expedition from Jardine-Matheson and Company, reported after interviewing a "blue-button" Mandarin in Kishen's company that most of the cabinet flunkies on hand enjoyed opium "in the secret chamber." After a rather noisy six-hour session between Charles Elliot and Kishen, it was agreed that the British would vacate Chusan City and Peiho—remaining at Tinghai—while Kishen took their parley chop to the emperor, and elicited a response. Significantly, they slated their *next* war conference for Canton in the Flowery Land: "Kishen mentioned that a commission was to be appointed to start immediately for Canton," Jocelyn gloated, "to investigate the conduct of Lin, whom they blamed as the cause of the present trouble."

If Lin was in bad trouble, he showed no signs of moderating his anti-opium zeal. In Canton, he was now rumbling about mass executions unless the people straightaway gave over their revolting indulgences. If the volume of drug shipped from India to China that year is any indication—40,000 catties by official record alone, not counting American *afyon* and the fly-by-night smugglers that so pestered Matheson—Lin's crackdown just added fuel to the flame. Now he was sullenly growling:

> The criminal smokers of opium were allowed a year and a half, wherein if they failed to reform, whether officials, soldiers, or people, one and all are to be strangled. . . . To complete the period, there only remain about one hundred days. Death will then stand before your eyes.

This wallposter went up on the morning of September 27; on the afternoon of the same day, an Imperial chop arrived advising Lin that his powers as special commissioner for the port of Canton had been given over to Secretary Kishen. Lin was still Kinchae by title, but Kishen would be speaking for the emperor henceforth in all dealings with the Huang-Maou. It was a muddle so distracting that Lin, in one last grand gesture before Kishen arrived, sent nine war-junks and one thousand five hundred troops to Macao, to attack the *Hyacinth*. Captain Smith made a shambles of them; and when the emperor heard about it, he called for the return of both Lin and Teng to Peking "with the speed of flames" to answer "for the trouble."

Now Kishen beckoned to the British from the Flowery Land. The tars and sepoys of the expeditionary fleet were happy enough to move down to Canton from Tinghai: the Yangtze delta was a sump of "pestiferous exhalations," and no less than 448 of them had died from malaria and dysentery there in the last four months. Admiral Elliot, on the other hand, was dead set against this shift of scene. His orders came direct from Lord Pam, and they stipulated specifically that the co-plenipotentiaries were to do their negotiating from the mouth of the Yangtze, not the Pearl. A nasty rift developed between the Elliots over the proposal to follow Kishen southward to Canton, but the malaria resolved it. Admiral George was laid out so heavily with fever that Captain Charles drafted a notification by which the admiral handed over his commission on account of "sudden and severe illness," and signed it himself. Admiral George was back in India before he had the strength to object to this, and Kishen no longer had two plenipotentiaries whom he could play off against each other.

In Canton Elliot straightaway asked for Hong Kong as a permanent duty-free lodgement for British traders. Kishen pleasantly temporized that he had no personal objection to the idea, and would refer it to Peking.

In Peking, Lin Tse-hsu and the Mandarins were vengefully blackening Kishen's reputation, and the emperor was swinging back to their way of thinking. When the suggestion to cede Hong Kong arrived, Tao Kwang reacted by calling off negotiations and ordering Kishen to strangle the Huang-Maou one and all. In January 1841, then, Kishen moved reinforcements into Canton, to the Bogue forts flanking the exit from Whampoa. Elliot regarded this as provocative, and the sepoys took the forts with terrific slaughter. Stunned, Kishen exceeded his office and reopened negotiations, to preserve heavily populated Canton from being shelled from her own forts.

Within a month, Elliot announced that he and Kishen had settled the "Convention of Chuanpei." Hong Kong was now a dominion of the Crown, its European and Chinese citizens under the protection of the Queen, though they were to be "governed according to the laws and customs of China, every description of torture excepted." The Celestial Throne was assessed at 6 million in Spanish dollars in indemnity for Lin's opium confiscations, and Whampoa was reopened to British trade, "pending Her Majesty's further pleasure."

It was the final straw for Tao Kwang. Kishen was ordered back to Peking in chains, and a heroic mobilization of six thousand troops from Szechuan, Hupei and Kweichow was ordained. Two special military commanders, "Pacificators General," were appointed to lead the host into the Flowery Land to "quickly carry out the work of attack and extermination."

Elliot, hearing of this through Hong gossip, sailed the whole fleet into Whampoa, sank forty junks, and put the Bogue forts completely out of action. By the time the first of the Pacificators, seventy-year-old Yang Feng, got to Canton, the water was covered with British warships, and the hills overlooking town bristled with British artillery. Yang, who in former years had exterminated whole populations of Yunnanese rebels, philosophically sat down for long, civilized negotiations under the British guns.

"A war more unjust in its origins," fumed William Gladstone when he heard about this, "a war more calculated to cover this country with disgrace, I do not know and I have not read of." The occasion was the formal declaration of war against China, which was belatedly declared only after the chronicle of Elliot's bloody adventures, four months over, had been received in London. Gladstone, as Peel's most promising *protege* in the Tory wing, disgustedly observed that most pro-war votes came from "patriotic" backbenchers who favored continuing the conflict simply because it had begun. This was not William Gladstone's idea of patriotism.

> The right honourable gentleman opposite spoke of the British flag waving in glory at Canton. That flag is hoisted to protect an infamous contraband traffic; and if it were never hoisted, except as it is now hoisted on the coast of China, we should recoil from its sight with horror.

But the hostilities had commenced, Imperial ambition ruled the day. The Melbourne administration was heavily pressured by influential free-trade advocates, and the honourable member from Ashburton in the Commons, Joseph Jardine, who'd promoted the notion of occupying the Yangtze delta; and even after Jardine stopped pushing for it, having learned that it wasn't fit for European habitation, the Yangtze remained a prime priority on Palmerston's list of war aims.

When Pam heard that Charles Elliot had pulled out of Chusan, then, he was annoyed. Without Shanghai, all the other concessions in the Chuanpei Convention appeared to Pam to be almost worthless.

So Charles Elliot was royally repudiated for his exertions in China, literally. Wrote Victoria to her uncle King Leopold of the Belgians:

> The Chinese business vexes us much, and Palmerston is deeply mortified at it. *All* we wanted might have been got, if it had not been for the unaccountably strange conduct of Charles Elliot... who completely disregarded his orders and *tried* to get the *lowest* terms he could.

Charles Elliot had exceeded his office in any number of ways, and had still fallen far short of what his employers expected. In August he heard that he was being replaced by the distinguished India ambassador Sir Henry Pottinger of Bombay, and set about writing up his case on the way home. He did a pretty persuasive job of it:

> Between the 24th of March, 1839, when I was made a prisoner at Canton by the Chinese government, and the 18th of August, 1841, when I was removed by my own, we have turned a trade amounting to upwards of ten millions sterling, dispatched more than fifty thousand tons of British shipping, sent to England as much produce as would pour into H.M. Treasury, upwards of eight millions sterling, recovered from the Chinese treasury about 150 tons of hard silver, warded off from H.M. Government pressing appeals from foreign governments at particularly uneasy moments and on very delicate subjects, triumphantly manifested the prowess of the Queen's arms, and still more signally and with more enduring advantage established the character and extent of British magnanimity.

Impressive, but awfully frank. One doesn't hear much about Captain Charles Elliot after this in H.M. Foreign Service. Even Admiral George was rehabilitated to the point of taking on hardship posts—he was ambassador to the republic of Texas in the following year—but Captain Charles had no friends at all, it seems. Even the Mathesons were glad to see the back of him, being on wonderful first-name terms with Sir Henry Pottinger: "I have had two or three conversations with him," James Matheson wrote home, "of a very satisfactory nature."

When he negotiated the installment of a permanent British

consulate at Canton, Pottinger privately assured Matheson that "Colonel Balfour will give you as little trouble as he can, but it is advisable to be as independent of him as possible. We do not expect the consul to interfere with shipping outside the port of Amoy, so long, at all events, as they confine themselves to the sale of opium." If the opium runners should try smuggling in legitimate merchandise, that is, there'd be hell to pay.

Pottinger took a year to negotiate a settlement with the Chinese. The Celestial Throne's reparations totalled 21 million Spanish dollars: $6 million for the opium Lin had liquidated, $3 million which had been owed the British by Hong merchants, and $12 million for the expenses of the war. Hong Kong became a Crown colony proper, and the ports of Canton, Amoy, Foochow, Ningpo, and Shanghai were opened to British trade. Opium was nowhere mentioned by name in the Treaty of Nanking; the Chinese "need not trouble themselves whether our vessels bring opium or not," was Pottinger's phrase—implicity forbidding them to *search* for it on British ships.

He did in one instance throw a start into the opium traffickers, when he wrote to Pam, "I indulge a hope, a very faint one I admit, that it will be in my power to get the traffic in opium, by barter, legalized by the Emperor." *That* would have dropped the bottom out of the trade in short order. It never got further than the Emperor's chief negotiator, though, who would have been daft to suggest any such thing to Tao Kwang. "It is true I cannot prevent the introduction of the flowing poison," the emperor had realized, "but nothing will induce me to derive a revenue from the vice and misery of my people."

Tao Kwang was terribly chagrined. Everyone associated with this opium misery suffered by it. Lin Tse-hsu and the viceroy Teng together were stripped of rank and transported to Ili in the Cold Country; Ili was somewhere up among the Uighirs on the Mongolian-Siberian frontier, and people transported thither were just dumped out of a cart, penniless, among the tigers and Turks of the Tien Shan mountains. Kishen was condemned to death, but the sentence was commuted to exile in northern Manchuria, near frigid Kamchatka.

James Matheson gratefully quit the South China theatre after the Treaty of Nanking, and sailed home to take up the seat in

Parliament for Ashburton on Jardine's retirement. He was personally welcomed back by Lord Pam as a sort of war hero:

> To the assistance and information that you and Mr. Jardine so handsomely afforded us, it was mainly owing that we were able to give our affairs naval, military and diplomatic, in China those detailed instructions which have led to these satisfactory results.... There is no doubt that this event, which will form an epoch in the progress of the civilisation of the human races, must be attended with the utmost advantages to the commercial interests of England.

"I wish that the war had lasted a few more years," Matheson's son Alexander was already fretting in Hongkong, "as the opium trade did well, and may now be curtailed."

Yet there was no curtailing the opium trade. The new coastal ports provided by the Nanking Treaty turned into a bonanza for Jardine-Matheson, whose drug flotilla now enjoyed open access to them under the guns of the India fleet, and with the scarcely-disguised connivance of Crown port authorities.

The Canton Interest did not prosper under the new order of trade. In fact, the entire Celestial government appeared to go deeply into the red after the 1840 war with the Huang-Maou. The Europeans had a severe "legitimate" trade deficit to make up, and they did it with a vengeance. After Great Britain had extorted all these "extraterritorial" concessions out of the emperor—all those wide-open treaty ports with permanent consulates and factories—the rest of Europe demanded nothing less. Tao Kwang conceded extraterritorial privileges to the French, Germans and Russians, hoping at least that all these Huang-Maou would take to cutting each others' throats over the indispensable exports of the Inner Land. Instead, they mainly just took to hauling in opium, and taking away hard Chinese bullion.

By the mid-forties, thanks entirely to opium, China was some £2 million sterling in debt to the rest of the world. "This year will be long remembered in China for the depression which has existed in trade, with the single exception of opium," David Jardine—Joseph's son—recorded in 1846. Alexander Matheson backed up this appraisal: "There is a scarcity of money in China," he explained to the ever-querulous home office when remittances dropped; "$21,000,000 in Sycee have been taken from China to England in the last three years."

Inflation in specie-starved Guangdong brimmed over into unparalleled malaise and resentment. Authority was corroded to the extent that well-organized pirate gangs began terrorizing the East China Sea, compelling the opium firms to invest a thoroughly annoying outlay in shipboard ordnance. Jardine-Matheson's monthly company bulletin—candidly titled *The Opium Circular*—kept up an avid account of the progressively bizarre developments in the Flowery Land, since drug demand and drug price were bound to be influenced by them. Guangdong was precipitating, from the sounds of it, into a bedlam of armed factions, shooting it out with each other over idiotic controversies like land reform, women's rights, the drug traffic, and an incomprehensible range of religious issues.

Thirty million people, at conservative estimate, were killed in the course of the Taiping Rebellion between 1850 and 1865. The name "Taiping," meaning "Heavenly Grace" (or "the Hairy One," depending on intonation), was adopted by one Hung Hsiu-ch'uan of Guangdong, who was persuaded by the Christian missionaries that he was descended from Jesus, Confucius, Lao Tzu *and* the Buddah Guatama, all at once. The consequent charisma of this syncretic messiah was such that his militant followers occupied for a while all the great Yangtze cities, almost to the sea. Since they were ferociously antidrug, David Jardine was much perturbed: "The insurgents, it is said, have recently taken the important Malwa market of Tientsin at the entrance of the Pei-ho. We feel it will cut demand at Woosung as dealers are worried about distribution."

The Taiping cultists were ultimately "subdued" in 1865 by the British schoolboy idol Charles "Chinese" Gordon of Khartoum at the head of the Ever-Victorious Brigade—an improving saga of pity and terror which is, alas, pretty irrelevant to narcotics. Not *everything* that happened in China in the 1800s revolved around the abominated opium trade. For one thing, the already huge Chinese population had quadrupled in the course of one hundred years (from 147 million in 1742 to 400 million in the 1830s). This rather sudden population boom was an enormous factor contributing to political upheaval and social unrest, as well as a tremendous incentive to smoke opium, if only to feel alone in that throng. So it was certainly not the drug trade all by itself that prompted the dissolution of the Chinese Empire, though devotees of Karl Marx will emotionally argue otherwise.

> That a giant empire, containing about ⅓ of the human race, vegetating in the teeth of time, insulated by the forced exclusion of general intercourse, and thus contriving to dupe itself with delusions of Celestial perfection—that such an empire should be overtaken by fate on the occasion of a deadly duel, in which the representative of the antiquated world appears to be prompted by ethical motives, while the representative of overwhelming modern society fights for the buying in the cheapest and selling in the dearest markets—this, indeed, is a sort of tragical couplet stranger than any poet would ever have dared to fancy.

The esteemed London correspondent for the New York *Tribune*— between brawls in Hyde Park and broods in the British Library— pumped out plenty of fantastic hackwork like this in the early fifties. Horace Greely would buy anything that reflected badly on the British Empire, and he paid by the line. He might not go for Marx's famous equation of religion with opium, but if Marx was only knocking "the Christianity-canting and civilization-mongering British Empire," pushing "that soporific drug, opium" on the hapless coolies, Greely would be glad to run it.

Marx was not exactly wrong in his analysis of what ailed China, only about seventy years ahead of events. Briefly, it was his conviction that the West—specifically Britain, for the sake of Hoss Greely—was systematically dismantling the classic feudal social structure of Imperial China in order to create a measureless population of helpless consumers for Western manufacturers. They were doing this with opium, and succeeding apace, because the illegality of the opium trade was making poor people wealthy, impoverishing the rich, draining the Empire of legitimate currency, fostering inflation, diverting funds from sensible development, comprehensively eroding China's economic fabric. As the age-old hermetic integrity of Chinese society fell apart, European piecegoods would replace native Chinese handicraft industries, and the East would be slave to the West. This didn't really happen until the 1920s—those Chinese handicraft industries were infinitely more durable than Marx would give them credit for—but the idea was intriguing.

Karl Marx did not much dwell on the pharmacological properties of opium, being entirely obsessed with its economic properties. It was the illegal *trade* that was poisoning China, not the
drug itself. "Before the British arms the authority of the Manchu
dynasty fell to pieces; the superstitious faith in the Eternity of
the Celestial Empire broke down; the barbarous and hermetic
isolation from the civilized world was infringed. . . ." Revisionists
in latter years have portrayed Karl Marx in the unlikely role of
an anguished humanitarian crying out against the enforced drugging of a nation of Celestial innocents. In truth, Marx personally
regarded opium as just one intoxicant among many, furnished to
the proletariat like gin in Britain, to shut them up; he only taxed
the benighted Chinese administrators for their foolish, inflexible
refusal to scientifically employ it as *their* control agent.

> The Chinese, it is true, are no more likely to renounce the use of
> opium than are the Germans to foreswear tobacco. But as the new
> Emperor is understood to be favorable to the culture of the poppy
> and the preparation of opium in China itself, it is evident that a
> death-blow is very likely to be struck at once at the business of
> opium-raising in India.

Once again, the Marxian analysis was only flawed by being about
three dialectical jumps ahead of real events. The emperor Hsien-
feng, who succeeded to Tao Kwang in 1850, was literally brought
to the ultimate legalization of opium in China only at the business
end of a cannon-barrel.

Hsien-feng, as you might imagine, was appalled at the condition of the Heavenly Realm when he ascended the throne: paramilitary cults carving up the south, barbarians aswagger through
all the coast towns, opium everywhere, Mandarins in the Squeeze,
and a whole new subpopulation of *noveau riche* tradesmen and
investors whose families had never amounted to trash before.
Directly he took vigorous corrective action on all fronts. In the
matter of opium, he reminded all the land that any sort of contact
with the foreign mud for smoking was a capital offense, and the
executioner's axe was whetted and ready. Sublime with com-
passion, he ordained a twelve-month period of grace over which
all addicts were expected to detoxify completely, or heads would
roll by the millions; the families of opium violators, he added,
would be sold into slavery.

Naturally the Mandarin faction was delighted with the emperor's zeal, especially when he retrieved poor Lin Tse-hsu from the Cold Country and set him to work pacificating the religious "crazies" around Hunan. Even better yet, magnificently better, Hsien dispatched to Guangdong Province as the new viceroy one Yeh Ming-chan, an old associate of Lin's. Though barred by international treaty from giving the Huang-Maou their proper deserts at the garrote pillory, the Viceroy Yeh fancied he could make things blessed sticky for them. Since the Flowery Land was abroil with desperate sectaries, armed and excitable, it was perfectly convenient to keep the local Huang-Maou perpetually terrorized by vigilante mobs and secret societies.

As time went on, incidents of supposedly unprovoked assault on allegedly innocent Europeans increased. The vigilantes were necessarily indiscriminate, pestering Europeans of every sort, from every nation, diplomats and drug movers and cotton factors alike. Protests were lodged in high places, and eventually the temptation abroad grew intolerable to manufacture another profitable war.

Lorchas were sitting ducks for the coast pirates: clumsy fat-bottomed Western-style hulls fitted with cranky paper junk sails, hauling heavy merchandise between Hong Kong and Whampoa. Most often they flew the British flag under Hong Kong registration, comprising an all-Chinese crew under a British master. In the autumn of 1856 a pirate gang waylaid the lorcha *Arrow* in Chuanpei Bay, appropriating all her opium and kidnapping her master for ransom. The viceroy Yeh refused to take action, professing himself to be confused about the proper nationality of the *Arrow*. For no justification other than this (and because the balance of trade that season was swaying in favor of the Black Tea Men), Great Britain launched the second Opium War. And this time the French republic insisted on joining the fray.

The action was much briefer this time. Steamers and schooners of both European navies were dispatched to Shanghai, and sailed right up the Grand Canal to Peking, where they burned down the Imperial summer palace—the venerable Yuan Ming Yuan, the grandest museum of all civilization, site of hallowed artifacts dating back to the Bronze Age. The Emperor Hsien, surrounded by the most preposterous engines of modern war, consented to send a negotiating embassy to Tientsin. James Bruce, the earl of Elgin, settled for an indemnity this time of £20,000,000 sterling—sufficient to tilt the trade balance away from the Chinese forever, which was the point of the whole undertaking. The remaining coast ports—Newchung, Formosa, Swatow, Tengchow, and Kiumgchow—were opened to trade with special privileges for British and French mercantilists. And a commission was appointed to sensibly legalize and regulate the opium trade.

"Opium," the Tientsin Treaty proclaimed in one quick line, "will henceforth pay 30 taels per picul* import duty. The importer will sell it only at the port."

It is said Lord Elgin legalized opium over his personal better judgment, and this may well have been true. But he despised the opium upstarts who were lobbying to keep the article securely contraband. With an annual volume close to sixty thousand catties of drug, and their whole operation geared to an optimum cash turnover, the British drug barons were quaking at the prospect of formal duty fees, tariffs, quotas, quality inspections, and all that bureaucratic nonsense. It took eight months to get all the details suitably worked out—Lord Elgin had to haggle down the proposed opium duty by fifty percent—and when the evil day came, David Jardine took it with cautious equanimity. *The Opium Circular*, August 1858:

> It is definitely arranged that the article is to be legalised subject to a duty.... This will not come into operation until the new tariff does, which may not be for some months yet. The immediate effect should be to increase demand for the drug rather than otherwise, but it will no doubt also encourage the growth of native poppy.

Sure enough, within a year the merchants of Swatow were discovered to be sophisticating good Jardine-Matheson Malwa with inferior Chinese opium. More ominous yet, buyers for the Swatow Opium Guild were booking steamship passage to Calcutta and speculating on opium at the auction block. Dismal times were at hand for Jardine-Matheson.

They were getting pressed out of the trade at both ends of the connection now. In previous years Jardine-Matheson had enjoyed

*130 gm. silver per 100 chests.

the nimblest and most well-armed merchant fleet in the China Seas, and offered to other merchants the singular advantage of having their cargos underwritten by the Bengal Insurance Company. With the 1850 opening of the Peninsular and Oriental steamship line, all these advantages were lost. David Sasoon and Sons now effectively enjoyed a fleet fully equal to the *Red Rover* and her expensive sisters, and anon there were spacious Sasoon factories in all the treaty ports besides Amoy. And the Sasoons were much closer with the Indian producers than Jardine-Matheson could ever be.

The Sasoons had a pedigree stretching back before the sixteenth century, when the Inquisition had run them out of Spain for being Jewish. David Sasoon's father, Shaykh Sasoon ben Salih, had prospered so mightily as a merchant banker in Turkey that the local Pasha had several times jailed him for no other reason than to extort ransom from the family. David, the firm's prolific patriarch—he had twin sons and a grandson on the same day in 1841, at age forty-eight—set up operations in Rajputana, Central India, in the thirties, just as the Malwa growers commenced wholesale opium exports, and the Honourable Company's monopoly was opened up to independent investors.

Unlike Jardine-Matheson, the Sasoons exploited the post-Company *laissez faire* bonanza with an eye toward the long term, and never specialized in opium to the point of neglecting any other commodity that could turn a profit, however slim and chancy. When most of the other traders stepped out of the Indian cotton business, the Sasoons made a point of rescuing impoverished Indian growers with loans for seed money, and in this way they cut out the necessity of dealing with producers thirdhand through Bombay. In the fullness of time, when the Sasoon-supported cotton growers found they couldn't sell enough of the crop to make the loan interest, David and Sons were in a choice position to suggest alternative tillage. They would even advance money for the necessary opium development: irrigation, soil enrichment, dung and hordes of migrant harvesters at culling season. By and by, whole districts of the Native States were under poppy contracted to David Sasoon and Sons for harvests years in the future.

"Silver and gold, silks, gums and spices, opium and cotton, wool and wheat—whatever moves over land and sea feels the hand or bears the mark of Sasoon and Co." By 1850, when the Peninsular & Oriental opened its bottoms for unlimited Sasoon cargo, the family already figured among the *creme de la creme* of several continents. Elias Sasoon, the second eldest son, presided over commercial operations in Bombay in the palatial Sasoon office-mansion on fashionable Malabar Hill. The front gardens afforded a splendid prospect of the broad emerald harbor, and the back looked out over the pestilential sewer-slums of the Untouchable district: a highly "motivating" location. The family's exclusive *soirees*—where the cosmopolitan colonial set were attended by Caucasian slaves from the Turkish markets—set the tone for every society season on the subcontinent.

It was during the second Opium War, the *Arrow* war of '56, that the Sasoons rudely elbowed Jardine-Matheson into second place on the drug exchange. No one was bidding much at the Calcutta auction that spring, apprehending much difficulty in delivering the drug on account of the hostilities in China. So it happened that three Sasoon brokers—E. Gubbay, E. D. I. Ezra, and S. Isaac—bought the entire Patna crop. This was moved via steamship to the extensive and well-guarded Sasoon factories on the China coast, and was housed there for months until the war was over and buyers were clamoring for opium at any price. After the subsequent landslide sale, a lot of Chinese drug merchants were in debt to David Sasoon and Sons, which lent the Chinese a splendid incentive to do business—legal, contract business—exclusively with the Sasoons in the future.

"The trade has altogether gone to the dogs," Alexander Matheson groused when his firm formally opted to abandon active drug speculation in 1871. This was not done hastily. The whole decade beforehand had been taken up with careful investments in respectable Chinese concerns, mainly railroads. The process was given a decided nudge in the mid-sixties, when the Taiping insurgents chased all the Huang-Maou out of their occupied territories. By the time Chinese Gordon and the Ever-Victorious Brigade had pacificated the Yangtze and the occupied treaty ports, key commercial postions which formerly had been held by Europeans were now securely filled by Chinese. With proverbial industry, the Chinese expanded development, setting up warehouses, wharves, and equipment of their own. Also they set up pawnshops and banks, in which Jardine-Matheson was also pleased to invest.

After '71, Jardine-Matheson announced that the firm "now looked to opium only for freight, charges, insurance and storage"—but Sasoon and Sons quickly managed to squeeze them out of those categories also. After that, David Jardine and Alexander Matheson retired to England, leaving non-family staff to handle Asian operations. Matheson succeeded his father as the Honourable Member from Ashburton, and Jardine converted his capital into that securest of all investments, an internationally-renowned art collection.

In 1872, the same year the Sasoons came into possession of three-quarters of all the opium in India, the eldest son became a peer of the realm of Great Britain: Sir Albert Abdullah David, companion at hounds to the Prince of Wales, later Edward VII. Sir Albert, with brothers Ruben and Arthur, were continual confidants of the Royal Family through the *fin de siècle*—proof that Victoria and Edward weren't the least bit antiSemetic socially, though they did shamefully snub the Rothschilds. "Opium trading was still considered *unexceptional* and apparently less noxious socially than vulgar profit-taking on the Exchange," allows a Sasoon biographer. "Besides, their mercantile eminence in India and the Treaty Ports lent them a semi-imperial cachet among the guardians of protocol at Buckingham Palace."

It was homegrown Chinese opium that very gradually eased the Sasoons, the last of the great opium barons, out of the trade. The volume of the drug shipped out of India grew all the time—90,000 chests in 1870, 105,000 in 1880—but the prices diminished as vast districts of Szechuan and Yunnan went under poppy. Chinese opium was always derided as a strictly commercial commodity, much inferior to the imported India drug, though this may well have been pure Huang-Maou propaganda. Lab analyses from the period show that Szechuan opium turned up a higher morphine content than the choicest Malwa, perhaps explaining why in the early eighties, Szechuan production was "greater than the whole Indian crop, Malwa, Patna and Benares put together." The Chinese drug was "all but universal" in central China, the London *Times*'s Shanghai correspondent reported. Imported opium appears to have been a sort of status symbol among the better circles simply because it cost so much more than "commercial" Chinese opium:

> Indian opium is consumed in the provinces adjacent to the treaty ports, and, being an expensive article as compared with native opium, is mostly smoked by the well-to-do classes. The common people in these provinces smoke the native drug.

The last Sasoon opium season was 1890; the April shipment was valued at £111,000, but what with import duties and overhead, and the general downward-tending profile of India sales over the past decade, divestment was clearly in order. Also, opium-running was quickly acquiring a violently disreputable aura in all the better circles; it was a combination of deteriorating cash flow and real shame that prompted the Sasoons to give the trade over to penny ante independents at the advent of the nineties.

Morphine was abroad now in the Central Land, for another thing. It was carried thither in the early eighties by the pious field workers of the Medical Missionary Association of China, an Anglo-American fundamentalist outfit who peddled it to converts and pagans alike as "anti-opium pills." This can only be accounted for by absolute ignorance; the medical journals in America and Europe had been devoting plenty of copy space to the causes and treatment of morphinism, ever since Dr. George Calkins in '71 had published his epochal *Opium and the Opium Appetite*. No one of authority any longer fancied that just because morphine was the pure chemical extract of opium—the active therapeutic ingredient consecrated by the technological prestidigitation that went into refining it—that morphine would be non-addictive, an excellent detox agent for opium addicts. Yet the benevolent pastors of the Medical Missionary Association, with aggressive dioceses everywhere throughout the Central Land, commenced moving in untold crates of morphine around 1881.

Of course they eventually realized what they'd done, well after the serpent was in their garden. Still, the 1886 convention of the Medical Missionary Association of China placed the blame for the unprecedented addiction epidemic squarely on everyone but the Association. In a magnificently synergetic analysis, Dr. H. W. Bourne of Shanghai fingered the Jesuits and equivocal Chinese converts together as the agents behind "the new evil, viz., morphia-eating."

They have developed the habit of morphia-eating instead of opium-smoking. The native Christians and ministers, in some parts of China, have become in the habit of selling these pills, in the first place, with the desire to suppress opium smoking, but they have found that they made money by the sale of them. I am positively told by men of Canton, Amoy and Swatow that the native Christians are becoming deteriorated by the habit of expecting to make money and enrich themselves by the selling of these remedies, and that their first object, that of enabling the opium-smokers to be cured, has vanished from their view. I am further credibly informed that in South China morphia is being known by the name of *"Jesus opium."*

"Jesus opium": while it's certainly not inconceivable that the Jesuits infesting Guandong and Yunan could have devised some positive use, by their lights, for morphine addiction in the interest of some great religious objective, most likely this slander originated from the understandable urge on Dr. Bourne's part to simply pass the buck. Missionaries of all sorts and every doctrine characteristically passed the buck for their lack of success in Christianizing the Celestial Realm. China, with eons of continuous culture behind it, just did not go over wholesale to Jesus like neolithic Pacific Islanders and American Indians, whose previous deities had been their grandfathers. Even those Celestials malleable enough to imbibe the superstitions of the West tended to fuse them into weird doctrinal syncretisms like the Buddhist-Christian-Taoist creed of the Taipan rebels. This, very naturally, was attributed by the missionaries to opium. And so they brought in morphine by the case, as a cure for opium.

All in all, by the end of this most calamitous century, there were many people in Peking who profoundly regretted that the Imperial edict of 1524, which rewarded with death any foreigner who stepped on Chinese soil, had ever been repealed.

SEVEN
AMERICAN AFYON

When the right sort of wind is blowing, the Afyon women go out to the fields and collect the poppy-sap. The wind of early summer on the high Anatolian plateau of Turkey, gently stirring the last remaining poppy petals in the late afternoon, is just right for this. When the green capsule is scored twice longitudinally, the culling woman holds the stalk upright for a moment and the milk issues out by itself, drawn forth from the little wounds to meet the cool, stroking breeze. Just a dab of it emerges: If the wind were any stronger the sap would smear and be lost, but the right sort of wind draws it out, fixes it there on the lance-grooves, and begins drying it right away. The Turkey poppy is not a high-yield cultivar, twenty pounds per acre being optimum. As it sits out in the wind overnight the sap turns pearly, then rosy, then nearly brown. When the women come back to scrape it in the morning—dew is not a hazard in Afyon province after the middle of June—the opium already looks pretty much like what the consumer will smoke or eat.

The opium and the petals are about the only parts of the plant which are not used by the Afyon women. The seeds go into their bread, the leaves go into their salads, the oil is used for cooking, the stalks are woven into sturdy fabrics for patching their ceilings, and the drained pods are chopped into fodder for cattle. Only the men in Afyon smoke opium at all, and not much of it. Most of it is fashioned by the women into standard two-pound loaves, wrapped in poppy leaves, and left outside to thicken in the breeze for a couple of days. Uncovered then, the opium loaves are lightly dusted with sorrel seeds—it keeps them from sweating to-gether—and laid in wickerwork baskets lined with linen for trans-port to the Black Castle of Opium.

Afyon-Kara-Hissar: the town is set around a thousand-foot sandstone bluff, atop which the said Black Castle of Opium sits, to preside over the gathering there each summer of all the afyon of Afyon province. This was an orderly, methodical, and care-fully-regulated enterprise around 1800, and had been so for almost eight hundred years. The opium chiefs in the Black Castle took in 150,000 pounds of afyon every summer, no more, and no less, and stored it there. In late autumn they distributed seed among the selected Anatolian poppy villages for the November sowing, so that the plants would develop roots all winter, and quickly bring up precisely 150,000 more pounds for them the following summer. To ensure a steady, unfluctuating return on this in-vestment, the opium chiefs parceled the crop out carefully. All year long, at regular intervals, they loaded mule-caravans with afyon for the five-day trek down to insatiable, infidel, pestilential Smyrna.

Plague, pox and greed prevailed in Smyrna; nobody liked the place very much. Early in the eighteenth century Smyrna had supplanted Constantinople as the Ottomans' chief port of contact with the ferociously commercializing West; Smyrna, on the Med-iterranean, was more accessible to trade, and besides, Constan-tinople had been through enough horrors since the Crusades. Europeans who took up consulate posts in the "Sublime Porte" were carefully chosen from among people who had already had the smallpox. It was exactly there, in fact, in the 1720s that a British consul's wife, Lady Mary Wortley Montague, observed how Turkish midwives immunized children against the smallpox by intentionally inoculating in them cases of sublethal cowpox. With a once-pretty face scarred by smallpox gouges herself, Lady Mary took this unfathomable oriental notion back to England, where Dr. Edward Jenner became interested in it and invented inoculation. The ultimate extinction of the smallpox virus from the face of the planet would, hence, proceed out of Smyrna.

John Jacob Astor (1763–1848)
*Astor's American Fur Company was simply too big to smuggle
contraband properly. When, in 1817, one of his ships—the
Seneca—hastily offloaded nearly seven tons of drugs
in full view of the citizens of Canton, it precipitated the most
vicious Mandarin crackdown on the opium trade up to that time.*

Whenever possible, American ship captains preferred to moor out across the mole in Smyrna harbor, commercializing second hand with the Turks through the seasoned European consuls. The British were a great help with this, strangely, setting up decent transactions for just a "light consulage and dragonage fee." Lord Cornwallis himself, Viceroy of India after the American War of Independence, had ordained that Yankees ought to get favored-nation status at any port with a British trade presence, as long as they stayed orderly. This opened up all India to them, and by 1800, New England ships were regularly running bottoms full of pepper and tea from Calcutta to Smyrna. But of course they did not stay orderly.

Nearly half of all the opium that came out of Smyrna every year was bought up by the British Levant Company, strictly for carriage to Europe and the United States. British vessels were forbidden by Crown statute from conveying Turkey opium to the China market at Canton; to do so would also have cut into the Honourable East India Company's opium monopoly, and the Honourable Company was forever in sorry enough condition without that. But there was no law forbidding these Americans from running afyon into China, except for the law in China. Here was all this opium, standard grade and dependable quantity, buyable the year 'round at Smyrna. For Yankees like Thomas Hanasyd Perkins of Boston and James and Benjamin Wilcocks of Philadelphia, whose families had lately spent eight years running the British blockades off their own coasts, the temptation was flatly irresistible: smuggle this contraband into China under the noses of the *British* smugglers!

Boston smuggler Charles Cabot, in 1805, was clearly thinking along these lines, as he coordinated the commercial activities of a little fleet belonging to James and Thomas Perkins about the Indian Ocean. Standing in at Borneo he found the locals starved for opium, so he dispatched a ship to see if some could be bought at Penang, where the Honourable Company had warehouses. All he had to do was run up a phony Union Jack, he discovered, and they'd sell it freely, and let him move it anywhere. The Bornese were grateful and generous. A man could get rich, by heaven, if he were to get in on the ground floor at the Calcutta opium auction. "I intend to purchase Opium at the Company's sales

& proceed to the eastward," Cabot ambitiously wrote home to Boston, "where I have no doubt of being first at market." The earliest return mail, however—six or eight months later—instructed Cabot to drop everything immediately. He was to batten down the hatches, stand off for the Cape of Good Hope, and "make a voyage to the Mediterranean to procure Opium."

The James and Thomas H. Perkins Company of Boston was clearly anxious about the James and Benjamin Wilcocks vessel, *Pennsylvania*, which had just set out from Smyrna for Batavia in the Dutch East Indies with over sixty-five hundred pounds of Turkey opium. Everyone immediately heard about it—these Yankees had perfected industrial espionage along with the art of blockade-running—and nobody believed that the dirt-poor Maylays of Batavia were going to absorb all that opium in one batch. Benjamin Wilcocks of Philadelphia had lately been appointed official United States consul at Canton—that's Wilcocks of James and Benjamin Wilcocks, mark you—so it was obvious that the *Pennsylvania* was truthfully bound for Canton. A second Wilcocks ship, the *Sylph*, subsequently left Smyrna with quicksilver, Spanish dollars, and Turkey opium. The rush was definitely on, and the Boston Perkinses were not about to be left out of the scramble.

Thomas Hanasyd Perkins sent out his favorite nephew that summer to Canton: John Cushing, just sixteen years old, clerk to Perkins's permanent Canton supercargo, Ephraim Bumstead. Apprehending that the youth might need some wholesome diversion in the austere commercial compound on Thirteen Factories Street, Perkins sent after him a complete Shakespeare—"a library in itself," he guaranteed the lad. Cushing also carried urgent instructions to keep a special eye out for "information regarding the article of Turkey opium." Specifically: "Is it to be got on shore with little risk? What is the price to the Mandarins for getting it on shore?" Since it only cost two Spanish dollars per pound on the Smyrna docks, Perkins had high hopes for afyon: "if as much in repute in China as the Opium of India, great profit may be made on it."

Poor Bumstead promptly died of the cholera at Canton, so it must have been the precocious John Cushing who brought off the coup that followed. When Charles Cabot's boats finally made

Whampoa, stuffed with Perkins and Company afyon, so much of it went straight onto the black market that opium prices at Canton were depressed for the rest of the season. The Wilcocks brothers' Philadelphia opium ships, meanwhile, sat in Whampoa Harbor full of carefully-stored drug, unable to unload it at a decent price, and missing out on bargains at other Asian ports— bargains that were picked up by the Perkins vessels that had quickly dumped all that opium on Canton for minimal profit, and had then headed out.

This was a pretty canny commercial maneuver for a sixteen-year-old boy to execute, even John Cushing. But going by later developments, it's reasonable to assume that right from the first in 1805, Cushing was a protégé and confidant of Houqua, the richest private individual in the world.

Houqua, *capo di tutti capi* of all the commercial Hongs in Canton—the CoHong Guild—was already richer than John Jacob Astor was ever going to get. He would undoubtably have been the emperor's number-one henchman, had it been any empire but China. Houqua had people all over the world squirming under his corporate thumb, since literally *all* the tea that came out of China passed through Houqua's fingers. Everything that went in or out of the Celestial Empire, aboveboard or contraband, was the property of Houqua whenever it was on the dock at Whampoa. As a result, mercantilists in Boston, Baltimore and Bristol, London and Lisbon, Manchester and Madras and Madrid—were *all* in debt to Houqua. Very deeply in debt, a lot of them.

China needed hardly anything, after all, because it produced nearly everything in gross abundance. So any Western merchant company that could land a factor's compound on Thirteen Factories Street was in an excellent position in terms of receivable commodities. Tea, rhubarb, dye, silk, porcelains, camphor, sandalwood: these Houqua sold and loaded at his pleasure, in abundance. Steel, cast iron, opium, ginseng, ebony, *beche de mer*, cottons and furs: these he bought and unloaded when he cared to, which was not nearly often enough to suit the Westerners who did business with him. People who traded with Houqua's CoHong tended to get a lot of Chinese merchandise from him at first, and to set up in consequence a lot of extremely far-flung and complicated trade arrangements with the major European markets, which were always anxious for Chinese produce. Once the merchant got suitably overextended, of course, Houqua would proceed to tighten up the supply of merchandise; the tea harvest in Fukien would be "delayed" because a typhoon had washed out the bridges, or a dreadful mulberry blight would "redistribute" the Szechuan silk market. The poor Huang-Maou commercialist, having inevitably already taken a few expensive shipments from Houqua on credit, would discover that all the money he'd made in Europe was *owed* to the renowned Hong grandmaster. Houqua would simply make out a chop for thus-and-so a sum, calculate the interest on it, and suggest that the delinquent merchant commence running in an occasional load of hard-metal Spanish dollars to effect those interest payments. He wasn't ordinarily out to ruin anybody; Houqua simply liked to keep people under his thumb.

So Houqua's thumb was felt as a physical presence in banks, offices, and counting-houses the world over. If he'd been a Mandarin with connections in the Forbidden City, the Chinese right now might own the light by which you read this page. However, it *was* China where political Mandarins were enjoined by caste barriers from dabbling in commerce. In China, Houqua was just a sleazy profiteer and usurer—something more degenerate than a pimp, really—and the more money he made, the more evidence there was of his moral degeneracy, and of the mortal greed of the idiotic Huang-Maou who did business with him. The Celestial Emperor would not have eaten from a plate on which Houqua's shadow had fallen.

The opium business for Houqua was just another way to selectively ruin the thieves who came to Canton to trade. The records of opium shippers show that by 1805 they were already pulling a moderate amount of silver bullion out of the CoHong, who paid for it in exchange for smuggled opium. But the opium bullion was always Indian sycee, which the East Indiamen were now sorrowfully running in regularly to Whampoa, to make up the interest on *their* very sizeable CoHong chop. By contrast, the Spanish dollars that entered Canton did not go back out in exchange for opium, ever; *they* were recognized international currency, mined out of Peru and stamped in the Spanish royal mints, buying a recognized dollar's worth of merchandise anywhere in the world. Sycee bought less per weight of silver than Spanish dollars, and bought rather less anywhere outside the British Empire than anywhere within it. Houqua took in and kept the real money, and let just enough of the fishy Indian metal flow back, in exchange for opium, to keep these drug-running Huang-Maou murdering each other over it.

In this article of opium, some *other* Hong agent would negotiate with the Western commercialists, never Houqua. No one in any of the Hongs ever physically went near the opium themselves, either for smoking or for commerce. The eyes and ears of the emperor were everywhere, and most heavily on these smarmy moneychangers of Whampoa Harbor.

So when John or Thomas H. Perkins of Boston wrote to their European buyers things like this—"Our friends Houqua and Perkins and Company have recommended in very strong terms the purchase of a large quantity of opium"—you have to assume they were only showing off their very privileged commercial intimacy with the richest private individual in the world. Certainly no one else but their precocious nephew, John Cushing, ever seems to have profited nearly so handsomely from dealing with Houqua over such a very long term. As long as Houqua was on top of the trade in Canton, James and Thomas H. Perkins stayed head and shoulders above everyone else in this article of Turkey opium.

It wasn't very good opium, compared with Patna or Malwa. Since this Turkey opium was the very article that was being used by Europeans and Americans throughout the century, it's interesting that Chinese smugglers mainly used it contemptuously to *cut* their India drug, just as they used molasses and dung. But it was profitable enough.

By 1812, John Cushing of Perkins and Company was also Houqua's agent in all his dealings elsewhere in the world. At Canton, Cushing attended to all the port fees and permits for incoming ships from many nations, warehousing their legitimate cargos and brokering them through the Hongs, berthing and scheduling and overseeing their receivables; arranging the midnight opium transfers in utmost secrecy, *cumshaw* and all, so that the Mandarins, the British, and Benjamin Wilcocks were all equally in the dark; gathering commercial intelligence from ports all around the world, plotting how to beggar the rivals of Houqua and Perkins in places thousands of miles away, months and years in advance.

Cushing does not seem to have been the sort of chap much

given to idle vacationing, not even with sybaritic Macao just a day's sail down the Pearl River, across the outer lighting in Chuanpei Bay. No women or distilled liquor were allowed in the closely-watched enclave along Thirteen Factories Street, and without special permission, no Huang-Maou trade factor was suffered to set foot in China anywhere but the commercial square, or the Whampoa docks. You had to have an inborn immunity to more things than the cholera to put up with twenty-three years on Thirteen Factories Street, as John Cushing had.

But Cushing appears to have been entirely content with business, and the company of people like Wilcocks, the other European and Parsee factors, and the motley sailing crews that had to be bivouacked in the trade compound while their ships sat in Whampoa for weeks and months on end sometimes. The various factors, although they spent most of their working hours trying to ruin each other's companies, got along very well personally.

After the War of 1812, Cushing picked up handsome brokerage commissions from the Boston firm of Bryant and Sturgis, along with Joseph Peabody of Salem and John Donnell of Baltimore. Benjamin Wilcocks also handled Peabody's business occasionally. About the only United States firm that would have nothing to do with Cushing or Wilcocks—precisely because it *would* inevitably entail moving opium—was the venerable New York tea-shipping house of Olyphant and Company. Remorseless Quakers, the Olyphants had a factory all their own on Thirteen Factories Street; Cushing and the rest called it "Zion's Corner."

As time went on, and these Boston and Philadelphia houses visibly fattened on opium bullion, the magnificent John Jacob Astor of New York City decided to dip heavily into the trade. Astor's globe-girdling American Fur Company, never given to doing things by halves, bought nearly *ten tons* of Smyrna afyon in 1816 and 1817, and tried to broker it all through Wilcocks in two big batches. Wilcocks certainly knew what a fiasco that would cause, but he doesn't appear to have advised against the project; he was probably conniving to turn the tables on Cushing, and wreck the market for any incoming Perkins's drug for the season.

So to everyone's astonishment, in the summer of 1816 the American Fur Company's enormous *Macedonian* put in at Jackass Point, carrying 110,000 Spanish dollars, 1.190 tons of Wisconsin ginseng, 450 chests of Madagascar ebony, 133 chests of quick-silver—and over 5,000 pounds of Turkey opium. Normally, when any such impossible cargo of opium descended on Canton the carrier was prepared to sit for a good while at Whampoa, doling it out parcel by parcel, so that the price shouldn't entirely fold under, and so that not too much of a midnight stir would be raised at the off-loading berth. But the *Macedonian* was on a tight itinerary, being part of the fabulous Astor industry that coordinated everything from the seal harvest on Kamchatka to the boiling of *beche de mer** in Patagonia, and so the opium was off-loaded hastily and with only a minimum pretense to secrecy.

And if that was not embarrassing enough, things became *really* tense the following summer when Astor trebled the dose and shipped in nearly seven tons in his *Seneca*. All this opium in one bottom was enough to not merely kick the Turkey and India prices out of kilter, but to rupture the whole impossible Squeeze apparatus, with its unwritten but exceedingly precise traditions of *cumshaw* and long-distance haggling. Astor was just too *huge* to move contraband properly. Enormous wickerwork baskets of sorrel-dappled afyon loaves were left sitting on the docks in broad daylight, prompting mixed indignation and horror in the Hoppo's bribe-takers.

On a subsequent occasion an Astor boat, trying to sell a load of Persian opium to the Hongs, was turned down flat. If Turkey opium was just so much molasses in the estimation of Houqua, Isfahan juice was more on the level of dung. Astor decided that if the confounded coolies were going to turn into *connoisseurs* over this inefficient article, then he'd just not trouble himself with it any more. The American Fur Company at the time had the corner on moving Turkey opium from Britain to New York, where Astor advertised opium auctions in the local papers, all entirely legal and ordinary. This perfectly respectable merchant therefore stepped out of the China opium trade.

But the damage had been done. Just a few weeks after the

---

*Literally, "sea slugs": *Gastropodia pulminofera*, a shell-less mollusk that inhabits seawater in the Southern Hemisphere. Gathered during its shallow-water spawning season, boiled and dried, *beche de mer* supposedly has aphrodisiac properties. The Chinese believed that it "wonderfully strengthens and nourishes the system and renews the exhausted system of the immoderate voluptuary."

Seneca departed—about the time it should have taken for the gossip to reach Peking, and the emperor's outrage to echo back to Canton—the Mandarins cracked down, the first domino in a chain of events eventually leading to the seige of the foreign trade factories and the Opium War.

A Baltimore brig called the *Lion*, skippered by one William Law and stuffed with Turkey opium, didn't help by mooring up at Whampoa about this time. Supposedly the *Lion* wasn't carrying opium at all, but only bullion, an installment payment on some enormous debt which her owners, Minturn & Champlin of New York City, owed to Houqua. But the New Yorkers, teetering on the edge of ruin anyway, had brilliantly plunged most of that bullion into purchases of Smyrna, and directed poor Captain Law to fleece this insidious Oriental who was aggravating them so exceedingly from the other side of the globe. Law had instructions to fawn and grovel extravagantly before Houqua, painting the firm's insolvency in the grimmest light he could. Once "the fears of the creditor" had been suitably aroused, they told Law, he was to give as little of that Turkey to Houqua as he could to cover their debt chop, and try to sell the rest to some other Hong *capo*.

That Law actually tried this shows how little these New Yorkers knew about the opium industry. Of course, the instant he said the obscene word "opium" in Houqua's presence, with witnesses on hand, the audience was at an end. Law had a terrible time getting rid of the *Lion* opium. It took weeks, parceling out small bundles of "this troublesome article" to whatever fly-by-night smugglers had the courage to move it off his notorious ship. Then after a few other opium ships drifted in, all at once prices went through the floor, and Law ridded himself of the rest at a song. The whole affair, said Law, was "little if anything better than to have shipped dollars from New York."

This troublesome article was again the source of American embarrassment in the autumn of 1817. Captain Christopher Gannt, the Baltimore skipper who had sailed the first big load of *Pennsylvania* opium into Canton a dozen years before, was moored in Macao Roads on the Donnell & Co. *Wabash* when a gang of pirates overwhelmed him one night. They killed some of Gannt's crew, and took off with $7,000 worth of silver bullion and a ton and a half of Turkey opium. When Wilcocks heard of the outrage he exploded, and went straight to the viceroy, demanding satisfaction. It took a month, but the Mandarins hunted down the gang leaders, and tortured them into disclosing the location of their lair—where, of course, most of that *Wabash* opium was still sitting.

This "occasioned not a little disgust on the part of the Viceroy," Wilcocks wrote to the Secretary of State. There were canquings on Chaoyin Street that month, floggings and stranglings, and a flock of sorrowful Hong flunkies heading off for the cold country in oxcarts. Houqua himself was obliged to publish a series of fierce proclamations on behalf of the CoHong, solemnly warning the Huang-Maou that further outrages of this sort would not be countenanced by the Divine Majesty of Celestial Reason. Wilcocks translated them for the State Department, but he was no grammarian:

> Foreign opium, the dirt used in smoking, has long been prohibited by an order received, it is not allowed to come to Canton: If it be presumptiously brought, the moment it is discovered, it inevitably involves the Security Merchant; and the crime of the said vessel, bringing the prohibited dirt for smoking into Canton, will also be assured.

If Houqua was now reduced to trembling obedience to the Imperial will, obviously the opium trade at Canton had become a mortally dangerous criminal enterprise. "The competition will be less next year at Smyrna," Cushing jubilated to the Perkins's buyers in Leghorn, Italy. They were to plunge a few hundred thousand pounds sterling into opium, raid every Levant Company auction from Smyrna to Marseille to London: "go very extensively into the business" before larger and awkwardly respectable companies like Astor's thought twice about what the ferocious Mandarin crackdown really portended.

Twenty thousand pounds of afyon went on Perkins's *Ophelia* at Gibraltar, and at Smyrna forty thousand more went aboard the *Bocca Tigris*—a brig named for the very stretch of the Pearl River in which she would be sitting for the next few months, parceling out her opium stingily to offloader gangs. "No time should be lost" in buying up all available Turkey, Cushing urged the Leghorn agents, "as the first arrivals will put the others on

the scent." The idea was to gather at least a year's supply of the
drug and then let it sit around Whampoa, "kept on board until
an opportunity offers to sell it deliverable alongside:"

> From the intention of the Chinese to be very strict about Opium,
> the competition you fear we think will not exist. *We know of no*
> *one but Astor we can fear*. It is our intention to push it as far as
> we can.

Over the next four years Cushing pushed it to the highly profitable
limit, benefiting from the new drug crackdown. The Hong masters
now kept resolutely in the background in this article of opium.
Smuggling negotiations were conducted entirely through the non-
Chinese wharf gangs, who haggled prices on behalf of "Clubfoot"
or "Cockeye"—the *noms du contraband* adopted by Houqua's
minions. It took a good while for the very respectable supercargos
of the Honourable East India Company to get properly confidential with these murderous Malay, Bornese and Filipino mafiosi.
In the meantime, the Company's enormous wholesale warehouses
at Black Butter Bay, out past Macao, sat packed with unsalable
India opium. These were grand times for interlopers like Cushing
and Wilcocks, who got on well with these pirates, as well as for
two young independent British shippers named Joseph Jardine
and James Matheson who commenced moving Malwa opium into
Whampoa about this time.

By 1820, Cushing was advising the Perkinses to put a lid on
Turkey imports. No more than three tons of afyon should be
sitting in Whampoa at any given time, that being the evident
saturation point for demand. Altogether at this point, James and
Thomas H. Perkins were buying about half the Smyrna crop each
season, and their imports to Canton totaled between one-third
and one-half as much as the British were smuggling. They would
have been content with that from the looks of things.

But the Honourable Company was not prepared to tolerate any
such sycee drain from the starving millions of India, to the detriment of the proceeds of their extremely rickety corporation. In
self-defense, the Company sent troops into Malwa, the western
poppy-growing regions around Rajputana, and opened up a new
auction dock at Bombay. They aimed to pull on these scrabbling
Yankee interlopers, *en bloc*, the same pirate ploy the scrabblers

were always pulling on each other: flood the market for a couple of seasons with so much of the drug that buying prices would plummet, the "men of little capital" would lose their shirts, and the Honourable Company in the long term would wind up with the whole smuggler's industry at Canton.

When this was tried on such a large scale—in 1820, the Company dumped four thousand double-decker catties of Patna and Malwa onto Whampoa, all in a bundle—of course something grotesque happened. *China absorbed it!* The Hongs bought that enormous concentration of India opium, along with the Turkey opium the Americans were moving, and the prices not only stayed firm, but more of the drug was invited.

Even the Yankees were a little shocked at the way the Chinese appetite for opium appeared to *quintuple* over the next few years. Before 1820, the Hongs kept the demand for the India drug down to less than four thousand catties in well-spaced-out, regular shipments. Ten years later, *twenty thousand* catties of Patna and Malwa were moving in on a slipshod, irregular, but very profitable schedule. American imports of Turkey opium tried to keep pace—in 1825 Thomas Perkins nearly ruined his company with mass purchases of Smyrna afyon, against John Cushing's advice—but the prices for Turkey stayed pretty much the same, even though they kept moving in more of it. At the peak of the Yankee trade, in the late twenties, even though they were handling more afyon than ever, it didn't amount to a *tenth* of what the Company was smuggling.

Houqua, it appears, discreetly stepped out of the opium market in 1821 after the next Yankee opium scandal—and with him went any prudent limits on demand from the Canton interest. With the *Emily* affair the Americans became so visible and notorious in this article of Turkey opium that the viceroy of Guangdong believed Turkey itself to be a territory of the United States. Since it was his Mandarins whose heads rolled whenever the emperor blew up over things like opium, the viceroy in that year decided to kick the United States and British drug-movers entirely out of his bailiwick. And thus the *Emily* incident went down in history.

"The hottest persecution we remember," Liverpool opium pirate Holly Magniac called it, and Magniac had seen a few things in his years around the South China Sea. The *Emily*, a schooner out of Baltimore owned by John Donnell, tied up at Whampoa in early spring that year bearing a little tin, for appearances' sake, and a massive portion of the last Smyrna crop. Cushing, afraid she'd oversell and ruin prices for the coming season, persuaded *Emily* captain William Copeland to broker it very slowly, bit by bit, through Donnell's Canton supercargo, Griffin Stith. Thus the *Emily* was still sitting in Whampoa on a hot day in September when one of her seamen—a Sicilian deckhand named Francis Terranovia—got into a terrible argument with an old Chinese lady on a sampan lying alongside. Terranovia hit her on the head with an olive jar, it seems, and she fell into the Pearl River and drowned.

The viceroy appreciated the lady's sacrifice; it was just what he needed. When his investigators showed that the *Emily*'s whole cargo of "foreign tin, hardly worth anything" wouldn't have covered half her five-month dock fees so far, he concluded, "it appears the vessel came for no other purpose, but to sell Opium. Infinitely detestable: Rightly did heaven send down punishment and cause Francis Terranovia to commit a crime for which he was strangled."

Terranovia was duly garroted by the Mandarins after a notably fair trial, time and place considered. No testimony for the defense was accepted—no interpreter for the defendant was provided, for that matter—but at least it was conducted in public, and nobody was tortured before the last few minutes. The Mandarins actually conceded to hold the proceedings on the *Emily*, and stooped to haggling formally with Wilcocks, who submitted a stiff protest on behalf of the United States State Department. To no avail: The defendant was convicted and strangled, and all Perkins and Company vessels were directed to leave Whampoa Harbor for the time being. The Hoppo's top *cumshaw* collector, a socially prominent Mandarin, was convicted, queued, canqued, and exiled to the cold country. Two CoHong junks were seized with East India Company opium in the Bocca Tigris, and their crews fared even worse.

If the *Wabash* crackdown was a smuggler's windfall, the *Emily* affair was a typhoon of new profits. Since in quaking observance of the Celestial Throne, the Mandarins were never again about to let drug ships moor up in Whampoa, Cushing followed the British opium traders and stationed a fat-bellied Perkins's ship,

Cadet, thirty miles downriver at the new drug depot at Lintin. Without Houqua to coordinate the buying end, demand turned wide open, and business boomed.

To handle Turkey sales, Cushing went into business with John Sturgis of the Boston Sturgises, and opened a peculiar sort of bank on Thirteen Factories Street. The buyers for Clubfoot and Cockeye came to Perkins & Sturgis now to learn the approximate quantity of Turkey opium that might be lying off Lintin, and haggle out a suitable price. They would presently be given a coded chop from Perkins & Sturgis, entitling them to pick up thus-and-such amount of *"gum"* at Lintin, for whatever the cumshaw fee was in Spanish dollars. The price of the drug itself was never entered, and in fact Perkins and Company was pretty secretive about all the sycee they were robbing from the Honourable Company; but at $150 in sycee per chest minimum, in a *bad* buying season, well—the Perkins's restaurant chain is today one of America's more secure investments.

Young John R. Latimer of Philadelphia, arriving in Canton in 1824, was audibly scandalized, at first anyway, when he observed the godfatherly tactics that Cushing's operations deployed to keep watch over all the Turkey opium in China.

> If they were advised of a quantity coming to others, they put the market down by forcing a sale at something under their selling prices—when the new parcel arrived the agent had to come into some arrangement with them to sell conjointly... or be obliged to dispose of it, at much below what the quotations just previous to his arrival had led him to expect, and then immediately after he was sold out, and before his Drug has been delivered, great to his mortification, the market rises without apparent cause.

Poor Latimer started out with any number of disadvantages, thanks to the general incompetence of his employers. James and Benjamin Wilcocks had been solidly under Houqua's thumb for five years, ever since Benjamin's father-in-law back in Philadelphia had accepted a few large cargos of legitimate Chinese goods on credit. It took Latimer years to become trusted by Houqua—who hardly dared *speak* to an American any more—and get the chop canceled. In the meantime he had to maximize the one advantage the Wilcocks firm enjoyed, which was a very warm relationship with Jardine-Matheson and Company of London and Bombay, the up-and-coming new non-Company opium shippers. Through them, Latimer got an entree in to the prominent Bombay shipping firm of Hormuzjee Dorabee, and the Calcutta brokerage house, Alexander and Company. Before long, Wilcocks and Company was making $20,000 per year on opium commissions out of Calcutta alone.

It is to Latimer of Philadelphia, who clearly had no shame at all, that we owe most of the more precise statistics about the United States trade in Turkish opium. He kept proper ledgers, unlike Perkins and Company, since he was the underdog, and it was his aim to sweep the Boston concern off the water.

In this endeavor, Latimer was abetted by young Samuel Russell of Providence, Rhode Island, who came to Canton the same summer and set up the factory of Russell and Company on Thirteen Factories Street. He went into business with an old China hand, Philip Ammidon, supercargo for the venerable Baltimore house of Brown, Benson and Ives. (Brown and Ives had the distinction, in 1796, to run the first crate of India opium straight from Calcutta to Baltimore.) While Ammidon courted the Parsee drug shippers of India, Russell opened up fruitful areas of co-operation and corruption with Jardine-Matheson.

"It is generally in our power," a Jardine-Matheson circular advised the American firms presently, "to remit funds to England on more advantageous terms than can be effected in Bombay." These wholly unscrupulous privateers, to get around all inhibitions posed by the Honourable Company's government-backed monopoly, began washing their opium sycee through the London bank accounts of the American firms, which were impervious to Company scrutiny.

Before long, Wilcocks and Russell were suitably established to join in on the lucrative mother-ship opium trade at Lintin Island. About the time John Latimer put a Wilcocks mother-ship full-time at Lintin—the *Thomas Scattergood*, serving the Bocca Tigris from 1829 to 1831—the Yanks began falling out with Jardine-Matheson. Running their extremely sophisticated lookout system from the Kapsingsmoon Point in Hong Kong (see Chapter 6), Jardine-Matheson and Company started trying to edge their co-smugglers out of the trade. The East India Company's opium monopoly was on its last legs; Joseph Jardine was in Parliament now, lobbying forcefully for the complete opening of trade to independent shippers, and even London's very prestigious Dent and Company had gone heavily into opium carriage. Whenever the Honourable Company's monopoly should fold, these British buccaneers were preparing to scuttle the Yankee corsairs.

All the Americans agreed it was time to take the money and clear out. Cushing brought in some Boston relatives in 1829, to take up the traces on his retirement. The most promising of the lot was young Robert Bennett Forbes, who replaced Sturgis as supercargo for the Lintin mother-ship operation. His brother, Thomas Tunno Forbes, took up the overall business from Cushing, and was soon after drowned in a typhoon. He left a will handing over the Perkins combine to Russell and Company. Young Bennett Forbes, out at the malarial Lintin depot, put up a fuss over this development, so Cushing came back in on the first available Perkins and Company ship (the *Bashaw*, hauling one thousand crates of afyon) and settled things.

Cushing and Samuel Russell were bosom chums by now, both incredibly wealthy and set to retire. In view of the surviving Forbes's youth and inexperience, Cushing confirmed the transfer to Russell. Russell, having by this transfer gotten the whole Turkey trade in his pocket, retired himself, and went home with Cushing to an easeful old age. (Or so he hoped: actually he went bankrupt shortly after founding Wesleyan University in Provincetown, now in Middletown, Connecticut.) He left the trade in the hands of his assistants, William Law and Augustine Heard.

Law was not particularly clever, but Augustine Heard was every bit a Russell protégé, and began advertising among the Parsee factors of Calcutta that the *Lintin*'s bottom was available for opium storage at rates cheaper than the Company storeships: *free*, in fact, as long as they factored their merchandise strictly through Russell and Company. Out at Lintin, young Robert Forbes spent two years stuffing afyon loaves and Patna cattyballs into canvas sacks, for moonlight transfer to the nightmare pirate praus that issued up silently out of the fog, with dried human heads and hands decorating the gunwales. He made $30,000 each year, according to Law, and got $20,000 in shares in the *Lintin*. It was his great nephew William Cameron Forbes who launched the perfectly respectable investments journal of the same name.

Latimer carried on fruitfully at Canton for six years after Benjamin Wilcocks went home in 1827. Augustine Heard simply could not abide his partner Law, who was abrasive as well as stupid, and continually asked Latimer to take over the company. Perversely, Latimer refused to accept the whole Russell operation on a platter, and instead carved away two-thirds of their Turkey trade before he retired himself in 1834. He officially stated it was the malaria that prompted his departure, but it was much more likely the lapse of the Company monopoly. As a final disservice to his kinfolk and nation, he sold his entire combine—including Wilcock's half—to Jardine-Matheson. He got out with a satisfying "competency," as he put it, and became a gentleman farmer in Delaware.

Russell and Company went heavily into tea in 1834—which must have both heartened and frightened the Olyphants of Zion's Corner—and concentrated mainly on European sales for the next two decades. In times when the British opium trade was the object of the emperor's greatest displeasure, the Russell people would enthusiastically haul in Patna, Malwa, Turkey, Isfahan—whatever they could buy, wherever they could buy it, for as long as the crackdown lasted.

As a rule, though, the New Englanders followed the pessimistic advice of Samuel Russell, who left Canton just as the drug prices went through the floor, thanks to the sudden descent of British privateers on Lintin Island: "The consumption of this article appears to be gradually decreasing, and we should not think it in the future a safe article of remittance." With so much India drug available now, the Hongs did not need Turkey for the purpose of adulteration.

It was much safer—and infinitely more legal and respectable—to simply pick up opium at the Levant Company's Smyrna and Marseille sales, and move it to the medicine-makers of the good old United States of America. The sales of this article appeared to have an extremely promising future in this very *nervous* young republic.

EIGHT
NERVOUS WASTE

My own conviction is, that if a man will take to stimulants, the juice of the poppy is as harmless as any other source of excitement; and then it has this strong recommendation, it never makes a man foolish, it never casts a man into a ditch, or under the table; it never deprives him of his wits or his legs. It allows a man to be a gentleman; it makes him visionary, but his visions create no noise, no riots; they deal no blows, blacken no one's eyes, and frighten no one's peace. It is the most quiet and unoffending relief to which the desponding and distressed, who have no higher recourse, can appeal.

The Reverend Walter Colton
"Turkish Sketches," 1836

The chief and primary cause of this development and very rapid increase of nervousness is **modern civilization,** *which is distinguished from the ancient by these five characteristics: steampower, the periodical press, the telegraph, the sciences, and the mental activity of women.*

George Beard
American Nervousness, Its causes
And Consequences, 1881

America was a great market for opium. In 1840, the New Englanders ran in so much opium—24,000 pounds—that it came to the attention of United States Customs, who put a duty fee on it, raising the price to $1.40 per pound wholesale. Within ten years, imports trebled to 87,000 pounds. By 1860, the price had quadrupled to $4.50 a pound; that year the United States imported 105,000 pounds of the drug. In 1870, America had upped its intake fourfold: 500,000 pounds of opium paid $2.50 duty, and around 25,000 pounds *more* were smuggled in by enterprising West Coast schooner captains. Considering that most of that 1870 opium was boiled down to morphine sulphate to be injected with hypodermics, as likely as not, by a population of less than forty million souls—it's not surprising that around that time thoughtful Americans began to seriously wonder if the nation might have a slightly unwholesome fondness for narcotic drugs.

"Because it is insinuating," 1870s addict William Rosser Cobb was to say of opium, "because it makes no noise in its progress, men have been silent about its infernal ravages. Alas! its very silence is ominous of its strength. The silent forces of nature are those which are most potent." It was the lament of a whole country that seemingly woke up one day to discover that it had been addicted to morphine for quite some time already.

No one could have imagined it in bright, peppy, optimistic 1833, when *Blackwood's* magazine of New York confidently predicted,

> as a matter of comfort, that we are not to expect, either in Christian Europe or in America, to see the consumption of opium ever become so universal as in Mahometan countries, where the use of wine is forbidden to the true believer.

Between Jesus and manly alcohol, and general white Anglo-Saxon splendidness, America would certainly abide uncontaminated by this effeminizing oriental luxury. The *Blackwood's* reporter therefore urged that the drug be developed on a trim cost-efficient Yankee basis. Domestic cultivation was suggested, but turned down, even though some fairly high-powered experimental poppies had been nurtured out of Vermont soil.

> Our poppy plants are probably too slow in their growth, and possess too little juice or succulence, to yield a satisfactory return

to the opium-gatherer—were the uncertainty of climate and the dearness of labour alone not sufficient to preclude the idea of our entering into competition with the Eastern producers of the drug.

So with characteristic American ingenuity, *Blackwood's* came up with a brilliant technological solution to the challenge. Opium could be *stretched*, most wonderfully, with just a little laboratory work.

> Besides familiar substances such as gum, mucilage, resin, fat, caoutcouc, &c., it contains morphine, narcotine, codeine, narcine, thebaine, opianine, meconine, pseudomorphine, porphyroxine, papaverine and meconic acid—eleven peculiar organic compounds, which occur in greater or less quantity in nearly every sample of opium!

Actually there are twenty-four alkaloids in opium, most of them pharmacologically inert in isolation, but the only one that was of material significance to *Blackwood's* was the first one. Morphine—"this pure chemical compound, the composition of which is fixed, and the physiological effects constant and certain"—was the solution. Three times stronger than opium, it stood to stretch each pound of drug three times further. And yet more satisfying to the high-tech American imagination, the same laboratory process yielding morphine also yielded codeine, thebaine, and papaverine: a little hocus-pocus with test tubes, acids, and filters, and each pound of drug went maybe *twelve* times further.

Morphine tablets, ointments, solutions, tinctures, suspensions, and clysters were on all the drugstore shelves by the 1850s, gradually easing out the traditional crude preparations of laudanum. This elicited the approval of the medical community generally. Ever since Thomas De Quincey in England had so graphically described the peculiarly romantic horrors of chronic opium-eating, literate doctors had noticed a tendency in some patients to go on taking laudanum long after their immediate physical afflictions had been alleviated and cured. Asthmatics who took it to clear their lungs at the onset of acute attacks might start to feel attacks coming on four or five times a day, day after day, for years. People with dry coughs would start coughing again—and *sniffling* now—whenever their last dose of opium wore off. The bellies of diarrhea sufferers would commence to

The first recorded case of nervous-waste syndrome resulting from opium smoking was a "sporting gentleman" named Clendenyn who met his downfall in San Francisco's opium dens. This illustration accompanied a newspaper account of his sad tale circa 1880.

rumble. Melancholics grew doubly melancholic without their medication, manics went twice as manic. Snakebite victims, tetanus survivors, mild burn cases—long, long after the medical condition disappeared, would just keep taking this rather vile-tasting medicine, with the kind of phenomenal daily regularity you'd never see with cod-liver oil.

On the other hand, these cases were extremely rare in proportion to all the people who took laudanum, even for weeks and months on end, who were only too happy to stop taking it as soon as they were well. Communication among doctors in the United States was still minimal; not many systematic observations were being traded. Some people appeared to react differently from *most* people to opium; that's all anyone could figure out. This is where medical knowledge of addiction stood for a long time in the United States. Not many doctors were convinced at all that addiction, in the rare cases it occurred, was a very troublesome phenomenon.

Early on, Dr. Samuel Armor of Long Island owned that "typically bilious and melancholic" patients seemed to respond unwholesomely to opium, while "the sanguine and mixed temperaments" took it only as medicine. Even for the diminishing number of physicians who still believed in Galenic biophysics, this was a vague and unhelpful observation. The proprietor of Rush Medical College—an Illinois quack factory that degreed its doctors via the U.S. Postal Service—lucidly concluded, after long and penetrating observation:

> I have always noted that persons affected with opiates in a manner *not* intended, are invariably poor excreters.

In the mid-1800s, though, American doctors were much more interested in the new hypodermic techniques for morphine injection than they were in any of the drug's consequences. First developed by Dr. Alexander Wood of Edinburgh, the syringe went through several rapid developments, vastly improving its efficiency and accuracy (See Chapter 3). The hypodermic technique was being touted by the entire European medical community as a significant improvement over oral opiates, but it was in America that the new device aroused the most curiosity.

It was still years, though, before Lister taught doctors to *wash*.

For years yet, doctors were injecting people with each other's contagious diseases, and *causing* tetanus by leaving track-sores untreated. As late as the 1870s, at the New York City Clinical Surgery Medical College, Dr. Alfred Post was clearly persuaded that it was the *dose of the drug* which caused infections at the injection site; he got around the problem, therefore, by applying injections more *liberally*.

> I attribute this immunity of my patients from local irritation to my manner of giving injections. I raise a fold of skin, pierce it with the needle, inject a drop of the fluid, pass the instrument a short distance, inject another drop, and so on to the end. In this way, the liquid is diffused and much less violence is inflicted than when the fluid is injected in one mass.

It could have been worse. Doctors dreamed up no end of intriguing injecting styles once Dr. George Wood of Philadelphia had determined that it hardly mattered *where* you injected a person just so long as the opiates got into the body.

> A sensation of fullness is felt in the head, soon followed by a universal feeling of delicious ease and comfort, with an elevation and expansion of the whole moral and intellectual nature, which is, I think, the most characteristic of its effects. There is not the same uncontrollable excitement as from alcohol, but an exaltation of our better mental qualities, a warmer glow of benevolence, a disposition to do great things, but nobly and beneficently, a higher devotional spirit, and withal a stronger self-reliance, and consciousness of power. Nor is this consciousness altogether mistaken. For the intellectual and imaginative faculties are raised to the highest point compatible with individual capacity. The poet has never had brighter fancies, or deeper feelings, or greater felicity of expression, nor the philosopher a more penetrating or profounder insight than when under the influence of Opium in this stage of its action. It seems to make the individual, for a time, a better and greater man.

The above was written by Dr. George Wood in his *Treatise on Therapeutics* (1868), one of the most widely-used mid-century American medical texts. Though Wood himself first injected morphine around 1852—maybe the first American to do so—he was in this passage speaking strictly of raw opium. In this he also had considerable experience, since his wife had been a laudanum addict for ten years.

Whatever Mrs. Wood's experience, opium certainly never lost its honeymoon lustre for Dr. Wood. It could, he allowed, promote in certain weak-willed characters a "total loss of self-respect and indifference to the opinions of the community; and everything is sacrificed to the insatiable demands of the vice." It's not known what Mrs. Wood thought of that portrait, or if she ever put herself successfully through his detoxification mode: "a diminution of the dose being made every day, so small as to be quite imperceptible in its effect," he prescribed, "leading to a cure in somewhat more than a year." By this extended stepdown, Wood swore, "This evil habit may be corrected, without great difficulty, if the patient is in earnest."

Morphine was another matter entirely for Wood. He prescribed it for such broad categories of affliction—"pain, insomnia, and nervous irritations"—that there couldn't be much he didn't use it for. Like most physicians, he considered opiates to be "stimulants," and morphine was both more effective and safer than opium in this respect—"less liable to provoke irregularities of mental action and, with an equal excitant influence on the faculties and feelings, to derange them less frequently, and in less degree."

Moreover, since it was safer and more efficient than opium, in terms of subcutaneous administration by hypodermic, this pure white powdery alkaloid drug could just do no wrong, in more eyes than in Dr. Wood's. The clean, powdery alkaloid could be accurately weighed and measured down to the hundredth of a grain on late-model apothecary scales, and a given dose would always have *exactly* the same physical effect in people of similar body weight. Of course there were always *some* doctors who had to insist that morphine, like opium, would appear to weaken in effect if administered to the same individual over a period of weeks, necessitating progressively augmented doses; but as late as 1868, the medical school textbooks were still insisting that something else in opium besides morphine caused tolerance development. Isolate the morphine scientifically from that other thing—those other things, actually—and morphine would surely not diminish in effect, like crude opium, with repeated administrations.

Morphine, anointed and hallowed by the most austere prestidigitations of advanced chemical science, just could not be the same murky substance that had catapulted Samuel Taylor Coleridge screaming out of his sleep every night. By Wood's time, the count of opium alkaloids was around twenty: it was surely one of the *others* that constipated, and another that gave people the midnight horrors, and a third one yet that made them go sniveling back to their laudanum like a dog to its vomit. It was probably a fourth ·alkaloid that intoxicated them, too: "The singular pleasure of the opium consumer," everyone was confident, would be absent with morphine, or at least attenuated to a therapeutically decent degree.

Some gave up on the notion early, with vast regrets. A Dr. Phillips, in 1866, advised the New York Academy of Medicine that he had personally discontinued the practice of administering morphine hypodermically, "from a desire to check the tendency to self-injecting." Inevitably, some patients *would* leave the doctor's office, after getting an injection or two of morphine, and stop into a drugstore on the way home and buy a shiny hypodermic kit all their own, along with specially-prepared patent vials of injectable Magendie's Morphia Solution. This was bound to sour a few conservative professionals on this grand new technological synergy of alkaloid and syringe. But doctors more dedicated to the American cult of progress shrugged it off. *Some* patients put themselves through grueling high-colonic saline enemas three times a day, for no reason at all—though *most* patients wouldn't. Some patients invented preposterous imaginary maladies, and insisted on being continually treated for them at considerable pain, risk and expense—though *most* patients didn't. If there was this new sub-category of morphine self-injectors, was there anything new or particularly significant to that? Who could blame anyone for developing a certain measure of fascination for this ultra-efficient, and forbiddingly elegant new device for the subcutaneous administration of pure alkaloid drugs? Professor H. H. Kane waxed lyrical in *The Hypodermic Injection of Morphia*, 1880:

> The glass cylinder and metal cased instrument, when properly made, is probably the best, as it is strong, the fluid in the cylinder can be seen, bubbles of air detected, and any dirt or crystallized morphia can be seen and readily removed... The instrument may be graduated on the glass or on the piston rod... Messrs. Codman

& Shurtleff of Boston are making a most excellent instrument, all metal, so tempered and jointed as to be perfectly accurate, airtight, of even calibre, easily cleansed, and strong enough to withstand any ordinary blow without injury.

As realistic notions of sepsis gained ground after the Civil War, and doctors and patients in America learned to wash themselves on other occasions than ritual baptisms, secondary infections subsequent to morphine injections became much more rare. As hypodermic technology advanced, with ever-thinner needles causing ever-milder tissue trauma at the injection site, it all really began to qualify as a felicitous new leap in the evolution of the healing arts.

As the needles got better, though, people started blundering into veins with them. "Any part of the arm or leg may be selected," Dr. Kane carefully counseled, "avoiding of course those situations where there is liability of wounding a vein."

The difference between subcutaneous and intravenous administration is pretty conspicuous with opiate alkaloids. Around 1860, Dr. George Jones at Cincinnati had begun hitting veins by accident.

> The first time I became somewhat alarmed; the patient threw up her arms, complained of suffocation, giddiness, excessive fatigue, a severe tingling sensation flowing the course of the circulation. The countenance was at first livid, then flushed; the eyes became unusually brilliant; slight muscular twitchings, profuse sweating, with cold extremeties, and in a few minutes complete relaxation followed by a deep sleep, which lasted a few hours, when she awakened, feeling, as she expressed it, "ever so much better."

He had given her an overdose. Presumably the woman had a rather low order of tolerance to morphine—or was getting an uncommonly stiff dose—or she probably wouldn't have gone into such a profound and refreshing coma after the first flush of traveling prickly heat. For people wholly unaccustomed to opiates (what few remained so late in the century), the effects were, presumably, even more dire whenever the needle tip strayed into a vein.

Overdose therapies, methodical and highly inventive, came much into fashion thereafter. Early on it had been noticed that the belladonna alkaloids—atropine, hyoscamine, and scopolamine—had a peculiar synergy with opiates. Administered alongside morphine, belladonna extracts kept the pupils from constricting and the breathing rate from slowing quite so much, and conspicuously diffused the terrific mental exhilaration about which Dr. Wood of Philadelphia was so keen. Since they antagonized these few signs of opiate intoxication, the word went out that the belladonnas were full-fledged opiate antagonists, and they were incorporated into all sorts of overdose remedies, addiction cures, and general opiate quackery. (See Chapter 12) Physicians also variously guaranteed that mercury and strychnine were useful in the event of "morphine poisoning." Some actually injected overdose cases with "aromatic spirits of ammonia," and swore that the victims survived in spite of it.

The best overdose remedy, naturally, was prophylactic: avoid veins—simple enough. But in the event of accidents, Dr. H.H. Kane came up with a truly brilliant prophylactic device: the tie-cord.

> I am firmly convinced that no physician should be held free from blame in case of accident where he has not had a ligature or tape loosely encircling the arm above the point of puncture. At the first intimation of danger this should be pulled tight and kept so for several hours.

In case of an accidental intravenous, that is, you could sit back for a good long while, releasing the tie-cord every few minutes or so, experiencing a peculiar episode of traveling prickly heat all through your body each time you did this, which not all patients found wholly unpleasant.

With the equivalent of some 500,000 pounds of opium, mostly processed into pure alkaloids, circulating through the United States in 1870 alone, it can be pretty confidently projected that a good deal of it was being self-administered, intravenously, tie-cord and all, by people who had been through a couple of accidental overdoses, and grapsed the *point* of it all. "The tendency to self-injecting" hit an all-time high in the 1870s and 1880s. Never before or since have so few Americans taken so many opiates. It was dreadfully obvious by now what was going on, and a timely reaction set in. Dr. Robert Bartholow, *The Hypodermic Method*, 1879:

The introduction of the hypodermic has placed in the hands of man a means of intoxication more seductive than any which has heretofore contributed to his craving for narcotic stimulation. So common now are the instances of its habitual use, and so enslaving is the habit when indulged in by this mode, that a lover of this kind must regard the future with no little apprehension. It may well be questioned whether the world has been the gainer or the loser by the habit of subcutaneous injection.

"Epidemiology" is an ill-advised concept to apply to social patterns of drug use,* but if the conditions were ever ripe for a morphine "epidemic," it was over the last quarter of the nineteenth century in America. Morphine sulphate was exceedingly cheap, much cheaper than alcohol for the euphoric tickle it gave you, and every pharmacy and general store carried preparations of it cal- culated to appeal to every sort of person alive, whatever the individual emotional quirk or physical ailment. There were lower- proof opiates like laudanum and codeine, in tasty syrups and candies, to inculcate in novices of any age an appreciation of opium's particular extra-therapeutic properties, and to insidiously lead them, through a succession of higher-proof nostrums, to morphine itself. Anyone who visited nearly any physician, for any complaint from toothache to hemorrhoids to consumption, could count on coming away all atingle with traveling prickly heat. Availability, purity, and social acceptance of morphine were at an all-time high, price at an all-time low. And from 1875 to 1890, the land sustained a series of economic "panics" that really amounted to one long, hideous depression. If the prevailing the- ories about drug epidemiology in the late twentieth century were strictly applied to the late nineteenth century, you'd have to con- clude that the only people who *didn't* get hopelessly addicted back then had to be sociopathic aberrants or endocrinological freaks.

Throughout the 1870s, the opiate use in the United States grew

---

*In 1938, when the first methodical studies of drug addiction got under way at the Lexington Narcotics Farm in Kentucky, Dr. Lawrence Kolb submitted to the Public Health Service a study on the "epidemiology" of heroin use. It was sent back for revision: "Drug addiction," a PHS supervisor cannily noted, "is not a contagious disease." This has been largely forgotten in all the excitement since then.

at a rate considerably steeper than the general increase in population. The appearance of pure, cheap, cocaine hydrochloride was everywhere enthusiastically greeted, and sales of more traditional pharmaceutical highs like chloral hydrate, ether, and cannabis tinctures suddenly took off on a handsome surge. Americans were eating, drinking, smoking, injecting and clystering up more drugs, and more varieties of drugs (alcoholism was also a national scandal) than ever before, or ever since.

Addiction finally became a bona fide medical problem, in 1871, when Dr. George Calkins published *Opium and The Opium Appetite*. Addiction was no longer something that could be trivialized by the scintillant high-tech glamour of pure alkaloid extractions and gleaming glass-and-brass surgical instruments. The proportion of people unable to get off morphine after being exposed to it—morphine being three times stronger than opium—had to have risen at *least* 300 percent, and Calkins' estimate that probably every fifth American had this disease may not have been wholly unrealistic. Once addicted, most of them were bound to be seriously worried and inconvenienced by it; and since their attempts to kick it at home would only give rise to an exquisitely revolting and scary complex of influenza symptoms, they would naturally consult doctors for help. Most doctors, Calkins knew from experience, would simply send these people off to their colleagues who ran local pharmacies, to fill regular morphine prescriptions.

Scandal and recrimination animate every line of Calkins' prose about the opium appetite.

> This gentleman, now of middle life, having suffered much from a diseased ankle, was advised (professionally) to use morphine hypodermically. The immediate effect being found most soothing and satisfactory an indefinite continuance was suggested; and now, after a habituation for two years, the invalid is hopelessly delivered over, an abject slave to the habit, enervated in body and enfeebled in mind. The thigh of the afflicted limb is literally studded with punctures, to be counted by the score.

For two months this unfortunate man had been subjected to the elegantly-conceived detoxification therapy of a New York physician, that is, a gradual daily stepdown of his morphine dose, accompanied each day by a higher dose of atropine, opium's

"antagonist." To no avail though, as he "still continues on, writhing as helplessly as if, Laocoön-like, he were wound around in
the coils of some monster-serpent."

High-tech glamour cast no dazzle into Calkins's eyes. Morphine was just as addictive as opium, and addiction once contracted was a degenerative physical disease condition, probably
incurable. Calkins was not sanguine at all about the opium appetite; laudanum-takers especially were prone to manifest shocking and abrupt physical maladies—sudden "colloquiative diarrhea" leading to expulsion of "steroraceous bile"—at odd
moments, especially after they'd gone a day or two without their
medicine. At about the same time, these addicts would contract
"hyperesthesia," reacting with pure physical agony to every foot-
step, every door-slam, every church-bell note from the outside.
Calkins made gloriously morbid reading for health-conscious
American hypochondriacs everywhere. There were a lot of them,
most of them were already addicted, and Calkins guaranteed all
a fatal "crisis" sooner or later—"it may be in three weeks, or
perchance not under three years."

Doctors certainly should have known the calamities attendant
on the abuse of this drug: an inexorable buildup of the "*moribific
leaven,*" Calkins called it, which decayed and slew its victims
as remorselessly as consumption and undulant fever. Even among
the laity, surely just about everyone now had seen sick people
take morphine, sometimes *for years on on end,* and then die.
How, therefore, should anyone of ordinary wisdom and reason
ever go anywhere near it?

"This being eminently an age of *novelties* and experimenta-
tions," Calkins began—and therewith launched the "modern
times" theme in drug-abuse etiology. The fault was largely in the
times, Calkins boldly affirmed, and after him a legion of practitioners and drug addicts took up the refrain: "Stimulation is the
cry. Our people stimulate too much, and one stimulant paves the
way and calls for another, each successive step calling for something stronger." Calkins's generation beheld the dawning of the
Age of Anxiety, and *that* was why people were taking drugs. All
previous hypotheses to explain American inebriety—sex, hered-
ity, even the Civil War—could be taken up and subsumed into
this "modern times" theme. And it seemed to *help* a good deal

to do that, when addicts and doctors alike went searching for the cause of this lamentable state of affairs.

Virtually no one of the times, interestingly, blamed the addiction epidemic on the simple fact that there are always a lot of people who just like getting high. Hardly anyone thought to put down on paper what morphine felt like, and what could possibly be in it to attract anyone. This had to wait another generation. In his 1923 autobiography—*Thirty Years in Hell, or the Confessions of a Drug Fiend*—Col. D.F. McMartin recaptured it pretty vividly in a few passages. Full of years, wisdom, garrulity, and obviously very few sincere regrets, this retired drug addict and lawyer, recalled the point of it all with vivid clarity. For the intellectually-disposed person, opiates confer a unique

> capacity of unraveling abstruse cryptograms that would puzzle ancient and modern dogmatists, indulge in recondite investigations, delve creditable in the mysteries of the alchemists, converse in icy algebraic symbols, deductive and inductive ratiocination, expand the meaning or moral of signs and tokens, the mystery of the unobtainable, the procession of the equinoxes, the acceleration of gravity, and even decipher the hieroglyphs.

Unlikely as it may sound, opiates also confer this selfsame feeling upon people who are stupid. This is why they classed opium as a "stimulant" for so long, despite all the physical evidence that it was really a depressant. Yet it certainly had the property—with long-term use—of comprehensively depressing a lot of people.

"That stimulation will not be considered a benefit," Civil War addict "Anon" confessed in his 1876 drug autobiography, "which is followed by reaction and collapse." He attributed the cause of his addiction to the war, and specifically to the Confederate guards at Andersonville, who injected wretched Union prisoners of war with morphine, against their knowledge or consent, to tide them through starvation and dysentery.* "I sing only the 'pains of opium,' its 'pleasures' I have yet to see," confessed Anon.

---

*A great many late-century male addicts, and their prescribing physicians, dated their habits to the war. It *had* been the most important episode in peoples' lives, and certainly it was a more dignified alibi than vicious curiosity, uncouth acquaintances, or an over-prescribing physician. But opium and morphine use did not really start to rise sharply until some five years after Appomattox, meaning that the war had nothing to do with morphinism.

He attributed to morphine nothing but depression—"general effeminacy, sickness and misery." Far from intellectual reverie, it promoted an icy and regretful indifference to himself and society, a lot of sitting indoors with thick, dull, neutral books. Plagued by nightly horrors, vague fears of losing his job and not being able to afford his habit, Anon felt strangely *conspicuous* withal, and avoided company for fear of somehow being "a mortification to himself and a grief to his friends."

"It is not *pleasure*," J.D. Bulkley firmly stated, "that drives forward the confirmed opium-eater, but a *necessity* scarce less resistible than that Fate to which the pagan mythology subjected gods not less than men." Bulkley, a doctor of divinity, was, in 1840, the first American addict on record to write a detailed drug confessional. Bulkley didn't dwell much on the euphoria, or the physical depredations of the drug. Withdrawals were mildly disagreeable, he allowed, but the *really* disagreeable thing was simply knowing he was an addict.

Bulkley had first begun to take morphine tablets to treat some unspecified but chronic complaint; once addicted he stepped down to laudanum, which he had to continue for years and years, before giving it up. His years as an addict, he recalls candidly, "were as healthy as any, if not the healthiest years of my life." But he'd never felt comfortable with opium, which "weakens or utterly paralyzes the lower propensities, while it invigorates and elevates the superior faculties, both intellectual and affectionate." Curious, this. The suspicion begins to form that Dr. Bulkley may have been medicating away some fairly troublesome interior difficulties, especially when he generalizes about the opium addict: "He is in a different *sphere* from other men, and *in that sphere* he is sane."

This suspicion of underlying psychic disorder is supported by the prime cause to which Bulkley lays all his vague discontents: "nervous exhaustion" he called it, a fashionable mid-century euphemism for "the accursed habit of nervous abuse, which *little* innocent school-boys are taught by their depraved elders in school." Drug abuse was merely a certain consequence of self-abuse, the substituting of one sensual vice for another. Masturbation certainly followed the same abominable behavior pattern: "It is usually continued till the unfolding reason and conscience open the victim's eyes to the true nature of his habit." But by then it's too late. All poor Bulkley could do was switch in mid-adolescence from masturbation to opiates—and to the vice of chewing plug tobacco, about which he was only scarcely less self-recriminative.

For FitzHugh Ludlow of Schenectady, "nervous waste" was both cause *and* effect of substance abuse in general. "A feeble childhood soon exhausted its superfluous activities," he discreetly confessed in *The Hasheesh Eater*, 1857, "and into books, ill health, and musing I settled down when I should have been playing cricket, hunting or riding." Son of a fire-breathing Bible-thumping abolitionist-evangelist, Ludlow exhibited telltale nervous waste signs throughout life.

The Hasheesh Eater—which really bespeaks more the intoxication of precocious literary talent running amok rather than having anything to do with actual cannabis hallucinosis—was Ludlow's endeavor to emulate Thomas De Quincey. If ever there was a Romantic devotée, it was Ludlow. Since he wouldn't have had much in Schenectady to write about that was Romantic, at around the age of eighteen he began testing out various mind-altering medications in the shop of an apothecary friend. He investigated chloral hydrate, ether, and opium with indifferent results, before he took a few tastes of what he called "hasheesh"—tarry brown alcoholic tincture of cannabis, what we today call "hash oil." The brand name was Tilden's C. Indica Extract; it sold for six cents a bottle.

The visions and meditations of *The Hasheesh Eater* comprise a sort of *Reader's Digest* review of Romantic literature and philosophy. Grand spectral processions, beautiful houris, and the solemn patriarchs of ancient religions and religions unknown populate Ludlow's imagination. Demons, machines, Mandarins, monuments and tabernacles pullulate, in settings that sail from the Great Wall of China across the Hindu Koosh into the labyrinthine bowels of the earth at the indent of a paragraph. Uneasily he reassures himself, time and again, that it's all just for unscientific experiment's sake; surely he will never do it again. But boredom and lassitude supervene, with a replenishing fascination for the drug.

On graduation from Union College, having solemnly foresworn stimulants, Ludlow spent a "long and severe winter" teaching in

Watertown, on the yonder side of the Adirondacks in the arctic Saint Lawrence Valley. There being no "hasheesh" in that frigid wilderness, Ludlow discovered that he could do all this glorious fantasizing himself, *sans* drug—whether or not he wanted to. The spontaneous visions, swarming suddenly up into consciousness in the full light of day, populating the world with delights and monstrosities, infused him not with panic, but with "self-convicting pangs"—"I have broken my vow! Alas! Alas!" The ecstacies and obscenities now were succeeded by depression and disassociation, a revulsive impatience with the material world for not being as romantically phantasmagoric as when he was out of his mind. Ludlow was clearly in a precarious state at this point, "the only hasheesh-eater this side of the ocean." It was very good for him, come spring, to get back to New York, where there were people he could abide.

All this, mind you, was the work of "hasheesh," leading Ludlow to opine that a person was endowed by God at birth with a finite reservoir of "nervous energy," and that any unusual "stimulation"—such as drugs or sex—consumed an inordinate amount of this physical energy, which once spent, could never really be replenished. Already prematurely exhausted by childhood "superfluities," how much more energy must Ludlow have spent with tincture of cannabis? The question persecuted him physically: He died at age thirty-four of tuberculosis.

The economics of "nervous energy" were as grim and intractable as any commercial system that could develop under industrial capitalism. Whatever short-term gain the drug might offer, in terms of medicine or recreation, the long-term drain on one's energy represented a drastic and terminal reduction of fixed capital. Look at what happened to poor Coleridge:

> He exhausted by mighty draughts all his credit at the bank of healthful life, and that is a corporation which never permits us to overdraw. Up to the very last deposit of blood and sinew, nerve and spirit, prompt payment will meet every demand; then comes the crash, and the bankrupt nature is no longer seen on the 'Change.

Never mind that Coleridge's balance of payments stayed topside for sixty-two years, despite a pint-per-week demand from his Old Blackie. He didn't write anything certifiably Romantic over the last twenty years, so what was he worth to Ludlow? Old Black Drop laudanum had cruelly exacted its due in nervous energy, which Ludlow inevitably interpreted in *sexual* terms: "emasculation of the will," and "a spiritual unsexing." These were the economics and biophysics of nervous energy in the industrial West, and these economics *always* get worse before they get better.

The nervous-waste epidemic peaked right about the same time as the drug-abuse epidemic was blossoming, and they were wedded into one glorious psychopathic whole by Anthony Comstock. Comstock gave his name to a whole era in American Puritanism after Congress in 1873 awarded him absolute license to travel all over the country with the United States Postal Service, apprehending smutmongers and drug doctors anywhere he personally chose. Renowned today chiefly for his heroic exertions against what he took to be obscenity, Comstock also happened to harbor a morbid obsession about drugs. Anything you might inject, sniff, swallow, smoke, rub on, or pour into your body was as threatening to Comstock as anything you might look at or read while masturbating. This random selection of Comstockery will illustrate the syndrome better than any imaginable psychobiographical commentary:

> Fathers and mothers, look into your child's face and when you see the vigor of youth failing, the cheek growing pale, the eyes lustreless and sunken, the step listless and faltering, the body enervated, and the desire to be much alone coming over your offspring; when close application to work or study becomes irksome, and the bouyancy of youth gives place to peevishness and irritability, then seriously look for a cause. It may not always be the case, but in many instances it will be found to come from secret practices, which have early in life sapped the health of mind and body.
>
> ...Our youth are falling by the wayside. Lives that otherwise might shine as the stars in the firmament are shrouded in a veil of darkness, with horrors to the victim's mind which no one can describe.
>
> ...The effect of this cursed business on our youth and society, no pen can describe. It breeds lust. Lust defiles the body, debauches the imagination, corrupts the mind, deadens the will, destroys the memory, sears the conscience, hardens the heart, and

damns the soul. It unnerves the arms, and steals away the elastic step. It robs the soul of manly virtues, and imprints upon the mind of the youth, visions that throughout life curse the man or woman. Like a panorama, the imagination seems to keep this hated thing before the mind, until it wears its way deeper and deeper, plunging the victim into practices that he loathes.*

These are the robust cadences of exuberant, animated self-loathing projected onto a socially-accepted scapegoat. Comstock drove at least a half-dozen people to suicide in his life with his righteous witchhunting, and confessed himself jolly about it any time it happened. It made him feel jolly for months on end when a little old lady in Greenwich Village, whom he had twice checked into the Tombs for printing up her imaginary trysts with the Archangel Michael, heard he was going for a third warrant and stuck her head in her gas oven. Drugstore proprietaries he rarely bothered to prosecute, preferring to just go in with an axe and destroy any premises where drugs of which he disapproved were said to be sold. Mainly he disapproved of contraceptives and abortificients—rye ergot and quinine suppositories—though later in the century he became the terror of opium dens in Chinatowns on both coasts. And in the nineties, when he learned that a lot of mail-order patent medicines contained substances associated with nervous waste=—like morphine—he swung his weight as special postal inspector to discourage national periodicals from accepting ads for them. Drugs were just as good an excuse for censorship as sex.

As the self-abuse and drug-abuse epidemics synergistically blended, though, the inevitable paradox was dimly glimpsed. If opiates suppressed the carnal appetite (as they most certainly did), and in doing so presumably conserved the limited reserves of nervous energy which were *known by science* to be irreplaceably diminished by the catastrophe of orgasm—wasn't that a point in their favor, then?

George Calkins seems to have apprehended this paradox, when he regretfully disapproved of cold-turkey detox as a morally ac-

---

*Cf. az-Zarkashi (Chapter 2) But Comstock couldn't possibly have read az-Zarkashi, whose writings were strictly in Arabic. It just comes naturally.

ceptable morphine cure. "The perturbative method," he called it. There'd be nothing wrong with it, except that male addicts had a tendency to shed *sperm* during it. To be sure, he noted, this nasty reaction didn't appear to be aggravated by any pernicious species of physical pleasure, but some lost quite a bit. In an era where a teaspoon of semen was officially equivalent to a gallon of arterial blood—and was not only forever irreplaceable, but vital to the function of the organism—the "perturbative method" could theoretically damage the body as much in three days as morphine could in as many years. Calkins therefore discouraged it on humane and economic grounds.

Others even attested to the *advantages* of addiction, on moral grounds. Confessed addict Reuben Eubank—*Twenty Years in Hell* (1903)—allowed that his libido had embarrassed him frequently in his youth, though never over his two decades on the needle. Contemporary morphinist William Cobb, a newspaper editor, stated that it was the only beneficial property of the vicious drug: "Opium has only scorn for the lustful."

Ludlow in the fifties had confidently predicted that the national tendency to nervous waste was surely going to get worse, basing his reasoning on the new science of genetics. As Ludlow saw it, because dad had had to squander his nervous energy in the scramble for advancement, the typical American child "inherits a constitution least of all fitted to bear these draughts upon it. The question of his breaking down is just a matter of time." With each new generation in the nervous republic, the tolerance to intoxicants like opium would necessarily lessen; and with each generation henceforward, the time will come earlier when its avatar runs out of nervous energy, and then, "The devil stands at his ear, and suggests opium."

Ludlow did not invent this scenario in a hashish delirium. All the most progressive and thoughtful figures of the day were devoted to some such concept. By their lights, the susceptibility of white people to opium was rising steadily in proportion to that of other races as modern times evolved. People with dark complexions, like the Chinese, resorted to opium for the euphoric feeling, pure and simple, because—it was surmised—they weren't *noble* enough to get anything better out of it. And because of that these nonwhite races, with their seeming immunity to the effects of intoxicants, came to be perceived as a grave threat to the American middle class with their supposed increasing vulnerability to nervous waste syndrome. Improving author C.W. Post wrote in 1897: "Very many of these celestials and Indians are mentally and physically inferior, and they go on smoking year after year, and seem not very much the worse for it. It is your finer natures that suffer, deteriorate and collapse. For these great and terrible is the ruin."

So it was that opium—not morphine—emerged finally as the magic scapegoat that neatly sewed things up. In 1891 President McKinley solemnly signed a new tariff law imposing savage prison penalties on any Chinaman who might try to sneak opium past the Customs shore patrols. The domestic drug epidemic had already peaked and subsided midway through the eighties—total imports in 1890 were down to 93,667 pounds, legally—but it made people feel reassured that something was finally being done about the Chinese and their revolting smoking opium.

The evolution of the Chinese drug prejudice is so fascinating it gets an entire chapter to itself here, the "Yellow Peril." There were innumerable persuasive reasons why Americans just then should have hated and feared the Chinese, and this was one of them: it took the onus off middle-class morphine to focus popular resentment on opium. William Cobb, morphinist newspaper editor, gave morphine credit at least for reducing sexual concupiscence, and even lowering the crime rate. Morphinists "do not descend to low practices of any kind; they are not dishonest; they aim to deport themselves well; they do not harm anybody save themselves; they do not fight, or brawl, or commit murder." Just as it obtruded the sex drive, pure-alkaloid morphine, administered *via* surgical syringe, dimmed the allure of criminal profit for the satisfied addict. It was the necessary vice of the "scholarly, refined and aristocratic" elements of modern times. Whereas, no one smoked opium but from "wantonness of desire," to *facilitate* criminal and concupiscent inclinations.

> The smoker is absolutely without shame. He is a creature given over to his own lust, walking after the flesh, and has no desire to get out of a slavery that brings him no sense of degradation.

Any 100-percent degradation-sensible American would at least go for a cure once in a while. By the nineties, there were cure clinics all over, advertising quick, complete, confidential, and permanent detoxification for anyone with the money to afford it. All of them were lying on every single count, and widely known to be lying, but that didn't put any dent in the demand at all. (See Chapter 12.)

It was the thing to do now that the Chinese had been hauled into it all. Whole volumes of horror stories about the health hazards of morphine couldn't have done it—health is about the last thing anyone considers in deciding whether or not to abuse any drug—but prejudice persuaded people to go for the cure right away. A lot of them kept going back, too, faithfully and regularly, for the rest of their lives.

NINE
YELLOW PERIL

At ten o'clock at night the Chinaman may be seen in all his glory. In every little cooped-up, dingy cavern of a hut, faint with the odor of burning Josh-lights, and with nothing to see the gloom by save the sickly, guttering tallow candle, were two or three yellow, longtailed vagabonds, coiled up on a sort of short truckle-bed, smoking opium, motionless and with their lustreless eyes turned inward from excess of satisfaction—or rather the recent smoker looks thus, immediately after having passed the pipe to his neighbor—for opium-smoking is a comfortless operation, and requires constant attention. A lamp sits on the bed, the length of the long pipe-stem from the smoker's mouth; he puts a pellet of opium on the end of a wire, sets it on fire, and plasters it into the pipe much as a Christian would fill a hole with putty; then he applies the bowl to the lamp and proceeds to smoke—and the stewing and frying of the drug and the gurgling of the juices in the stem would well nigh turn the stomach of a statue. John likes it, though; it soothes him, he takes about two dozen whiffs, and then rolls over to dream, Heaven only knows what, for we could not imagine by looking at the soggy creature. Possibly in his visions he travels far away from the gross world and his regular washing, and feasts on succulent rats and bird's-nests in Paradise.

Chinatowns of the American West were a tourist attraction from the very beginning of the Gold Rush days. When Samuel Clemens penned the above for the Virginia City *Territorial Enterprise* in 1865, he was dutifully filing his set-piece description of opium smoking in the Oriental quarter, a requirement for every cub reporter on every territorial gazette.

Plain contempt, unmixed as yet with hate or fear, was the prevailing flavor of American racism directed against the Chinese throughout the Gold Rush epoch. It was the Chinese who dug the most difficult mines and moved the ore out to the refineries, labor so cruelly backbreaking and lethally hazardous that no white man in his proper senses would consider it. The Celestials were imported specifically for the purpose, whole clans and townships of them, after the 1848 gold finds. Mostly they came from the eastern provinces of the empire, peasants and artisans from Hunan, Anhwei, Kiangsu and Shantung. They were leaving behind the endless series of calamities that tortured China through the last half of the century—the breakdown of Imperial authority, incessant feudal warfare among petty regional despots and terrorist cults, the total collapse of the ancient irrigation systems and consequent famine, with pestilence thrown in. So they were ready for anything when they got here: conditioned to feudal serfdom and the hermetic Confucian family-universe, they made for a splendidly tractable and efficient work force, and they kept rigorously to themselves. As long as the whites needed them to open the mines and get the ore rolling, the Chinese were merely a mildly repugnant necessity.

By the time Clemens filed his Chinatown set piece in 1865, things had already begun to change. All the really big gold mines had already been plumbed and put into production, so the Chinese were no longer welcome in them. Once the shafts were blasted into the vein, struts and beams safely installed, and narrow-gauge track lines laid in—once the really dangerous phase was complete, and the bodies of the coolie cave-in victims had been transplanted to the local Confucian cemetery—then the whites righteously took over the operation, usually with a vengeance. In the 1850s, white miners at the Maryville, California gold fields passed a local ordinance banning Chinese from the county as soon as the shafts were laid; and in Coal Creek, Washington, they expeditiously burned their Chinatown to the ground as a signal that coolies no longer need apply.

Increasingly through the 1860s, then, the 50,000 Chinese on the Pacific Coast clustered in the boom towns like Virginia City and San Francisco. When they weren't being routinely worked to death, they had a brilliant facility for recreating eastern China's florid landscape and culture in the scrubbiest, least promising sections of the Pacific Coast. San Francisco's Chinatown was a glorious high medieval merchandise mart, its twisty cobbled avenues hung with crisply-lettered ideograph billboards, swaying over bazaar stalls all atumble with Peking ducks preserved in jelly, pickled eggs, dried and powdered ginseng roots, rhino horn aphrodisiacs, lemons, pears, tangerines, and delicacies even less familiar to whites. Most households kept peculiarly plump, short-haired dogs tethered in their gardens, maintained on an all-grain diet special for feast days. Lustrous balls of black and brown smoking opium were used as an exchange medium until, after being halved and quartered in successive negotiations, the final slices were smoked by the end consumers.

Somehow the coolies even managed to duplicate the clothes and architecture of Imperial China, passing about in scuttle-sleeved embroidered gowns and glossy skullcaps among ornamented pagodas and temples. They acquired oxen and enormous swine, and landscaped the neighborhood with terrace gardens, even irrigation ditch-canals wide enough to accomodate rafts and pirogues. They celebrated God after traditionally gaudy Confucian and Buddhist fashions, in grand temples outfitted with gaudy graven images, with thunderous clashing music, fancy fireworks, and costumed dragon-dances on feast days. Their environs were conspicuously clean, so proverbially clean that their laundries were patronized by the very same white people who, like Clemens, maintained and *believed* that the Chinaman lived in filthy squalor by natural inclination. Their Mandarin food was also signally nutritious and savory, compared to the greasy beef and white bread that comprised the Caucasian diet, and so their restaurants became famous along the coast.

The gap between what white people believed of the Chinese,

and what they saw with their eyes, was so enormous that it can hardly be accounted for even by innate American racism. What they saw with their eyes was as alien to them as the dark side of the moon, an incomprehensibly authentic medieval Oriental landscape, dizzying with exotic odors and music, populated with queue-tailed Chinamen and tiny-footed Chinawomen uttering melodious Mandarin and flat quacky English with equal facility. Just visiting Chinatown was as unreal for whites as the most preposterous fantasy which the Chinaman could possibly entertain over his burbling yen-hok. Under these hallucinatory circumstances, it was entirely possible to believe the most outlandish anti-Sinese libels, even though they patently contradicted the most concrete evidence of one's senses. When it became convenient to believe ill of the Chinese, it was entirely possible to do so with minimal effort. These people did smoke opium, after all—the legendary dream drug—and that in itself made them a little unreal.

It was accepted without question in the 1860s, then, that the Chinaman had robbed the whites of rightful employment on the new transcontinental railroad system. In fact, one of every five Chinese in the West was involved in railway construction, spanning ravines with trestles, blowing tunnels through mountainsides, shoveling level grades out of vertical mesa slopes, and laying endless leagues of steel rail across the salt flats and prairies. It was the Chinese who were trapped in the high Sierra blizzards, decimated by the Indians, bitten and stung and eaten by the wildlife; Vanderbilt simply couldn't find white workers crazy enough to take the job, especially at coolie rates, and so it was the coolies who built the railroads. The whites, feeling vaguely robbed of an epoch of heroism and sacrifice equal to that of the great 1850s covered-wagon migrations, never entirely forgave the Chinese. They were accused of robbing jobs no one else would have taken while they were available, and revenge was duly forthcoming.

By the early 1870s San Francisco's Chinatown had become sufficiently prosperous and populous that the city council prudently began enacting special local ordinances for Orientals. Chinese workers were forbidden employment in public-funded work pro-

During the 1880's, the most lurid examples of "yellow journalism" propagated by the Hearst newspaper syndicate portrayed opium as a drug used by Chinese men to seduce and enslave white women. When a federal ban on opium was finally passed in 1905, such accounts comprised much of the testimony on which the law was based.

jects, and Chinese people were enjoined from buying real estate or securing business licenses. What's more, a "Cubic Air Ordinance" was enacted, allotting 500 cubic feet of air minimum for every factory worker and apartment tenant in the city; it was enforced only in Chinatown. The jails themselves were in violation of the law, stuffed with Chinese to bursting. In an exquisite refinement of cultural sadism, it was decreed by the health department that all jail prisoners wearing knotted pigtails must, for sanitary reasons, have said pigtails removed; a sacrilege comparable to shaving a Lubavitcher rabbi.

So far this was only standard racism, nothing more pathological than racism in any other culture. After 1873, though, when the country plunged into a depression that would persist until the end of the decade, the Chinese came to represent something uniquely terrible in the American imagination.

It was utterly inexplicable, and entirely unexpected that the economy *would* fall apart in 1873, of all years. The railroads and the telegraph had been laid out everywhere across the land and everyone had been *promised* a fat new future because of it; nowhere to go but up. Then in 1873 the bubble burst, the bottom dropped out, and nobody had work at all. New homes were abandoned in the midst of construction, families dissolved, the cities swelled with drifters and whores and orphans, breadlines formed, and food riots broke out. This was decidedly not what had been scheduled for the glorious seventies; the schedule had been sabotaged somehow, by someone, and the little man was hungry for an explanation and a scapegoat.

Samuel Gompers had both. President of the cigarmaker's union in 1873, Gompers was brilliantly negotiating the coalition of transcontinental craft unions that would, in the next decade, coalesce into the American Federation of Labor. A Jewish immigrant from England, Gompers was acutely aware that the panic and ensuing depression were the consequence of Victorian industrialists' lack of vision; unless the new technology of production was actively shared with the workers, organized by craft unions instead of serf-like corporate labor squads, it would benefit no one at all. Gompers knew this, and knew it was only a matter of organizing a national labor coalition with real political clout—

and he also knew that if he said as much in public, he'd be jailed or shot as an "anarchist."

In a stroke of brilliance, then, Gompers conjured up the best of all possible scapegoats for America's misery—the Chinaman. It was a work of natural selection, since the big bosses were indeed using cheap coolie labor to thwart union organizers wherever coolie labor was available. Though there were still less than a thousand Chinese living outside of California in the United States, seventy-five of them were hired by a Massachusetts shoemaker especially to break a strike in 1870. In California the Chinese had for years enjoyed employment at the most routine, insipid, boring handicraft industries in the region. Now when times were tough enough that even the feistiest California romantics were ready to enlist for coolie labor at coolie rates, these jobs were abruptly perceived as prestigious positions which had been weasled away from the white man by the conniving Chinese.

Gompers's cigar workers pointed the way, being the first unionists to present their exclusion of Chinese from membership as a *moral* point. In 1874 Gompers sold the California factory owners on the idea of packaging their stogies with proud printed labels declaring "White Labor," with a special certificate in each box reading:

> Protect Home Industry. To All Whom It May Concern: This is to certify that the holder of this certificate has pledged himself to the Trades Union Mutual Alliance, neither to buy nor sell CHINESE MADE CIGARS, either wholesale or retail, and that he further pledges himself to assist the fostering of Home Industry by the patronage of PACIFIC COAST LABEL CIGARS.

This in fact was the *original* union label, the first of a long and proud tradition. The anti-Chinese sentiments were union code, an implicit challenge to employers who might try to break up unions by any such underhanded ruses as hiring coolies.

No one whatsoever objected to this, especially not the Chinese. Throughout this period of mounting anti-Chinese sentiment, well into the twentieth century, the Chinese bore up under it with magical stoicism. Their communities everywhere were rigorously nuclear, and as self-sufficient as possible. They had as little contact as they could with whites, by preference, and no aspirations at all within the white culture. Though unionists might squeeze them out of one deplorable category of industry, like cigar-making, there was always some equally deplorable category available to them. They simply didn't care for the things of the white culture, and so the vicious racism of the whites could in no way demoralize them and lead them into self-destructive hatred. Except for very sporadic anti-Chinese pogroms, the white authorities pretty much left the Chinatowns to themselves. Thus the Chinese made the finest scapegoats anyone could hope for.

By this time the West Coast Chinese population had doubled to around 100,000 obliging the authorities to enact a new raft of appropriate legislation. Mostly, these ordinances were enacted under "health code" stipulations, a Sacramento senate commission having officially decreed that the Chinese were physically noxious: "The whites cannot stand their dirt and the fumes of opium, and are compelled to leave their vicinity." The health laws succeeded well in keeping the coolies pent up in their Chinatowns (which is where they wanted to be anyway) and prevented them from taking over white peoples' enterprises (in which they had no interest at all), and legislators incessantly reminded voters of that every election year.

As early as 1874, San Francisco banned the passage of smoking opium in the city limits—not because of health concerns as such, but because it was believed that the drug stimulated coolies into working harder than non-smoking whites. As anti-Sino sentiment proved to be both politically expeditious and cathartic, opium evolved into the very totem of the American progressive movement: The legendary dream drug, opium became for whites the agent which made the Chinese at once so contemptuously subhuman, yet so insidiously industrious, cunning and all-corruptive. Nothing ordinary could be invoked to account for such a paradox, nothing short of some magic *drug*! Opium was the Chinese drug, and it was religiously banned all over the West.

Again, the legislation was purely cosmetic, leading only to occasional police raids on Chinatown opium dens whenever the police budget appropriation was due. Mainly the Chinese were suffered to maintain their accustomed vice, as long as the appropriate authorities were appropriately pacified.

For all the political and legal fireworks, life in the large urban Chinatowns passed mainly undisturbed from day to day. Occasionally a pogrom was visited on far-flung, tiny, temporary Chinese work camps. At the nethermost pit of the depression of the 1880s, indignant whites raided the Chinese camps in Los Angeles, Eureka, Jacoma and Rock Springs, Wyoming, and scores were maimed and lynched. But in the established Chinatowns, with their solid, imposing Mandarin cultural trappings, the Chinese were simply not perceived as a threat.

In fact, they were bigger tourist attractions than ever, offering all the exotic glamour of Hong Kong and Shanghai, and were infinitely more accessible. All things oriental were the perfect rage in this era, and the same cities which ostentatiously imposed repressive anti-Chinese laws also gloriously advertised their romantic Chinatowns to visitors in Chamber of Commerce brochures. The local press was equally schizophrenic. Cub reporters were still required to do periodic Chinatown sketches, deftly mingling the glamour of the Orient with the prevailing horror of Chinese and opium. When Sarah Bernhardt, with a covey of other Parisian actors, visited a San Francisco opium den in the 1880s, it was written up rather hauntingly in the *Examiner*:

> ... Suddenly they found themselves in a little ten by twelve apartment in which a dim candle burned. On the low banks around the room lay Chinamen, whose faces stood out in a cloud of smoke with ghastly pallor.
>
> "C'est horrible!" gasped the ladies.
>
> "C'est magnifique!" exclaimed Madame Sarah, pushing into the room with eager curiosity.
>
> A victim lay in a stupor before her. He was evidently marked for an early death. The tight skin seemed green and mouldy. His fingers were mechanically preparing a ball of opium for his pipe. His muscles seemed to act without the control of nerves. It was a sort of living death.
>
> "Il rêve!" exclaimed Bernhardt, leaning over him and peering into his countenance, as if to read his dreams.
>
> Then breaking away with a shudder she hurried to the door and out from the cloud of smoke and out to the cold air of the street.

It was obviously a dicey proposition, composing the proper sort of anti-dope tabloid propaganda for the William Randolph Hearst press. There was an irresistible demand by editors for peppy and original Chinatown pieces dwelling heavily on the menace of opium, but how could a reporter consistently fulfill it? If opium were some insidiously debilitating physical poison, conducing the gradual consumption of flesh and an early demise, then who could get suitably alarmed over its use by the abominated Chinese? It was generally conceded that the Chinaman had no place in the United States of America whatever. When the AFL was finally officially chartered in 1886, the delegates triumphantly called for the physical expulsion of all Orientals from America: "By force is the only way to remove the coolies and twenty days is enough to do it in." The newly-founded American Pharmaceutical Association made a big deal out of excluding smoking opium from their approved pharmacopoeia, officially declaring, "If the Chinaman cannot get along without his 'dope,' we can get along without him."

Still, some Yellow Peril formula was necessary if the proper sort of jingoistic fervor was to be maintained over the issue of the Chinese and drugs. And the formula was duly developed, at the advent of the 1890s, in the tabloids of William Randolph Hearst. It came to be called "yellow journalism," and it sounded like this:

Most of us know vaguely about the colony of Celestials that clusters about the lower end of our wonderful Bowery, but there are not many who know of the hundreds of American girls who are drawn into it each year from tenement houses and cigarette and box factories to become the associates of the Mongolian. They are attracted by the color of the life that they find there, and the opium habit soon takes a hold on them which they cannot shake off. As for the Chinamen with whom they live, it must be said of them that they treat these girls more kindly and allow them more money and a wider freedom than the roughs and their like of their own race, whose prey they might, in the natural order of things, become.

If 100,000 Chinese really couldn't ruin the job market for thirty million able-bodied white workers (this was beginning to wear thin, especially after the economy began to pick up), then there had to be something really supernaturally evil about them to account for all the hate that was focused upon them. White women in thrall to the yellow man's narcotic—that was the formula. The opium busts, after that, started coming thick and fast:

> A squad of policemen gave Chinatown a raking over on Sunday night last. They scooped in 34 pretty girls, none over 23 years of age, and the youngest 18. The prisoners had all been smoking opium, their associates being Chinamen and rough young men. One girl, not over 18 years of age, was found lying on one of the bunks, partly disrobed, sucking from a poisonous pipe, an ugly-looking Chinaman beside her. Someone gave a signal and the Chinaman escaped.

In the fullness of time, it was unnecessary even to invoke the "ugly-looking Chinaman," as the sex angle sold so well. Opium and white women provided a special libidinous thrill for Americans, touching off in them something deliciously morbid: miscegenation without sex, white womanhood ravished not by a competitive ethnic male, but a fantasy of some alien pharmacology. Everyone was horrified by this unspeakable prospect. When Congress finally passed a total country-wide opium ban in the next decade, the "white-woman story" was the very cornerstone of the expert congressional testimony on which the bill was based: "One of the most unfortunate phases of the habit of smoking opium is the large number of women who have become involved with and were living as common-law wives or cohabiting with Chinese in the Chinatowns of our various cities."

And if the yellow fiends were vicious enough to go after the white man's women with their seductive poison, what could keep them from going further and molesting *children*?

Every anti-drug campaign winds up with children; it's inevitable. The Sinophobe opium legend inevitably developed into this classic infantile hysteria. The San Jose *Mercury*, 8 October 1881:

> In the great city of San Francisco, boys, yes and girls, with the look of cunning, blasé old men and women, sneak out of vile alleys in the Chinese quarter and elsewhere, — out into the beautiful sunshine and refreshing sea-breeze, with such expression of weariness, duplicity, vice, and recklessness combined on every face, that the busy passer-by stops to pity and abhor.

The foolish, misguided, crazy boy—deceiving father, mother, employer—who deems it something smart and clever to "visit a joint" or "to hit the flute." The poor young fool stifles both conscience and his nostrils, and pretends to look approvingly and with the eye of a connoisseur on the box of deadly poison, and holding in the flame the dirty bowl charged with the prepared, perforated ball, draws death, dishonor, and disease in one fatal inhalation eagerly into his system. It is the road to speedy decay and rapid dissolution. An idolatry that has slain more thousands than Juggernaut. It is the curse of China. An impending evil, that, transplanted here, if not rooted out, would, before the dawn of another century, decimate our youth, emasculate the coming generation, if not completely destroy the white population of our coast.

This theme was most violently developed by none other than Samuel Gompers. In 1902 he composed a tract titled "Meat vs. Rice. American Manhood vs. Asiatic Coolieism—Which Shall Survive," as part of a lobbying effort for renewal of the Chinese Exclusion Act.

Chinese laundries, Gompers had determined, were everywhere pullulant with white orphans and kidnap victims, "tiny lost souls" forced to "yield up their virgin bodies to their maniacal yellow captors." Too righteously impassioned to keep up any consistent tense, Gompers raved on:

> What other crimes are committed in those dark fetid places, when these little innocent victims of the Chinaman's wiles were under the influence of the drug, are almost too horrible to imagine— There are hundreds, aye, thousands, of our American girls and boys who have acquired this deathly habit and are doomed, hopelessly doomed, beyond a shadow of redemption.

The occasion of this delirium was the pending renewal by the United States Congress of the Chinese Exclusion Act, which banned the entry of Celestials into America from 1896 to 1942.* By this time Gompers, regarded as something like a saint for his profound moral committment to American working men and

---

*It was lifted when China became necessary to the Allied effort in World War II; in 1942 also, Chinese Americans finally won the right to vote.

women, was just as profoundly committed to the Yellow Peril myth. "The superior whites," he said, "had to exclude the inferior Asiatics by law, or if necessary, by force of arms...The Yellow man found it natural to lie, cheat and murder and 99 out of every 100 Chinese are gamblers...The maintenance of the nation depended on maintenance of racial purity. It was contrary to the national interest to permit cheap labor that could not be Americanized and could not be taught to render the same intelligent service as was supplied by American workers."

Sinophobia, at bottom, was wonderfully apt for a host of purposes in American politics and culture over this era. There was a fundamental irrationality to it, of which everyone was perfectly aware, but against which absolutely *no* one spoke; only for the Chinese was it inconvenient, and the Chinese neither enjoyed any political power nor did they seek it. As the United States grew increasingly isolationist and xenophobic, politicos got far reciting patriotic Yellow Peril myths; their inventiveness in fabricating new twists to it effectively demonstrated how fervent was their love for America. This irrationality is with us still, as Dr. Thomas Szasz points out: "Significantly, while no educated person still believes the ugly nonsense heaped on the Chinese for decades by leading American authorities, most educated persons still believe the ugly nonsense heaped on opium."

In 1911 an access of irrationality was reached in the California Supreme Court, in the case of an opium defendant named Yun Quong. Quong had challenged the constitutionality of the state's anti-opium law on the simple due-process grounds that the statute had no relation to reality. Yun provided abundant evidence that opium had never harmed him or caused him to harm anyone else or to steal or destroy property. Whereat the Court, in upholding the conviction in spite of everything, put into legalese the convenient aberration which still, to this day, makes drug legislation a very special category of jurisprudence:

> The validity of legislation which would be necessary or proper under a given state of facts does not depend on the actual existence of the supposed facts. It is enough if the law-making body may rationally believe such facts to be established.

The key word is "rationally." It would have been madness for the court to have thrown out the California opium law that year, in which all the most solid national authorities, from Congress to the medical establishment, were gearing up to slap a national ban on the import of opium. The Hearst press was campaigning for it madly; the papers were spilling over with Yellow Peril. A judge would have been totally irrational to risk his career by admitting to the harmlessness of opium. One of the most prominent anti-opium gong-bangers just then was Colonel Charles Blinn, a veteran narcotics agent on the San Francisco Customs dock. Blinn was bursting with sheer American exuberance as he described for the papers, time and again, how he combed every Chinese ship that fell into his clutches, just to enforce policy:

> Leave it to the Chink when it comes to smuggling hop...For instance, while you're breaking your neck peeking into a ventilator the Chinks are standing by, empty-faced, giving you the ha-ha. Probably while you're ripping up things in the galley the No. 1 boys, gliding around in their soft felt slippers, are shooting the five tael tins down into the engine-room, and when you're busy sticking your prod into a boiler tube the Chinks are shifting the dope into the music box in the social hall...The Chink has the game down to a science. If you had 100 secret service agents sitting in rocking chairs around the deck and a dozen searchlights beaming over the ship the slippery yellow men would be getting the contraband off just the same; which means no disrespect to the service. They're regular sleight-o'-hand performers, these Chinks.

The relentless circular reasoning here—the less drugs the round-eye finds, the more he's justified in terrorizing the slant-eyes— also holds in police circles to this day, in the very special area of drug enforcement. By this time, however, there actually did exist a Chinese opium-smuggling industry; local opium bans had made it necessary, and so at last the venerable Yellow Peril myth was more than just an ugly play of opportunistic rhetoric.

Authentic Chinese triads were moving opium into the China-towns of the West Coast and New York City at this time; the Hip Song Tong and the On Leong Tong conducted a lively and colorful competition, punctuated with plenty of classic drug-ring skulduggery, murder, and operatic violence. The police and press had a grand time too, turning up opium in consignments of hundred-year-old eggs, bird's nests, petrified duck, and fresh lemons. RAID CHINESE LAUNDRY, GET OPIUM...CHOP SUEY PLANT A BLIND FOR OPIUM...

Sinophobia pretty much ended by the 1920s, though Charles Dana Gibson would once in a while sketch a group of his immaculate girls inside an opium den, lolling their long pipes in their laps, gazing down in demure intoxication at their magnificent alabaster cleavage, idly accepting a light from the talented fingers of a sinister Mandarin attendant. Any time a white woman got arrested in proximity to a Chinaman, it still made the front pages. But the yellow peril was definitely passé by the twenties.

There were new sorts of drugs around by then. And there were new scapegoats.

TEN
THE FATHER OF
AMERICAN NARCOTICS
LAWS

*The great majority of the followers of the Prophet have fallen
into the use, or countenance the use of opium, and even the
hemp drugs.*

*With the cry, "There is no God but God, and Mohammed is
his prophet," and we may add, "If you do not accept this dogma,
a little opium will improve it," the Mohammedan Arabs, Persians and Turks overran India...*

The distinguished reformer Dr. Hamilton Wright—who also promoted the view that cocaine-sniffing caused southern Negroes to
commit mayhem and rape—had nothing against snide racial slurs
if they won converts to the anti-drug campaign he was waging
in 1910: as long as those slurs weren't against the Chinese.

Wright at the time was employed by the State Department
under President Taft, the second of three presidents he would
serve, as a semi-official (his salary came out of the secretary of
state's "emergency" fund) drug advisor. In this capacity he became a most influential figure in the drive toward drug prohibition. He was the "father of American narcotics laws" in the
eyes of most historians, but his mission in 1910 involved more
than just drugs.

Wright had convinced his superiors at the State Department
that it would be a fine idea to court favor with China—and, it

was hoped, win valuable trade concessions—by staging showy international opium conventions, enacting strict domestic drug laws, and otherwise demonstrating American support for the Celestials's newly rekindled drive to stamp out opium smoking. So for obvious diplomatic reasons, his influential 1910 propaganda tract—*The Opium Problem: Its History and Present Condition* (cited above)—in stark contrast to documents of a similar nature written just a decade before, portrayed the Chinese *only* as innocent victims, while cannily fingering a nice safe scapegoat, the Arab, as the real source of the Oriental drug epidemic.

In Wright's revision of history, the Honourable East India Company was relegated to the status of a "trading machine, somewhat conscienceless," having merely taken over a "widespread" trade from their Arab predecessors. However, he charged, the British still bore the *moral* responsibility for the opium problem (the Arabs presumably having no morals), and in his speeches and papers he tirelessly exposed the shame of the Empire before all the world, on behalf of the exploited Chinese. This was just fine with the State Department if it pleased the government in Peking, and diverted their attention from such things as the Chinese-Exclusion Act.

Brash, loud, and aggressive (combining three exemplary virtues of Roosevelt-era manhood), Ham Wright was thought to be exceedingly good at his job by most people at the White House, though in far-off lands there were those who saw the father of American narcotics laws as the first Ugly American—manipulative arrogant, concealing behind a facade of good will a conviction that all foreigners were suckers and incompetents of a lower evolutionary order—and those at home, like Huntington Wilson, chief of the State Department's Far East Division, who viewed him as simply a schemer and a windbag.

By all accounts Wright was a prodigious talker. In countless speeches before civic and trade groups, he glowingly and voluminously portrayed the United States as China's salvation, and indefatigably spread the gospel of drug prohibition. To hear Ham Wright tell it, the Chinese had been wonderfully heartened in 1894, when a Royal Commission to study opium production in India was established, and miserably demoralized when the commission concluded that an opium ban would wreck the Indian economy, and that the drug didn't pose a serious health hazard anyway. Reason was only restored to the Orient in 1902, when the United States appointed its own commission to study opium use in the newly acquired Philippines (ceded to America along with Puerto Rico and Guam after the Spanish-American War in 1898). As a result, Congress had outlawed opium smoking among Filipinos and decreed systematic detoxification for Chinese addicts living on the islands. This, Wright declared, had raised China's spirits so mightily that "there was great joy in China. Her statesmen took heart and before long a movement was on foot to suppress the opium evil." Only in the wake of this American-inspired movement did China and Britain finally enact a treaty in 1906 to restrict the Sino-Indian opium trade.

It was an uplifting story of American efficiency, know-how, and derring-do amid the chaos of the Orient, but of course, not the whole story. For that we must backtrack to 1895. That year—with Russia, Germany, France, and Japan (in addition to Great Britain) carving out spheres of influence in China—John Milton Hay and Theodore Roosevelt conceived the "Open Door" policy, a bully bit of saber rattling, which demanded that China's treaty ports be opened to American commerce as well, and threatened armed intervention (in China) if they weren't. The "Open Door" was quietly accepted by the Chinese and the European powers with interests in the Orient, but the China trade coveted by the United States proved a more elusive prize. Ever since the Portuguese set up shop at Macao, the Chinese had wanted almost nothing from foreigners, with the exception of opium and since domestic cultivation of the poppy had been legalized after the Arrow War, they wanted far less of that. To make matters worse, after fifty years of foreign hegemony, the Chinese were in an understandable state of xenophobic panic.

American traders had never been able to command more than 10 percent of China's opium market anyway, so businessmen and diplomats—who'd optimistically seized on the idea of expanded foreign trade after the last of the nineteenth century panics in 1893, and had become even more vehement when America acquired the Philippines five years later—faced two sizable challenges: coming up with a product that would appeal to Peking, and the delicate problem of selling it to them. Their solution to the first challenge was to pitch the virtues of American know-how and expertise in the form of railroad technology, envisioned as a most lucrative gambit—if only the Chinese would listen.

As chance would have it, the answer to that problem appeared in the saintly persona of the Reverend Wilbur Crafts, superintendent of the International Reform Bureau, a missionary organization with outposts throughout the Orient. In 1900, Crafts was lobbying in Washington for endorsement of an international temperance measure to outlaw liquor and opium among "the child races that civilized nations are essaying to civilize and Christianize." Among these child races, Crafts included the Chinese and the Filipinos, who had just come under United States dominion. Crafts thought the evil of drink was paramount, but other members of the IRB singled out opium for their righteous ire, preaching not only that it was a source of moral degeneracy among the peoples of the East, but that it hampered world trade as well. The Chinese opium problem, in the opinion of one Reform Bureau member, Mrs. Joseph Cook, "despoiled the commerce of all nations by impoverishing and disturbing the largest market in the world." The Reverend Frank Gamewell deplored the impossibility of doing business with a nation whose citizens— though once renowned for their "industry, thrift, and a certain business honesty"—were now enslaved to opium: "The opium-smoker is proverbially unreliable. He loses energy and ambition, and disregards all obligations of business, home and society."

The International Reform Bureau, as part of a worldwide missionary and temperance movement, was daily growing in members and influence. At the same time, the movement for opium reform had revived in China, with the official blessings of His Excellency Tong Shao-yi who'd repeatedly announced that the Chinese government was "as much opposed to the Opium traffic as ever, although it is now largely produced by its own people, since they must have it." And in the Roosevelt White House this all began to suggest something like a viable foreign trade policy. Secretary of State Elihu Root endorsed the IRB—"As to Opium in China and liquors among the savage races," he stated flatly, "they are a disgrace to civilization"—as did Teddy Roosevelt himself. Their congressional collaborator, Henry Cabot Lodge of the Boston Cabots, pushed a resolution through the Senate in

*America's efforts to cleanse the Philippines of
opium smoking in 1905 were used by early reformers
like Hamilton Wright to encourage the passage
of domestic narcotics laws. Despite American
efforts, however, opium smoking in the Philippines—
as illustrated by this 1915 photo—continued apace.*

1901, forbidding the sale of alcohol and opium "to aboriginal tribes and uncivilized races." The provisions of the "Native Races" Act were later expanded, banning the sale of stimulants to "uncivilized elements in America itself and in its territories, such as Indians, Alaskans, the inhabitants of Hawaii, railroad workers, and immigrants at ports of entry." Railroad workers of course, meant the Chinese. The message to Peking was clear: If you let us build a railroad at least we are legally bound *not* to sell drugs to the coolies.

There is no indication that passage of the "Native Races" Act boosted our prestige in the Middle Kingdom, or inclined the Chinese to look with favor on American know-how, expertise and railroad technology. (The White House was inclined to think that it had.) However, it did serve as a precedent for a second federally enacted anti-drug bill, banning opium in the Philippines.

American control of the islands had gotten off to a shaky start: A Philippine independence movement had to be suitably crushed before the first United States commissioner could be installed in 1902. He was Episcopal Bishop Henry Brent, a heartfelt supporter of the IRB and their "Child Races" policy, whose abhorrence of opium was well known.

To Brent the opium poppy was a demonic apparition, awesome and deadly, which sprang from the ground to try the souls of Christian missionaries and their flocks in the Orient. "For rich, prodigal beauty, no field-crop under the sun can match it," he wrote in an issue of *Everybody's* magazine.

> The flowering poppy is vivid, dramatic, and passionate, like some superb adventuress alluring troops of lovers, and, vampire-like, sucking out their souls with her kisses.

Coincident with Brent's arrival, a fierce cholera epidemic broke out in Manila, and sales of opium—for medicinal home use— were brisk. Bishop Brent though, had not been called to minister to the bowels of these natives, but to their souls, and he expressed devout horror at the wide-spread indulgence in this filthy drug. Even so, the conclusions of the 1902 commission which he convened (and chaired) to recommend to Congress a suitable opium policy, were surprisingly moderate. They recommended the establishment of a temporary opium monopoly, with revenues accrued thereby to be used for education.

Their proposal was somehow intercepted by the vituperative Crafts, who promptly declared it an outrage, "pandering to the opium-craving of degenerate races." The commission was ordered to reconsider their proposals, but only one option was really open. Under pressure from the White House for the sake of the China trade, and from the IRB for the sake of the "Child Races" policy, Congress in 1905 voted an immediate ban on sales of opium to Filipinos. Chinese addicts living on the islands, who registered with the government, were to be detoxified gradually over a three-year period. Hospital cures were also offered, but out of an estimated 127,000 addicts only 10 volunteered—unaccountably—for treatment. In actual fact, the ban went unenforced—a follow-up study twenty years later indicated *no* reduction in native opium use—but it did send a message to China.

Ham Wright's assertion that America's action had precipitated the Chinese-British accords on opium, though, was quite unfounded. The basic formula for that treaty—the reduction of opium imports from India to China by one-ninth annually over a ten year period, accompanied by a one-ninth annual reduction of poppy cultivation in the Middle Realm itself—had been the topic of high level negotiations for a number of years. In 1906 the incoming Liberal cabinet solidly affirmed the treaty, and pushed a vote through Parliament condemning the Sino-Indian drug trade at last.*

However, a chance for the United States to assume a symbolic leadership role in the Orient, and in the area of opium reform presented itself when Brent proposed the formation of an international opium commission, to meet in Shanghai in 1909, made up of representatives of all the powers with material interests in the Far East. The Roosevelt White House applauded the idea. A serious set back in Sino-American trade relations had occurred when Roosevelt ordered American gunboats to China to break up an unofficial embargo of United States goods, organized in response to the renewal of the Chinese-Exclusion Act. Brent's proposed conference was seen as a way to appease Chinese anger

---

*"This House reaffirms its conviction," the 1906 Parliament declared, "that the Indo-Chinese opium traffic is morally indefensible, and requests His Majesty's Government to take such steps as may be necessary for bringing it to a speedy close."

by refocusing it solidly on Great Britain and the heinous drug trade.

A committee was formed to organize the meeting; it consisted of Brent, Charles C. Tenney, a retired missionary, and a young tropical disease specialist who had worked in the Orient—Hamilton Wright by name. Wright was by far the most vocal and active of the three in shaping the course of events to come. He immediately embarked on a national tour, preaching against the evils of opium, promoting the conference at Shanghai, and surveying drug use in America. He concluded that some form of federal legislation—at the time there were only a few cosmetic state laws—was needed to prove our sincerity to the conference participants, particularly the Chinese.

Wright proposed a ban on imports of smoking opium for its symbolic significance—only Chinese in America *smoked* opium—and *because* it affected only Chinese it was unlikely to provoke controversy in Congress, where federal regulations governing morals were thought by many lawmakers to be unconstitutional because they required police enforcement, traditionally the purview of individual states.

Dr. Harvey Wiley, head of the Agricultural Department's Bureau of Chemistry was quick to point out that Section 11 of the Pure Food and Drug Act, which he'd conceived and seen enacted in 1906, *already* prohibited imports of dangerous drugs. But Wright's symbolic law was embraced by his superiors, the most passionate of whom was Secretary of State Elihu Root, who sent a message to Congress urging the necessity "to have legislation . . . in time to save our face at the conference at Shanghai." The ban was enacted in January 1909, and Wright sailed triumphantly for China.

The International Opium Commission convened on February 1 chaired by Brent and made up of delegations from the United States, China, France, Germany, Great Britain, Holland, Italy, Japan, Austria-Hungary, Persia, Portugal, Russia, and Siam. Yet, however vigorously Brent and Wright lobbied for endorsement of the United States position that "there is no non-medical use of Opium or its derivatives that is not fraught with grave dangers, if it is not actually vicious," they found it impossible to rally general agreement that the drug was evil or even immoral. The

British wouldn't say anything of substance in the presence of India's representative, and Persia (the other major supplier of foreign opium to China), sent a local merchant to the meeting who listened with bland amusement and said nothing at all. The Shanghai Commission was able to draft only a vague agreement that opium should be "carefully regulated," and disbanded with only the United States and China expressing interest in reconvening in the future.

The conclusion was anticlimactic after all the hoopla, but Ham Wright had what he wanted. China was keen on another conference, and that was all that really mattered. But he also had obtained a consensus on opium reform, however insubstantial, which he felt made it "incumbent upon the American government to take a step that would convert the Declarations of the Shanghai Commission into international law."

This was Wright's way around the sticky constitutional states-rights questions blocking federal drug legislation. If the Shanghai Declarations were formalized as international law, constitutionally they would supersede state law, leading the way for passage of an "exemplary" domestic drug law, which Ham Wright was sure would really impress the Chinese.

Yet when he triumphantly—or so he thought—returned to Washington with his master plan, Wright was stopped short. A new administration was in office under the command of William Howard Taft, and though the Taft White House philosophically adhered to the same aggressive-ist foreign policy that characterized their predecessors, it was the opinion of some policymakers that a quieter, more cautious and canny approach might be more efficacious. This approach was favored by Huntington Wilson, chief of the State Department's Far East Division. Wilson was the first person Wright approached with his plan, and Wilson turned him down flat. Trade negotiations with China were in a *delicate* state, and he was fearful lest secret agreements be dragged into the open—in the emotionally-charged atmosphere of an anti-drug forum—by nations ill-disposed to both American drug policy and American manipulation of the China trade. Philosophy aside, though, Wilson didn't like Wright, and he was especially wary lest the abrasively outspoken reformer himself "kick over the traces."

Not one to be easily rebuffed, Wright went over Wilson's head to a man he found more sympathetic, Secretary of State Philander C. Knox, to whom he delivered himself of the opinion that:

> Our move to help China in her opium reform gave us more prestige in China than any of our recent friendly acts towards her. If we continue and press steadily for the Conference, China will recognize that we are sincere in her behalf, and the whole business may be used as oil to smooth the troubled water of our aggressive commercial policy there.

This made good sense to Knox, characterized privately by Wright as "a cold-blooded little fellow" who was just catching on to the fine points of "this opium business." Knox not only approved his plan for an international conference to be held at the Hague, but helped draft a new domestic drug law which they hoped would have the power of international law behind it.

The law envisioned by Wright and Knox, was in some respects still largely cosmetic and symbolic—a gesture toward China, an example of American know-how and goodness to the rest of the world—calling only for the registration and payment of a small tax on all opiates, cocaine, chloral hydrate and cannabis, and registration of all drug sellers. But the new law was hardly symbolic for violators, who faced up to five years in jail and a $5,000 fine.

To introduce the bill to Congress, Wright first approached James R. Mann—who seven years earlier had authored the "White Slave Act," America's first federal law governing morals. When Mann declined, he recruited Rep. David Foster of Vermont.

Proponents of the "Foster Bill" were bolstered during congressional deliberations by the release of the report of the Shanghai Commission. It was a sensational document, carefully prepared and for the most part written by Hamilton Wright, graphically depicting the opium evil as something America was heroically abolishing among the child races of the Orient, but could not yet control at home.

In addition to opium, the report reserved special venom for that "most appalling drug," cocaine, which according to Wright's text "is often the direct incentive to the crime of rape by the Negroes of the South." He hoped this racist horror story would be especially appealing to southern congressmen whose states rights sentiments had posed a real threat to the passage of drug legislation.* In response to the Shanghai report, Congress granted $25,000 to finance the first federal "efforts to mitigate if not entirely stamp out the opium evil."

However, opposed by the pharmacy lobby and proprietary companies—the Foster Bill provided no exemptions for patent medicines—the bill stalled despite an urgent appeal by President Taft to Congress to "see that its house is in order before the International Opium Conference meets at the Hague"; it was eventually killed. The Foster Bill did, however, lay the foundation for the Harrison Narcotics Act of 1914, which in turn sired most United States drug legislation since. And Wright had gained a great deal of support and prestige on Capitol Hill. One convert to his proposals, Representative Henry Finger of Mendocino County, California, even graciously offered to supply the Hague Convention with free wine, if Wright would get them to discuss cannabis. The weed was smoked in his district by "hindoos," Finger complained, and he was concerned lest they begin "initiating whites into their habit." Wright, apparently wary of losing the support of the temperance lobby, turned down Finger's offer.

As it turned out the Hague Convention was delayed until 1912, a turn of events which Ham Wright blamed on a conspiracy of opium-producing countries, when in fact Britain and China re-

---

*Alleged cocainomania among southern blacks was, at this time, a widely publicized and useful myth perpetrated by doctors, legislators and reformers. The American Medical Association had denounced "cocain-sniffing" among southern Negroes as early as 1900 in an effort to wrest control of the drug away from the patent medicine industry. For Wright's Republican congressional allies, cocainomania was also a highly effective ploy. With the failure of Reconstruction, a sizable bloc of southern Negroes had been disenfranchised who could otherwise have been depended on to vote solidly Republican, if the Bible-belt Dixiecrats had let them. But the Dixiecrats had relieved them of the power to vote, as one North Carolina congressman put it, "as the adult takes the pistol from the hand of the child." It was impossible to get federal agents to open the election process south of the Mason-Dixon Line, with the shibboleth of state's rights standing in the way: Police enforcement was felt by southern congressmen to be strictly the purview of states and localities. But if drug legislation was passed, it opened the way to federal enforcement of voting rights as well, and there were few southern congressmen who could long hold out against drug-control once the cocainomania scare was fully operative. That cocainomania led indirectly to civil rights enforcement in the South is wonderfully ironic considering the content of the cocaine propaganda. Dr. Edward Huntington Williams' "Negro Cocaine 'Fiends' are a New Southern Menace," an article which appeared in the Sunday *New York Times Magazine* in 1914, is a salient example. Williams charged that cocaine turned black men into veritable werewolves, consumed with violent homicidal

quired the extra time to work out the final stage of their opium ban. He was apparently still in a fine state of high dudgeon when he arrived at the Hague: The exceedingly mild-mannered Archbishop of Canterbury, an unwavering opium prohibitionist, was so miffed by his conspiratorial nagging that he urged the American delegation to dismiss Wright as "antagonistic." But Ham Wright persevered.

Turkey, Great Britain, Portugal, Japan, Russia, Italy, Germany, Persia, the Netherlands, the United States, and China attended the conference. England, aglow with the success of the Chinese accords, urged new measures prohibiting cocaine and morphine. Germany, protecting her burgeoning pharmaceutical industry insisted that a unanimous vote be required before any action could be initiated. Portugal demanded to retain the Macao opium trade, the Dutch demanded theirs in the West Indies, Persia wanted to keep growing poppies, as did Russia. France was ambivalent, and Japan denied *absolutely* that it was exporting morphine and hypodermic needles to China. Against this chaotic backdrop Ham Wright and the American delegation found it awkward to make much headway. Their righteous appeals to desist and reform were regularly rebuffed with allusions to America's own prodigious consumption of opiates, and its lack of domestic laws. The conference did patch together an agreement according to which signatories would "endeavor" to enact domestic legislation, and to control all phases of opium, morphine, heroin, and cocaine preparation and distribution (exemptions were provided for patent medicines with less than 0.2 percent morphine, or 0.1 percent heroin or cocaine). Since only twelve of the "46 Powers"

---

passions and, worst of all, invulnerable to bullets. He illustrated his point with the story of a police chief in Asheville, North Carolina, who was called out to arrest "a hitherto inoffensive negro" who was "running amuk" in a cocaine frenzy: "Knowing that he must kill the man or be killed himself, the Chief drew his revolver, placed the muzzle over the Negro's heart, and fired—'intending to kill him right quick,' as the officer tells it. But the shot did not even stagger the man. And a second shot that pierced the arm and entered the chest had just as little effect in crippling the Negro or checking his attack. Meanwhile the chief, out of the corner of his eye, saw infuriated Negroes running toward the cabin from all directions. He had only three cartridges remaining in his gun, and he might need these in a minute to stop the mob. So he saved his ammunition and 'finished the man with his club.'"

were present, though, the agreement could have no binding power until more signatures were obtained.

But Ham Wright saw the Hague Agreement as a mandate for strict domestic legislation, and he returned to Washington more determined than ever to get it. This time he recruited Francis Burton Harrison as his congressional liaison.

In its general outline, the Harrison Bill was very much like the Foster Bill, calling for the same harsh penalties, but making record-keeping procedures for doctors and druggists a bit easier. And, while banning morphine and cocaine in similar dilutions, it exempted patent medicines with less than ⅛ grain of heroin. Addicts, or anyone else for that matter, could still purchase heroin over the counter in drugstores for another ten years.

With the Harrison Bill pending, Wright left Washington to head the United States delegation at the second Hague Convention in July 1913. By this time thirty-four signatures had been collected on the agreement, mostly by Wright himself. This was still short of a majority, however, and the conference was adjourned without significant discussion. When the third Hague Convention convened in July 1914, there were still not enough signatures, the United States had still not passed domestic legislation, and Ham Wright was nowhere to be seen.

He was finally brought down by the venerable William Jennings Bryan, Cross of Gold populist and the new secretary of state under Woodrow Wilson. Accounts of the events leading up to Wright's dismissal have apparently been judged too trivial to be included in Bryan's papers and biographies, so it's impossible to judge the true dimensions of his loathing for Wright, although his actions speak pretty clearly.

After the second Hague Convention, Bryan brusquely objected to Wright's being continued as chairman of the delegation "at any price." But there were still those at the State Department who felt that Wright, despite his faults, was the only person qualified to lead the delegation at the Hague. So Bryan changed his strategy. He penned a note to the president in May 1914, stating that "the doctor looks like a drinking man." Coming from Bryan, one of the most ardent advocates of liquor prohibition, and a man of illustrious morals, this was a very serious charge indeed. The secretary followed up with a second letter asserting that William Phillips, the assistant secretary of state "also notes what I have reported on former occasions, viz. that Dr. Wright's breath smelt of liquor." Wilson's papers record that on June 6, Bryan demanded that Wright "take the pledge." Wright refused in a long memo to the president, and was promptly fired.

Yet even in disgrace, Hamilton Wright got what he wanted once more; the Harrison Bill was gaining momentum daily in Congress. One wonders what Francis Harrison, a notorious congressional drunkard, thought of the brouhaha that enveloped his White House ally. For the record, he said nothing, and in practice assiduously separated the comparatively safe issue of drug reform from the volatile issue of liquor prohibition.* The Harrison Bill passed smoothly the following winter, and Wilson signed it into law on Saint Valentine's Day, 1914.

Questions quickly arose, though, over the enforcement of the Harrison Act. Since the Hague Agreement lacked enough signatures to make it international law, it was felt in some quarters that federal jurisdiction in the area of drug reform did not yet supersede the policing powers of the states.

The only federal police unit at this time was a small contingent assigned to the Treasury Department to investigate income tax violations. The precedent-setting unit had only recently been installed, and only after much heated debate. The Treasury Department retained exclusive control over federal policing activities for another fifteen years, and in fact the Harrison Act was conceived, in part, as a tax measure simply because the Treasury Department's squad of T-men was available to enforce it. This at least was the firm opinion of the Treasury Department, which after 1914 replaced the State Department—whose attention was no longer focused on China and the China trade, but on rumblings in Europe—as the most active and influential federal agency in the area of "dangerous drug" control.

Enforcement of the Harrison Act was supported by some professional interest groups, and opposed by others on constitutional grounds. Drs. Lambert and Simmons of the A.M.A.

---

*Many supporters of Harrison's bill were likewise opposed to liquor prohibition; among them House Speaker Oscar W. Underwood, who viewed the Volsted Act as a "tyrannous scheme to establish virtue and morality by law."

supported strict enforcement, as did Frank Fredericks of the American Pharmaceutical Association (APhA). Writing in the *Journal* of the APhA, he commented that the Harrison Act's "purpose was to accomplish by federal powers what the states were unwilling or unable to do." Others, like James Beal of the National Drug Trade Conference saw the Harrison Act strictly as an information-gathering device, which, lacking the power of international law, was quite unenforceable. This, in fact, was the prevailing view until after the First World War, when everything changed.

At the behest of the American delegation, the Hague resolutions were incorporated into the Versailles Treaty ending the war, and the proponents of strict enforcement had the long-sought-after backing of international law. During the next ten years, the Treasury's Narcotics Bureau, headed by Col. Levi G. Nutt was expanded from 170 to 270 agents, its budget increased from $270,000 to $500,000, and some 75,000 people—including 25,000 doctors and druggists—were arrested for Harrison Act violations.

ELEVEN
HEROIN BOYS

There has developed a distinct class of heroin addicts, with a certain amount of freemasonry and cooperation among themselves. These latter are necessary to make it easy for users to procure heroin and to safeguard one another in the indulgence of a practice strictly forbidden by law. As a result, heroin addicts exist in large groups, the individuals of which know and help each other; in this way the habit is not only maintained but spreads rapidly. The majority of the present takers are boys and young men whose sociability has been developed in the gangs who later flock together in leisure hours at the dance halls, the movies and at that form of entertainment which they all seem to like best, vaudeville. For a long time the boys remain for the most part in good health, and all along they possess a fair degree of intelligence. Some examined by the Simon Benet test show mental defects, but the majority are not materially defective in intellectual qualities. Like most adolescents with social tendencies, they lack individual initiative, are imitative and easily led; they fall into the habit easily and, this is the tragic part of it, ignorantly and innocently. Once the habit is established, they lose interest in work, become late and irregular, throw up their jobs easily. Many are good workmen, but will only work for the purpose of getting money with which to buy heroin.

...Among the frequent misdemeanors charged against the

*heroin boys besides those directly concerned with the use or
possession of the drug, are stealing and destruction of property.
The customs entailed by the habit and the effects on character
of the drug itself are doubtless potent factors in forming and
holding together that criminal class which certain idealists do
not seem to believe exists.*

By these signs shall ye know them. This was the portrait of the
heroin addict in 1916, offered by New York neuropsychiatrist
Dr. Pearce Bailey in *The New Republic*: "They are generally
healthy and able to work, and are fairly intelligent. Many are of
engaging personality but, as often happens with personalities who
are engaging, they are unstable, suggestible and easily led." Bailey's sketch is the first intensive study of heroin addicts on record,
eminently accurate and compassionate: mainly poor urban immigrant youths scrambling for a living in an insecure and uncongenial job market, fleshing out their income with occasional
petty larceny, drawn by necessity into neighborhood gangs which
at once intensified their antisocial behavior and gave it a special
romantic flavor of adventure and camaraderie. Italian, Jewish,
Irish, Scandinavian: they were the original second-generation
ethnics.

Heroin itself, Bailey duly concluded, was only a predictable,
subsidiary adjunct of a culture so bitterly inescapable: "It would
almost seem that their desire for something to brighten life up
is at the bottom of their trouble and that heroin is but a means;
and that if this means failed them, they would turn to something
which might be worse." The idea of "curing" such individuals,
addict by addict, was obviously foredoomed, without some broad
program to refurbish and render tolerable a culture in which
addiction (and things worse) were fostered. Urban America,
though, looked thoroughly irredeemable to Bailey: "It would be
a happy philanthropy which would make farming attractive to
this class."

Philanthropy, though, was no more to be expected in connection with drug addicts in 1916 than it has been ever since. Heroin
addiction was quite a new thing in the year Dr. Bailey was writing;
new statistics just published by Bellevue Hospital showed that
in just the last two years, the admission rate for heroin addicts

seeking detoxification had soared from naught to nearly one thousand per year. Over the same two-year period, the admission rate for morphine addicts had plummeted from nearly one thousand per annum to zero. Since 1913, thanks to a landslide of federal and state legislation restricting the availability of morphine, heroin had entirely supplanted it, with a notable surplus, as the drug of choice among the urban netherworld.

The exclusion of heroin from the Harrison Narcotics Act (See Chapter 10), is only explicable in view of the ignorance of the self-interested reformers and legislators who bulled it through Congress in March of 1914. Hamilton Wright and Albert Knox of the State Department, IRS Commissioner Daniel Roper, and their collaborators on Capitol Hill, who'd engineered the move to replace doctors with federal agents as proprietors of the nation's "addictive" drugs and drug "addicts," simply were unaware of the fact that heroin is exactly as seductive and habit-forming as morphine; and easier to self-administer. They actually believed, along with quite a few practicing physicians, that heroin was a mild, non-addictive bromide useful in the treatment of respiratory ailments, and a promising adjunct for curing morphinists.

If they'd bothered to investigate, they would certainly have been a good deal more interested in heroin. It was admittedly a much newer drug than morphine, less than twenty years in use, having been developed as a sort of mega-aspirin in 1898 at Freidrich Bayer's Elberfeld Farbenfabrik works in Germany. In fact it was developed there by Heinrich Dreser, who in the 1880s had confected aspirin itself—acetylsalicylic acid—as an alternative to sodium salicylate, a previously-used analgesic which was, unfortunately, highly corrosive to the stomach. Substituting an acetyl molecular group for a sodium group turned out to be so stunningly effective that Dreser concluded he could do no wrong with acetyls. So in 1898 he took morphine and inserted two tiny strings of acetyls between its great big matching alcohol and phenyl hydroxyl groups. The result, diacetylmorphine, was tested out on sixty patients at an Elberfeld dyeworks, and seen to be much more than a mere headache remedy: cough, catarrh, bronchitis, emphysema, asthma, and even tuberculosis responded most marvelously to this new drug. Dreser's research team was stunned at the virtual absence of common morphine side effects

like nausea, anorexia, or constipation, and confidently therefore assumed that addiction would present no problem either.

Bayer accordingly dubbed it "heroin,"—from the German *heroish*, connoting a lot of power in a little unit—and sold it as proudly and assiduously as aspirin. Period newspaper ads for Bayer Heroin grandiously sang its virtues right alongside ads for menstrual and dyspepsia nostrums.

The recommended cough-suppressant dose was tiny, only three to five milligrams. Codeine was the opiate in commonest use as a cough nostrum, and considering the relatively higher doses that were needed to quell coughing, it was roughly ten times easier to overdose on codeine than on heroin, and this was Bayer's main selling point. But for only a little while. Within a few years after it went on the market, doctors everywhere were reporting some *phenomenal* side effects.

A single dose of it lasted only a few hours. For a person with a bad cold, then, as many as four doses a day might be needed for a couple of days running, after which the patient would typically report some dreadful sensations: cramps, headaches, soggy sniffles, profound anxiety and depression, lasting for a couple of days more. If the patient had any remaining Bayer Heroin in the medicine chest, he or she was all too likely to take it, and then take some more. It was the same pattern that had been seen with morphine for generations, except, where it took weeks and months to build up an addiction to morphine, one could pick up a full-fledged heroin habit in just two weeks.

By 1902, then, a heroin debate had commenced in the pages of medical journals. Physicians who'd experimented with heroin as a morphine step-down cure reported that it produced abstinence symptoms that were as bad as those arising from morphine addiction, if not worse, and accused their colleagues of creating "heroinists." Counterclaims, while conceding that heroin produced rapid tolerance, argued that abstinence symptoms were significantly less intense, and emphasized that heroin was superior to morphine for treating respiratory diseases, which it was. "Bringing charges against heroin," J.D. Trawick, a Kentucky physician, opined in 1915, "is almost like questioning the fidelity of a good friend."

The heroin debate was hot enough, though, to convince Bayer

to soft-pedal its Heroin campaign, distributing it mainly to whole-sale chemical companies to sell under various patented labels of their own.* Most effectively, the company ceased sending ad-vertising flyers touting the drug's manifold indications around to physicians. Doctors then as now derived virtually all their phar-macological know-how from drug-company ads, and in the ab-sence of a Heroin ad campaign, most forgot, or never learned, that such a drug existed.

At the turn of the century, when all this was happening, addicts, mainly bought morphine on prescription or in patent medicines. After 1910, as Ham Wright, the State Department, and northern Republican congressmen succeeded in promulgating anti-mor-phine laws, quite naturally morphine became harder to come by, with the natural result that users discovered heroin's superior virtues.

Some were introduced to it by doctors. In the wake of Dreser's original findings, there were scattered reports that heroin was a capital step-down cure for morphine addicts. Physicians who considered the five-day hyoscyamine "cure"—the most common detoxification procedure of the day—to be inconveniently messy and prolonged, were particularly keen on the two-day heroin cure as significantly tidier. Addicts tended not to go into hysterics or make messes when they were given diminishing doses of heroin; and when they left, they tended not to come back again very soon, which confirmed the idea that heroin was *the* detoxification adjunct for morphine. Such claims ceased abruptly after 1905, but not before the philanthropic Saint James Society had been persuaded to mount a massive campaign to supply free samples of heroin through the mail to morphine addicts who wanted to give up their habits.

Those addicts who attempted to detoxify with heroin learned, of course, that they could get just as high on heroin as on mor-phine, and even after controls had been placed on morphine,

*Early on, when non-Bayer brands of acetylsalicylic acid were being peddled in the US as "aspirin," Bayer sued for copyright violation. The Supreme Court ultimately dismissed the claim, ruling that Bayer had over-advertised the analgesic to the point that "aspirin" was now a household word. Bayer has never sued anyone for appropriating its brand name for diacetylmorphine.

heroin was still available *everywhere*. The *Journal of the American Medical Association* ran these remarks in 1913, the year a New York State law—the Boylan Act—banned all other commercial opiates:

> Dope users who found that police surveillance made it very difficult to secure opium, morphine and cocaine, soon learned that heroin could be easily obtained. No prescription is necessary. As a result they began using this drug, and the habit grew by leaps and bounds.

Even in places where local ordinances banned it (and long after the Congress belatedly banned it), heroin was a popular item with black-market peddlers, since its undistinguished grayish color makes it much easier to cut, with a wider variety of adulterants than pure white morphine.

Cases of heroin addiction among people who'd never been addicted to morphine were reported as early as 1903. An alarming number of these new addicts—at least the ones who showed up at Public Health Service detoxification clinics—were young, aged fifteen to twenty-five. In 1916, when Dr. Pearce Bailey wrote his article about them, the "heroin boys" constituted about one-third of the known addicts in Manhattan. For the most part they'd started out as chippers, occasional users snorting heroin with their friends, understandably unaware of its addictive properties. The fact that heroin was sniffable—requiring none of the messy and fearful hypodermic apparatus of morphine—considerably enhanced its recreational appeal.

"Any one with the price could go into nearly any drugstore and buy a packet of the pure drug," the anonymous "Leroy Street," a young addict of the period, recalled in his melodramatic memoir, *I Was A Drug Addict*. Until around 1910, says Street, he was a supremely typical white youth in Greenwich Village, living happily with dad and mom and little brother, a dedicated baseball player—until, at age fifteen, "low associates" among his chums introduced him to his first "blow" of 100 percent pure heroin. The next dozen years were hell, he righteously assures us, a succession of cold-turkey cures in the Tombs every time he got arrested, and a few voluntary detoxification attempts which even included the horrible hyoscyamine treatment.

In between bouts with the law, though—always for heroin possession—Street's experiences within the New York City drug milieu make for fairly agreeable reading. The folks around him were pretty much as Dr. Pearce Bailey described them, young men and women of respectable intelligence and decidedly appealing personalities, who used heroin for all the reasons Bailey presents—urban blight, boredom, peer pressure—and then some. "Respectable society" was, at the time, remorselessly fragmented and stratified, supremely rife with racial prejudices, and insufferably stiff-necked. Recreational drug use was not merely an escape *from* it, but a fundamentally affirmative rebellion *against* it. And this underlying factor, perhaps more than any other, influenced the evolving myth of the "heroin boys."

In 1916, as today, the number of occasional heroin users who didn't become addicted far exceeded those who did.* Even 100 percent USP grade heroin, used *only* on a Saturday night will not turn you into an addict; but it does have a way of climbing up on you, like the proverbial monkey. Of course, becoming addicted wasn't the worst thing in the world as long as heroin was legal and available; in blighted urban America, it even appeared in some ways entirely appropriate, until after Pearce Bailey discovered this sub-class of white kids on drugs. Dehumanized beyond redemption, and distorted into something supremely distressing, they were from then on destined to star in the next wave of anti-drug lobbying. Improving horror stories increasingly linked heroin to youth gangs, crime, and the threat of incipient rebellion. The New York City narcotics commissioner, Walter Herrick, reported with alarm that police raids on "cocaine orgies" were also turning up heroin—a drug, he assured everyone, that had the same fiend-producing powers as cocaine. Heroin, he asserted, caused youngsters to run amok. And since nobody at the time really knew *anything* about what heroin was or did, everybody believed him.

There were mitigating circumstances; these *were* uncertain times, peculiarly susceptible to the most paranoid fantasies. America was mobilizing for war, and the scourge of heroinomania

---

*In 1976, the National Council on Drug Abuse estimated that there were 7 million occasional consumers of heroin in America, at a time when there were some 700,000 addicts.

among the nation's draft-age young men was a subject of considerable worry. Rep. Henry Rainey, later to head the Treasury Department's Special Committee on Narcotics Traffic, was boisterously attacking heroin as "that German invention"—sentencing the addict to "sure death in less than 10 years"—insidiously perpetrated in America for the express purpose of winnowing the ranks of her fighting men. According to Congressman Rainey, some 80,000 draftees had been rejected because of heroin addiction. (Later records put the figure at about 3,000.)

After the war things became worse. Between 1918 and 1921 the country was shaken by a rash of Bolshevik bombings, violent labor strikes, and IWW (Industrial Workers of the World) agitation. This was no doubt the most openly "radical" three years of American history, since the Revolutionary War. And opium— in the form of diacetylmorphine—found a unique place in this scheme of things, in a way that would have had Marx spinning in his grave, for it was not the thing that kept the "people" down, allegedly, but what kept them marching, bombing, and agitating. In 1919 in New York City, the Mayor's Committee on Public Safety strongly implicated heroin in a series of political bombings, and elsewhere the drug was condemned as the tool of the left in coercing young people into sedition. Even Pearce Bailey, having served a time as the Army's chief neuropsychiatrist, abandoned his originally sympathetic stance to echo this alarm. He theorized that insecure, imitative and easily-led teenagers were seduced into radical doctrines for the same reasons they were seduced into the heroin habit.

> It is in them that mental contagion which spreads up to hysterical mass movements, spreads with the greatest rapidity, and in their minds sedition finds an easier route than realism ... suggestible, they easily become the tools of designing propagandists in spreading seditious doctrines, or in the commission of acts in defiance of law and order.

A like-minded law and order reformer baldly warned parents to beware lest their offspring take up heroin sniffing and "awaken to find that he has become a Bolshevik or an IWW."

Such grievous admonitions were inflamed by Representative Rainey's oft-quoted estimate that there were one million addicts in America in 1919. That figure, of course, was completely bogus—the only reliable estimate from this period, compiled by Public Health Service physicians Lawrence Kolb and A.G. DuMez in 1924, put the actual count at about 150,000—but it was taken quite seriously by lawmakers, newspapermen, and the public at large, and caused much alarm: who wouldn't be alarmed by the spectre of one million Bolshevik teenage addicts?

After World War I, a massive crackdown on doctors, pharmacists and narcotics addicts was launched by the Treasury Department, with predictable results—the expansion of black-marketeering in heroin and morphine selling at grossly inflated prices, the creation of a whole new criminal class composed of a few addicts who, denied maintenance opiates by doctors, were forced to steal to purchase the black-market product, and many more addicts who'd simply committed the "crime" of taking opiates habitually. Naturally the number of narcotic criminals in jails went sky-high: By 1928, fully one-third of the prisoners in federal penitentiaries were Harrison Act violators, for the most part addicts. Enforcement officials were quick to cite the sudden influx of addicts into prisons as evidence that a heroin-induced "crime wave" had swept the nation, in addition to everything else. The chief propagandist for this clever statistical fiction was Col. Richmond T. Hobson, Spanish-American War hero and arch prohibitionist, who'd turned his energies, after the passage of the Volsted Act, to the heroin problem. Thanks to heroin—a drug he swore most certainly caused "degeneration of the upper brain...in a few months"—the nation's crime rate had soared *900* percent! It was the nature of this perfidious substance, he blathered, to "change a misdemeanant into a desperado of the most vicious type." In light of this, Colonel Hobson warned young mothers to periodically check the food their children ate; and he also recommended:

> In using any brand of face powder regularly, it is a wise precaution
> to have a sample analyzed for heroin.

Hobson was echoed by a host of civic-minded Americans. An article in *Current History* magazine—"The Menace of the Drug Addict"—charged: "Heroin...is the most insidious and crime-inspiring of all drugs," and the *American Legion Weekly* published an article titled "Youth + Drugs = Crime" which characterized "insane daring, utter merciless and vicious cruelty" as the modus operandi of teenage criminal drug fiends, of whom the American Legion said there were two million abroad in the land.

There were a few dissenters: Kolb and DuMez disputed the claim that heroin had claimed millions of casualties, a smattering of writers pointed out that outlawing opiates, not the drugs themselves, was a spur to petty crime and expanded prison populations, and a few doctors still held that the fact that heroin didn't cause nausea and was incredibly effective for respiratory ailments made it an invaluable therapeutic.* But heroin apologists were far-flung then, and have been ever since. As early as 1920, the AMA House of Delegates forthrightly resolved

> . . . that heroin be eliminated from all medicinal preparations and that it should not be administered, prescribed, nor dispensed; and that the importation, manufacture, and sale of heroin should be prohibited in the United States.

This, of course, is precisely what did happen in 1924 when Rep. Stephen Porter, with the help of the Treasury Department, pushed a bill through Congress banning heroin, and plugging up the Harrison Act loophole airtight, and for good.

Once heroin was banned, statistics indicate that the numbers of youthful chippers and addicts declined drastically. Federal Bureau of Narcotics Commissioner Harry Anslinger revived heroinomania briefly in the early 1950s as a ploy to counter a New York Academy of Medicine proposal for heroin maintenance (See Chapter 12). In January 1952, he called a press conference to announce a crackdown which would, he confidently predicted, result in a "sharp reduction in addiction among teenagers." He had every reason for optimism: later statistics, released by his own department, indicate that at the time there were exactly 1,743 addicts under the age of 20 in all America.

---

*Today, with heroin completely unavailable to them, this remains a dilemma for doctors, particularly in some surgical aftercare cases where the vomiting that sometimes follows morphine injection might prove dangerous, even fatal to their patients, and in cases of intractable pain. This medical imbroglio even got the goat of syndicated conservative pundit William F. Buckley who wrote in one of his columns: "After seeing my dear mother and an aunt die of cancer and in such excruciating pain, even with drugs, it infuriates me to think our "progressive" country refuses to allow heroin to be used for medical purposes."

TWELVE
THE CURE

All through the year of 1925, Dr. Lawrence Kolb was injecting little white mice with the blood of humans. Dr. Kolb, who virtually fathered American addiction theories and treatment, over the nearly forty years he presided at the famous Lexington Narcotics Farm, got the blood from morphine addicts, courtesy of the U.S. Public Health Service in New York City; the white mouse was chosen to receive it, he explained, because "its small size made it possible to carry out the greatest number of tests with the limited quantity (of human blood) obtained."

As might be expected, the rodents injected with human addict-blood had a great tendency to go into convulsions and die, but Lawrence Kolb was happy to report to his supervisor, Dr. A.G. DuMez, that the survival rate among mice injected with human addict-blood was exactly equivalent to that of mice injected with blood from human non-addicts. This greatly pleased DuMez, since it indicated that there is no substantial difference between the blood of human addicts and non-addicts. Even if you took into account what was already known about blood types, immuno-suppressive responses and interspecies differences, Kolb's mouse tests provided the most impressive nail so far in the coffin of the equivocal "Autotoxin theory" of opiate addiction.

The refutation of the Autotoxin theory was not lightly undertaken. The Autotoxin had been central to American detoxification schemes since the great national cure binge of the 1880s.

It was an instinctive explanation for the existence of progressive tolerance to opiates and for withdrawal symptoms. The earliest Autotoxin theorists placed this anti-morphine agent squarely in the stomach. Constipation, after all, is about the only conspicuous physical complication that attends morphine addiction, and it does clear itself up most spectacularly within hours after administration is discontinued. An Italian doctor named Gioffriedi, contemplating this in the 1880s, came up with a compelling theory of addiction. Morphine, deduced Gioffriedi, obviously worked like a poison—a "toxin"—on the stomach lining, causing it to produce a corresponding counter-poison to neutralize it. This natural counterpoison—the Autotoxin—would inevitably have all the *opposite* properties of morphine. If morphine constipated, the Autotoxin would purge; if it made you feel positively *good*, the Autotoxin would make you feel positively *bad*.

This scheme hardly explained everything: the fact that most addicts eventually stabilize their daily intake at a finite, non-increasing threshold; or that withdrawals last three days, no more nor less, no matter what the addict's daily intake is. But the Autotoxin did provide a lucid, easily-graspable explanation for the more palpable syndromes of addiction. And it provided cure specialists with an alibi for that subtlest and most distressing syndrome—relapse to addiction, generally occurring within six months of a complete withdrawal.

Relapse was a continual thorn in the side of any professional cure specialist. The first cures with any theoretical basis at all laid great significance on the Autotoxin and tried vigorously to boost its activity during withdrawals. Strychnine was given abundantly, hypodermically, to stimulate the bowels to continual motion. Faradic and galvanic electrical shocks were applied to boost the Autotoxin's general convulsant properties. And most of all, the specialists provided heroic doses of belladonna alkaloids, since it was known, under the most advanced scientific precepts of the day, that the belladonnas were the closest thing in nature to the Autotoxin itself.

> *Not poppy, nor mandragore,*
> *Nor all the drowsy syrups of the world,*

Shall ever medicine thee to that sweet sleep
Which thou ow'dst yesterday.

Shakespeare in *Othello* remarked on the most obvious synergy
of opiates and the belladonnas; a moderate dose of mandrake
extract, which contains atropine and hyoscyamine and scopolamine, will make you as drowsy as a rather large dose of opium.
A *higher* dose of mandrake, though, will put you in a delirious
"waking" coma. Even before the Ice Age, belladonnas were used
world-wide in religious ceremonies. The drug promoted babbling
trances in shamans and other human oracles, and medieval women
commonly confessed, under Inquisition torture, to greasing
broom handles with mandrake salves, masturbating with them,
and flying to witch's sabbats with weird animals (See Chapter
3).

Belladonna had two salient advantages for the cure specialists.
Because it annulled morphine's mental clarity and euphoria by
replacing it with a drowsy, babbling disconnected stupor, it became established in science as morphine anti-toxin (artificial
Autotoxin), providing a conceptually elegant framework for ridding the body, once and forever, of every addiction-promoting
substance. And belladonna had the important advantage of keeping patients comatose: they wouldn't even *think* of sneaking out
of the ward, being entirely occupied in talking to their ancestors,
and flying through the sky with weird animals.

This treatment, in the very *best* cure spas, cost at least $100
a day—a phenomenal sum. Poor people, for $50 could spend
a few days of delirium in the public ward. But rich and poor alike
tended to become readdicted to morphine within a year. This, the
theorists explained, was obviously due to a residual amount of
Autotoxin still in the patient's body after detoxification which
could most certainly be eliminated by repeating the procedure.*

---

*The truly disadvantaged, who could only afford the mail-order nostrums offered in the
popular press, were nearly as thoroughly gulled. One self-cured expert offered a means
by which one could detox "quickly and painlessly," no medicaments involved at all,
through a simple mail-order course. The St. James Society charitably offered a "free trial
bottle" of something guaranteed to make you feel "as though life were worth living
again." It turned out to be heroin. In Chicago, the 1916 coroner's report on one Mrs. Mary
Willis, twenty, laid the cause of death to her secret-formula cure potion: "A chemical
examination of the brown fluid in the bottle labeled 'Dr. Weatherly's Remedy' showed
20.6668 grains of morphine sulphate (over one gram), per ounce."

Morphine itself was often an adjunct to the belladonna cure, which made some people skeptical. But those people just didn't grasp the full elegance of Autotoxin mechanics. A little morphine, now and then through withdrawal, *ought* to stimulate the client's stomach into manufacturing more Autotoxin. Augment that with atropine, keep the bowels churning with strychnine, administer regular and copious emetics and enemas—do this long enough, and you *ought* to purge a person's system of every last nanogram of drug and Autotoxin alike.

This approach irresistibly led to the promotion of the "bilious green stool" as the sovereign indication that one was cured of opiate addiction, forever, with no conceivable relapse liability. Exactly who came up with the green stool is still an issue of controversy. Some say it was Dr. George Petty, the most heartfelt exponent of compassionate medical treatment for drug addicts throughout this period. Others believe it was Dr. Alexander Lambert, of the American Medical Association, Theodore Roosevelt's personal physician, and an outspoken proponent of strict drug laws. (In 1904 Dr. Lambert wrote in The *Journal of the American Medical Association* (*JAMA*): "When this stool occurs, or shortly afterward, the patients often will feel relaxed and comfortable, and their previous discomforts cease.") Others credit Charles B. Towns, a Georgia insurance salesman who made a fortune dosing middle-class addicts with hyoscyamine and strychnine, and poking through their bedpans for the bilious green stool. Towns found out about the cure around 1905, he told *Collier's* magazine, from an anonymous benefactor he met in a New York tavern.

As he recreated the scene for *Collier's*, his benefactor said, "I have got a secret cure for the drug habit—morphine, opium, heroin, codeine—any of 'em. We can make a lot of money out of it."

"That's a job for a doctor," exclaimed Towns.

"It's a job for a man with an almighty nerve," responded the other. "You've got that."

Nerve he had, in abundance. Charles Towns turned the "bilious green stool" into the totem of an assembly-line cure technique that may have killed a few more people than it ever detoxified. Though the identity of his tavern benefactor was never disclosed, it was probably presidential physician Alexander Lambert. Towns and Lambert put their names together on a typically complicated and horrendous hyoscine cure in 1906. That year Towns used it to detox several hundred thousand Peking coolies to demonstrate America's sincerity in launching the Shanghai Opium Conference. Towns claimed that he cured four thousand Chinamen per day during his six-month sabbatical in the Inner Kingdom. He tried to set up an auxiliary clinic in Shanghai, but as he told the Shanghai Opium Commission, the outrageous rumor had sprung up among the Chinese that the Towns Cure always "killed within a year." In view of his impressive cure rate, though, the U.S. State Department credited the Towns method as "the most successful on record for the cure of the victim of the opium habit in any of its forms." Once Towns got back from China, Lambert wrote up the method for *JAMA* as the most advanced, effective and *compassionate* cure on the market, and within another year, there was a four-floor Charles B. Towns Hospital on Central Park West in New York City. Eminent addicts paid $330 a day for a private room, and the anonymous paid $75 per day for a bed in the open ward.

The Towns-Lambert method differed little from any other hyoscine cure: morphine was given for the first two days—to stimulate the Autotoxin—and the belladonna delirium was maintained for five days straight. With this regimen—the purges being especially violent and regular—the hallowed green stool was virtually guaranteed. Since the stool was the very signet of total detoxification, Lambert early on was estimating their cure rate at around 90 percent. "A little less than 10 percent returned to us for a second treatment," Lambert bragged. "A reasonable presumption being, that the ninety percent from whom we never heard further, who left our care, had no need to consult with us a second time."

As time went on, though, Lambert started distancing himself from Towns. For one thing, Towns gradually turned into a perfect crackpot, and before long was billing his cure as guaranteed to work for *any compulsive behavior*, from morphinism to nicotinism to caffeinism, to kleptomania and bedwetting. Lambert's defection from the Towns-Lambert Cure was also based on the need to revise his cure estimate significantly downward; as time went on, he began to notice that people kept coming back for the cure, cure after cure, for years on end.

The failure of the hyoscine cure was actually a boon to Lambert by then. Since the bilious green stool had been the very corner-stone of the Autotoxin theory, this represented proof that there *was* no Autotoxin irresistibly compelling addicts to step up their doses, and inflicting them with withdrawals whenever they stopped. The possibility that there was no Autotoxin stirred the developing drug-control lobby in Washington, of which Lambert had become a powerful leader in the twelve-year interval between advocating the Towns Cure and disavowing it.

During this period the drug-control lobby had engineered a number of pioneering laws regulating the patent medicine and pharmaceutical industries, resulting in a significant drop in the availability of opiates and American opiate consumers. Of these the most significant by far was the Pure Food and Drug Act of 1906. It was the brainchild of Dr. Harvey Wiley, chief chemist for the Department of Agriculture in Washington. A full-blown toxicophobe, Wiley was eventually fired by Theodore Roosevelt for continually sniping at the president's penchant for saccharine over sugar, but not before rallying his support to this new law. The immediate effect of the Pure Food and Drug Act, requiring contents labeling on patent medicines, was spectacular. Once the public knew what went into these preparations, fully one-third of all consumers stopped using them. Of course, significantly more of them didn't stop using opiates medicinally, and there remained a bottom line proportion of nervous-waste cases who simply *wouldn't* stop compulsively using opiates no matter how loudly their dangers were broadcast. Without a ferocious Auto-toxin prodding them on, this seemed a plain vicious indulgence, a quest for kicks and inebriated escape—a strictly *psychological* and criminal condition. The cure, therefore, envisioned by Lambert and the drug-control lobby in Washington, would be to pre-vent their access to narcotics through force of law.

In 1914 during debate on the historic Harrison Narcotics Act, Lambert and Dr. George Simmons, the editor of *JAMA*, launched a series of articles portraying drug addicts as a sociopathic sub-stratum of reprehensible weaklings with no more excuse for their indulgence than chronic masturbators. Lambert put his own name to most of these pieces; it was fairly well-known among doctors that Simmons had gotten his M.D. from the Rush Medical College mail-order school, and started out in Nebraska running an abortion clinic*, so he remained assiduously in the background on sensitive issues like the Autotoxin.

Dr. George Petty and his friends passionately defended the Autotoxin, entirely aware that they were actually defending drug addicts from dehumanization and oppression by the Washington drug-control lobby which was resolutely revising medical science in order to make drug addiction a federal crime. The Autotoxin doctors published innumerable case histories of the "family" addicts they were treating, people who behaved just like everyone else around them, except for the problem of getting dreadfully ill if they went for a certain period without injecting morphine. These people were simply vulnerable to the Autotoxin, whether they became addicted in youth from "vicious curiosity" or in consequence of medical therapy for painful afflictions.

These Autotoxin defenses provide a sentimental last look at American "family" addicts, the last generation of them who could seek maintenance treatment from family physicians, without fear of being turned in to the police.

> The constant use of narcotics produces a condition in the human body that physicians now view as a definite disease, which diseased condition absolutely requires a continuous administration of narcotics to keep the body in normal function...

The 1917 conclusion of New York's Whitney Commission, a panel convened to study narcotics addiction and its control, was the ultimate swan song of the Autotoxin theory, which by now had been sensibly relabeled "the disease theory" of addiction, in contrast to "the psychological theory" of addiction, so much in favor in Washington. No sooner did Dr. A.G. DuMez report to the Treasury Department that he was unable to find "the elusive Autotoxin" in the bloodstream of addicts than a number of the New York City doctors responsible for formulating the Whitney Commission policy were arrested on conspiracy and overprescription charges. Before long it was sheer professional suicide to

---

*After he got "respectable," Dr. Simmons conducted a twenty-year *JAMA* campaign against birth control in all its forms.

disagree with the Treasury Department on theories of drug dependence.

Immediately after the Harrison Narcotics Act went into effect in 1914, 124,000 physicians registered with the Treasury's Federal Narcotics Bureau as purveyors of morphine, along with 47,000 pharmacists and 1,600 drug companies. The project of overseeing these drug sources was an immense one for the new narcotics squad—especially after the Great War diverted their efforts—but they set out ambitiously with a series of test cases. They were, at first, thwarted in the courts. In 1917 a federal court ruled in the case of the *United States* v. *Jin Fuey Moy* that a physician could provide narcotic drugs to an addict, providing he did so in "good faith," that is, by prescribing a dose that was lower than that which the addict had been taking. The following year, when the Treasury's Federal Narcotics Bureau applied directly to the Supreme Court to extend their powers beyond overprescription by doctors, and be granted the right to arrest anyone simply caught *in possession* of illegal drugs, they were again turned down. Chief Justice Oliver Wendell Holmes opined that Congress would have to "strain its powers almost, if not quite, to the breaking point in order to make the probably very large proportion of citizens who have some preparation of opium in their possession criminal and subject to serious punishment." But when the Supreme Court ultimately—in the midst of the heroin-omania scare in 1919—decreed that it was illegal for any private doctor to prescribe opiates to an addict "for the sake of continuing his accustomed use," addiction itself effectively became a crime. To celebrate this development, the Treasury set up a special Narcotics Bureau as part of their promising new National Prohibition Administration. Col. Levi G. Nutt (see Epilogue), coordinated the department, with the help of 170 enthusiastic narcotics agents.

Physicians conversant with morphine addiction marked this all clearly. An agonizing choice was presented: they either cut off addicts they'd been treating for years, or risk losing their licenses if the Treasury drug squad decided to put them on their ever-more impressive arrest list. Dr. Lawrence Kolb, years later reviewing the F.B.N.'s arrest statistics in its first doctor purge, estimated that virtually all these physicians prescribed for "pa-

tients whom they saw as having a desperate need for the drugs."
Few of these doctors—25,000 by 1938—ever went to jail,
though. The narcotics agents would most commonly mount a
"conspiracy" prosecution, citing the doctor for conspiring with
the patient to funnel drugs to the street for resale; the doctor
would then turn state's evidence, and get off with a ruined reputation, while the patient did a long stretch of hard federal time.*

Lambert now was proclaiming the very latest Freudian theories
whenever he discussed drug addiction. It was basically due to
overweening "egoism" that anyone took opiates at all, Lambert
assured Nutt's Federal Bureau of Narcotics. Addicts took drugs
to get a sort of pharmacological sex thrill, an artificial stimulus
substituted for the honest, naturally born id. To provide a cure,
you only had to "irradiate and sublimate the libido which he is
so wantonly wasting on the fetish of drug addiction." This could
easily be done by force, Lambert guaranteed, if the addicts were
only rounded up and placed in a secure location. The Federal
Narcotics Bureau implemented this therapeutic scheme with grotesque enthusiasm.

By this time there were nearly sixty public addiction clinics
all over the country—in New York, Louisiana, Connecticut,
Georgia, California, Ohio, West Virginia, Kentucky, Tennessee,
and Texas—mostly offering gradual step-down cures. Those
which emphasized "social adjustment" were the most popular;
"social adjustment" was a euphemism for "maintenance." Of
course none of these clinics could last, in the light of Colonel
Nutt's zealotry.

One clinic that offered "social adjustment" was located in
Shreveport, Louisiana, a city with forty thousand residents, a
symphony orchestra, five banks, two colleges, a cinema, and a
number of prominent drug addicts. Of the thousands of addicts
who passed through the Charity Hospital clinic run by parish

*The New York Academy of Medicine ultimately and comprehensively condemned this
atrocity. In 1963 it stated: "Dictation, threats, hounding and oppression from the narcotics
forces over the years, and still continuing, were so indelibly fixed in physicians' minds
as not to be easily forgotten or braved again.... So thoroughly has the smear job on
addicts been done, so outrageously but erroneously have they been depicted, that the
mere mention of their name has conjured up an image of dangerous criminals or
fiends.... This is what happens when revenue agents become dictators of medicine."

Coroner Dr. William Butler, the oldest was a Civil War veteran who showed up at the age of eighty-two with fifty-five years of regular intravenous morphine use behind him, quite upset because suddenly he was subject to years in a federal jail if the police found out. There was also a preacher of seventy-nine, addicted for sixty-three of those years, and an eighty-year-old housewife with a thirty-year habit. There were also four doctors, two retired judges, a lawyer, a newspaper editor, one of the Shreveport Symphony musicians, a printer, two glassblowers, a local oil-refining millionaire, and the architect who had put up most of the striking French colonial edifices of which the city is still patriotically proud. Almost all were white, though Shreveport was nearly half black. The female addicts outnumbered the male 3:1. Nine-tenths of them had been introduced to morphine by way of medical treatment, and never been able to shake it afterward.

People with chronic pain conditions, like colitis or bayou rheumatism, were generally classed as "uncurable," along with people who had been addicted longer than ten years; these addicts were maintained on an average of sixty milligrams of morphine per day—which had Levi Nutt in Washington clamoring for Dr. Butler's license. Of course, Nutt would have been determined to close Shreveport's clinic whether it maintained patients or not—it was Treasury policy to close down *all* sources of morphine, but Butler's policy of dispensing daily doses to cripples and Civil War veterans made him especially vulnerable. Or so Colonel Nutt thought at first.

F.B.N. undercover agents visited Shreveport doctor's offices, behaving like addicts, trying to wheedle prescriptions for morphine out of physicians who would patiently refer them to the Charity Hospital clinic. They also spent time at the hospital contemptuously noting every "curable" ward patient who got a dose of morphine. "Cases almost dead were called curable," Butler noted later. By 1921, using such tactics, the F.B.N. had harrassed and terrorized every public cure clinic *besides* Shreveport out of existence. Dr. Butler, though, refused to give up, even after the Charity Hospital dissolved the clinic at the urging of the Shreveport Board of Health, who spouted allegations and horror stories straight out of Nutt's press releases. "We must bring this matter to a crisis," announced the *Shreveport Times*, "and might as well close all, and let the people howl."

That would have conduced to a most unhappy situation in Shreveport had Butler not explained to the local police chief exactly what that would entail, after hearing him preach to a few bystanders that all addicts should be driven straight "into the river." Dr. Butler took the man out of earshot.

> I told him, "I'm going to violate the confidence of one of my patients now, because I did not like what you said in front of those other gentlemen. I want you to know that your mother is one of those patients that you would like to drive into the river."

That said, there was no local demurral when the clinic merely changed its name in 1921 and carried on operations without the Board of Health's official sponsorship. Dr. Butler now dispensed morphine on his own credentials as Parish Coroner, and the F.B.N. had to decommission him all by themselves.

It took them until 1925 to impanel the proper federal Grand Jury to listen to charges of overprescription by Shreveport doctors. Nutt's men managed to round up seven area physicians, four druggists, two heroin peddlers, and thirteen addicts, and by sundry legal manipulations managed to keep Butler in limbo throughout most of the year as an unindicted co-conspirator. He was later absolved of all charges, but the experience finally convinced Dr. Butler to close the Shreveport clinic.

Most other clinics around the country disappeared more obligingly after the F.B.N. began its crackdown. Levi Nutt himself visited Atlanta in 1921, generating headlines over the scandal that two local drugstores were handling over two hundred maintenance prescriptions made out by the Atlanta public morphine clinic. The clinic was assiduously detoxing everyone who entered it, except for 200 chronic pain and terminal disease cases, whom they termed "incurable." In a brilliant refinement of bureaucratic sadism, Nutt excoriated the basic notion of providing addictive painkillers to "incurable" cases, since, under the Harrison Act's wording, doctors were *only* to provide them to patients with an eye to an ultimate cure. If these cancer and tuberculosis patients couldn't be "cured" by morphine, it was obviously illegal to give it to them in the first place. Atlanta obligingly suspended all detox procedures after Nutt's visit, and four years later cut off all extant "incurables" cold turkey. Dying patients, at that point, went through sessions of bone-crunching withdrawals to help them along.

By 1925, all legal supplies of narcotics to addicts had been eliminated. That year the Supreme Court, in the case of *United States* v. *Linder*, reversed its 1919 ruling and allowed that doctors *could* supply tiny, regular, unprofitable doses of narcotics— maintenance doses in other words—to addicts, who were, the Court said, "diseased and proper subjects for such treatment." But by then family doctors had been thoroughly intimidated by the F.B.N. crackdown, and most ignored the decision. So by the mid-twenties, the Treasury's narcotics force had pretty much done with doctors and pharmacists, and—despite grand pretensions to begin hunting down "big narcotics rings"—turned its attention forcibly and exclusively to arresting street addicts, filling jails until they overflowed.

"I was the only so-designated staff psychiatrist," Dr. Victor Vogel recalls about the day Lexington opened, "and I'd never had any psychiatric training." Addicts came in "by the trainload" that morning in 1935, and undoubtedly the bucolic bluegrass hills of Kentucky, and the unbarred front facade of the Lexington Narcotics Farm,* looked much more congenial to them than the places they'd just left. For years, convicted addicts had comprised more than two-thirds of all prisoners in the federal penitentiaries at Leavenworth, Atlanta and McNeil's Island. Wardens and other prison officials complained vehemently about overcrowding, so in 1935, at the behest of Congressman Stephen Porter, most of the addicts were packed in railroad cars and brought to Lexington.

Once inside, the Lexington Narcotics Farm was the very ideal of a Works Progress Administration institution: squares within squares, the archetypal WPA layout for everything from universities and hospitals to jails and madhouses. The thousand-acre grounds at Lexington comprised a bit of everything: libraries and

---

*The unfortunate name, subject of jokes by addicts and visitors alike, who would inevitably quip, "Where do you grow the narcotics?" was changed to the Lexington Public Health Service Hospital within a year.

laboratories for the staff, a very extensive research hospital, cell accomodations for up to 1,200 inmates, and a bank of solitary cells fitted with restraint gear, inevitably labeled The Hole. There was also an extensive dairy farm, a furniture factory, a garment shop, and a squad of vocational counselors and social workers. There were tennis courts, a bowling alley, a gymnasium, a chapel, and an auditorium for weekly movies and stage shows. *This* was the place to get a *Cure*!

Hopes were exceedingly high at the opening. Stephen Porter had lobbied strenuously for the opening of a "humane" addict asylum, along with the Superintendent of Federal Prisons, who was frankly more interested in getting all these addicts out of his prisons than in whether they cured their addiction. The bill to set up an Addiction Research Center at Lexington had encountered in Congress only the most overwhelming disinterest: the number of addicts in the land was minimal throughout the thirties, and there were *much* more important and pressing topics of public concern. Once Porter had passed his narcotic farm bill, he gave Lexington over to his psychologist friends at the U.S. Public Health Service—namely, Dr. Lawrence Kolb.

> The hospital's approach to the treatment program is based on the assumption that, while physical addiction is a very important thing that must be cured, the psychological angles of the case are much more important; and on the belief that if the patient is to achieve permanent cure he must be relieved of his emotional difficulties, or taught to adjust to them without recourse to narcotics.

That's how it always was with Kolb. If the physical complications of addiction were only minimally grave or important—and Kolb, remember, had been in on disproving the elusive Autotoxin—then surely it was all just a kink of the imagination. Surely addicts could be readily cured by a little psychotherapy, and be guided into ways of handling their imagination that would not include narcotics. Hence the vocational shops, the gym and movies: it was all so much more *benevolent* than some overcrowded jail: That alone should set addicts on the high road to total rehabilitation.

From any addict's point of view, of course, this sort of reasoning inevitably contradicts itself. If addiction's not that important, then there's no sane reason for threatening junkies with incarceration in places like Leavenworth or Lexington for all its relatively benevolent appurtenances. Still, the Lexington doctors were always puzzled that nearly every addict who could physically do so left their care before the recommended departure date.

Addicts volunteered for the Lexington Cure often enough, above and beyond the steady population of convicts who were compelled to live there. Volunteer addicts even tended to revisit the place at intervals for subsequent cures; they did this so often that the administrators could never rate their "cure" statistics above 15 percent, even when they had to ask Congress to renew their budget appropriations.

The Lexington Cure itself was a model of simplicity. Addicts were taken off all opiates for a day until withdrawal signs set in, and then they were injected with 200-milligram doses (subcutaneously) every few hours until the signs went away. Once stabilized for a few days, the addicts were then stepped down gradually over two weeks, with hot baths to relax them by day, and chloral hydrate for sleep at night. Finally, they'd go on the ward, expected there to benefit from the woodworking, the milking, the bowling, the haymaking, the weekly movie and all the other things for the good of the mind. Of course they all left within a month or so of their last shot.

They didn't stay any longer after accredited apprenticeship programs were set up in the mechanical shop, sign painting and x-ray technology. They didn't stay any longer when they were "motivated" to earn "pay" in cigarettes. Threats of The Hole didn't keep them on the premises. They got bored and they left. And though the relapse rate was not a percentage point less for those who *did* stick out the six-month recommended stay compared to those who left early, still the Lexington doctors were always agitating to keep the addicts on the Farm for at least half a year.

At first, they tried to induce clients to stay by threatening them with legal action, but they quickly ran afoul of *habeas corpus*. The federal district court for Kentucky affirmed in 1936 that volunteers can't be locked up in the United States under any circumstances, even if they volunteer to go to a narcotics farm. So Kolb's staff lobbied the Kentucky legislature, and a law was passed making "habitual narcotic use" a one-year offense in that state. From that point forth, no one who'd gone through Lexington once could reenter without confessing to "habitual narcotic use" before a state judge and undergoing a mandatory one-year detox.*

Even with their dropout problem, though, the Public Health Service straightaway learned a great deal that was new about addiction and abstinence. Besides the addicts who came in off the street, there was a pool of ex-addicts who'd detoxified years ago, and had been sitting in cells ever since, drug free. From those two specimen groups, it was soon determined that withdrawal symptoms were about the same for everyone, according to the accustomed dose. After fourteen hours of abstinence, everyone would be yawning mightily. Gooseflesh, with hot and clammy flashes, was universal. People would sweat and show muscle tremors and an inability to sit still in one spot. They also suffered from stomach cramps that brought on diarrhea and vomiting in high-dose cases. In marked contrast to morphine's effects, their pupils would be widely dilated, their noses would be running profusely, their eyes would water no matter what their mood, their joints and muscles would ache arthritically, and they were liable to manifest sudden erections and ejaculations for no reason at all. They wouldn't be able to eat or sleep, and all would readily take an offered injection of morphine at this point, even if they knew they'd only be facing another three-day stretch of this misery after it wore off.

Still there were significant subjective differences. "Some suffer much but complain little," it was remarked, "while others suffer little but complain bitterly during withdrawals." First-time patients tended to complain the loudest; those who'd been through it before tended to await the third day with stolid patience.

The study of withdrawal symptoms provided fertile research ground on the narcotics farm. Within a couple of years, Kolb's associate Dr. Carl Himmelsbach had developed a way of graphing every visible withdrawal sign, together with corresponding blood pressure, heartbeat and temperature measurements. He called it,

*This was not realized to be unconstitutional until 1961, when the California Supreme Court put it in writing that drug addiction *per se* is not a crime.

A typical "K-1" addict.
Dr. Lawrence Kolb of the Addiction Research Center in
Lexington distinguished six discrete types of drug
addict. All, he found, were equally uncurable.

appropriately, the Himmelsbach Abstinence Scale, and with it he could precisely gauge the "opoid effect" of any drug on addicts and nonaddicts alike. The Himmelsbach Scale was used, by reseachers, for example, in 1944 during one of Harry Anslinger's more vehement antimarijuana crusades, to determine that marijuana has no addiction liability, and in no way partakes of opiate activity; since this was developed at The Addiction Research Center (ARC), it was never reported by the popular press, even to the point where Anslinger would bother to denounce it. When Drs. Harris Isbell and Abraham Wickler tested cocaine on the Himmelsbach Scale in 1953, contemptuously concluding that it "does not cause physical dependence," that also went unreported.

"There is an abounding area of knowledge which was developed at the hospitals and at ARC that somehow doesn't get to the outside world," Dr. Murray Diamond was marveling long after his retirement from Lexington, "it just doesn't get there." The 1941 study on addict IQs was a case in point. The addicts turned out to have a "slight but statistically significant" edge over non-addict jail convicts, and what's more, to be generally smarter than their own ward attendants. Though this never got out into the world, it complemented something Dr. Kolb and his associates had already determined: that the addicts at Lexington weren't criminals except by virtue of arbitrary statute. And most of them weren't even really sick, either physically or mentally. It was impossible, for this reason, to put them through any kind of successful "treatment."

Kolb and his mentor A.G. DuMez had been confident about the sort of people they'd be dealing with, before the gates actually opened at Lexington. They expected "addicts of the delinquent type, who spend a good part of their lives in prison." The antinarcotics laws and the narcotics squads had ordained this by making it extremely unlikely that sane, decent, reality-oriented people would ever willingly go near heroin. Kolb very reasonably anticipated dealing with psychopaths of an exceedingly predictable type.

One of the effects of opiates is the obliteration of mental conflicts and the uncomfortable pathological strivings that result from them. The tensions, both physical and mental, produced by these strivings are relieved, and under its influence the neurotic or psycho-

pathic patient feels free, easy and contented. The contrast with his
usual state is so great in some cases that he is actually happy.

As early as 1925, Kolb had traced out this portrait of the post-
Harrison addict, and dubbed it "Kolb-1." The K-1 had an abnormal drive to make it big in the world, impose himself on
everyone around him, and generally give vent to authoritarian
behavior. But lacking the intelligence, education, opportunity or
plain courage to do so, K-1 stewed in his own juices, gnawing
his own liver self-destructively with alcohol most often, until
heroin was discovered to be the ideal agent for neutralizing this
drive at the source. Most likely, Kolb speculated, it had to do
with infantile sexual aggressiveness being forcibly stifled through
life by a hyperactive superego. This would manifest itself perfectly in an affinity for this particular mode of anti-social behavior—taking illegal drugs—since that behavior would also defuse
K-1's tormenting sex drive.

If anything, then, opiates performed a social service by ob-
tunding the K-1's natural propensity to run amok when the inner
conflicts bubbled up to intolerable intensity. Kolb was uncom-
promisingly radical about this, in a country which largely believed
that heroin specifically *inspires* addicts to commit horrid crimes.

> There is probably no more absurd fallacy than the notion that
> murders are committed and daylight robberies and holdups are
> carried out by men stimulated by large doses of heroin or cocaine
> which have temporarily distorted them into self-imagined heroes
> incapable of fear.... The effect of addiction on the psychopathic
> murderer is to inhibit his impulse to commit violent crime.... No
> addict who receives an adequate supply of opiates and has money
> enough to live is converted into a liar or a thief by the direct effect
> of the drug itself.... The effect on an aggressive criminal is to
> make him less a murderer and more a thief.

So this was Kolb's broad prospectus: take these energetic but
conflicted K-1s; work out their blocking taboos; and liberate their
energies toward creative, positive ends.

Dr. Lawrence Kolb assiduously worked on this scheme all
through the twenties, but Lexington had hardly been open one
year before it was discovered that K-1s hardly showed up in this
population at all. Far and away the most broadly represented
group turned out to be Kolb-2s, the virtual inverse profile of the
driven, authoritarian, self-conflicted psychopath.

"As we recall our years at the hospital," Dr. Robert Felix remarked in 1974, "it seems that nearly all our patients were of this type." K-2s were mainly just people who'd fooled around with heroin for idle kicks, become addicted, and consequently found themselves in trouble. They'd gotten on in the world quite adequately before they became addicts, and then had to start hustling extra money for heroin, avoiding the police, and doing other antisocial things. In stark contrast to K-1s, they were exceedingly tolerant of other people's behavior, even police and Lexington psychiatrists; they put up little resistance to institutional attempts to modify their behavior, but because of their very flexibility, behavior-modification had no lasting influence on them.

There were six well-defined categories of "K" at Lexington, and these inoffensive K-2s *always* comprised at least 60 percent of the general population. K-1s were exceedingly scarce; real psychotics, it turned out, don't very often give themselves the luxury of disengaging their anxiety with euphoric drugs. K-1s made a lot more trouble on the ward than K-2s, of course, forever starting fights, attempting escape, and smuggling in drugs; as time went on, and priorities shifted at ARC, K-1 convicts were generally rejected on application and shipped back to civil jails.* K-1 volunteers were detoxed and encouraged to leave at the earliest opportunity. When it turned out that addicts of just about *any* K profile seemed invulnerable to psychotherapy—that is to say, *all* addicts—the whole notion of analysis was gradually abandoned. An ARC report in 1953 was positively snide about it, since by then the institution had gone wholly over to a behavioristic catechism:

> Many addicts deny any need of psychiatric assistance and many frankly refuse therapy. The drug addict has found something—morphine—that allays his vague and free-floating anxiety. To demand of him that he relinquish a tested product for the relatively unpredictable success of psychotherapy is to demand more than many addicts can give.

---

*K-1s were regretfully discarded as Cure prospects when it turned out that they didn't appear to mind withdrawals. They suffered the most and complained the least of the lot. How can a person's behavior be systematically remotivated when he responds like *that* to highly aversive stimuli?

K-2s would, of course, submit to psychotherapy amiably enough. It just didn't do them any "good." On the couch they could introspect as deeply as anyone else, set up problems for discussion, and free-associate fluently. But they could never be made to identify their drug-seeking misbehavior with any particular set of childhood traumas, or the distant father or the carnivorous mother. They could be prodded into acting out any variety of repressed emotions, but the catharsis didn't make them any less liable to inject heroin when they went back out into the world; they didn't take heroin out of guilt and tension. And K-2s relapsed with the same frequency as any other category of K; that is to say, in almost every case.

The K-2s at ARC were described as exhibiting "psychopathic diathesis," meaning that they behaved just like psychopaths (they took illegal drugs), for no good reason beyond simple pleasure seeking and pain avoidance. They injected heroin at first because it felt good, and eventually they were taking it just to avoid the unpleasant withdrawals. "Carefree individuals," Kolb finally typed them, "devoted to pleasure, seeking new excitements and pleasures, and usually having some ill-defined instability of personality that often expresses itself in mild infractions of social customs."

Their relapse tendency, he thought, seemed to indicate that these individuals had a special learning disability. If they couldn't learn from bitter experience to keep away from dangerous drugs, then there was a fundamental lack in them somewhere: "inferiors who are striving to appear like normal men," Kolb concluded. If only one could determine precisely what this learning deficiency consisted of, it ought to be possible to cure it.*

---

*Had he ever had the time to meditate on historical matters, Dr. Kolb could have profited much by the classic fourteenth century profile of *The Child* by Bartholomew the Englishman. Between the ages of around five, "when he is weaned from milk and knoweth good and evil," to about sixteen, the medieval child was a very model of psychopathic diathesis:

> *They lead their lives without thought and care, and set their hearts only on mirth and pleasure, and dread no perils more than beating with a rod, and they love an apple more than gold.... They are quickly and soon angry, and soon pleased, and easily they forgive; and because of tenderness of body they are soon hurt and grieved, and cannot well endure hard work.... Through great and strong heat they desire much food, and so by reason of excess food and drink they fall often and many times into various sicknesses and evils....*
>
> *Since all children are spotted with evil manners, and think of things that be,*

The trouble was, all the addicts who wound up at Lexington, of every K type, took it for granted that they *were* cured, once they'd gone through the Kolb-Himmelsbach step-down. It always left them feeling full of energy, and more self-confident than they'd felt in years—as long as they were on the ward, where there was nothing more difficult to contend with than psychiatrists and vocational-education teachers, trying to persuade them to pitch cow manure, practice commercial calligraphy, or lathe down ornamental chair legs. But in the invigorating afterglow of detox, they weren't about to put up with any such frustrating routines. So they launched straight out to do *important* things in their lives and were back on the needle, usually within a year.

When this came to light, the future looked bleak for the Addiction Research Center. By 1942, with a 15 percent cure rate at best, it was hard for the ARC staff to convince the Congress that the nation was perceptibly benefiting from the farm, the wood shop, the sign-painting studio and the expensive doctors and social workers at Lexington and Ft. Worth. Curiously, it was a particular type of "K" addict—the "con-man" addict—who inspired the solution to this dilemma. Dr. James Lowry, at the time Lexington's liaison in Washington, fondly recalls:

> I remember prewar addicts as being of a very specific type; they were con men, professional criminals and card dealers. I learned more from them than almost anybody I've been acquainted with in my lifetime. I found their lessons very useful, whether I was dealing with Congress or State Legislature, or anybody else in my consultative work.

---

and regard not of things that shall be, they love playing, and games, and vanity, and forsake learning and profit; and things most worthy they repute least worthy, and least worthy most worthy. They desire things that be to them contrary and grievous, and set more store by the image of a child than the image of a man, and make more sorrow and woe, and weep more for the loss of an apple, than for the loss of their heritage; and the goodness that is done for them they let it pass out of mind. . . . When they are washed of filth, straightaway they defile themselves again.

Just as church-window portraits of medieval children always show them as miniature adults, just so Bartholomew's generalization here has more to do with adults he perceived as "immature" than with actual children—very few of whom are *really* this sweet. It is people like this who irresistibly fire up in people like Bartholomew and Kolb the imperative compulsion to *teach*.

Dr. Lowry apparently learned his lessons well. ARC made it through the war by opening the narcotics farms to deranged army personnel. Addicts had to be kept to a minimum to make room for shell shock cases, but that presented no problem. There was hardly any morphine available for detox or research—it had more pressing uses overseas—and for the same reason, there was hardly any available on the street. At the end of the war, the national addict population was below fifty thousand; which would, you'd imagine, have obviated any demand for a federal narcotics farm that would never be able to "cure" more than a few hundred anyway.

By the end of the war, though, ARC had evolved a whole new *raison d'être*. Though the object of developing an ultimate cure was forever the stated objective of Kolb and his colleagues, an alternative goal had suggested itself, a goal more immediately practical, and infinitely more profitable.

"The bee without a sting" was the providential new objective: a nonaddictive painkiller, some pharmacological homologue of morphine which would abolish the agonies of illness and injury, but would somehow lack any properties that might inspire healthy people to take it for pleasure. It would be a boon to humanity which would only *incidentally* make a fortune for any company with a patent on it. Toward the end of World War II, when drug companies everywhere began looking for subjects on whom to test their fantastic wartime advances in painkiller technology, the narcotics farms provided an ideal laboratory.

Any time some industrial chemist came up with a new modification of the morphine molecule, it was routinely analyzed by the Himmelsbach method at Lexington. Most commonly, addicts would volunteer in groups of twelve to try out any drug which might have opioid properties and had proven to be tolerably nontoxic in rats, cats, dogs or monkeys. After stabilizing them on morphine, four of the twelve would switch to the mystery drug; four would be continued on morphine, and four more would get placebo saline injections. Fourteen hours later, they'd all be checked out for withdrawal symptoms by the Himmelsbach rating scale. The opioid effect—the degree to which the mystery drug prevented withdrawals—could thus be precisely graded.

If you've ever wondered why the United States never signed

that part of the Nuremberg Treaty which still prohibits the venerable Bayer Fabrikfarben from performing medical experiments on prisoners in German jails, perhaps one of the reasons was that about the same time the treaty was being signed, the Addiction Research Center was endowed with a handsome new budget by the National Institute of Mental Health (NIMH) primarily on the strength of its drug-testing program.

In 1945, then, Lexington's research wing was considerably augmented and new facilities installed to prosecute the search for the bee without a sting. Most of the bars were removed from the windows; The Hole was put out of commission—the new influx of pure-research professionals hadn't gone through medical school with the aim of working in a jail—and admissions leapt from less than two thousand to over forty-five hundred by 1950. Addicts actually *wanted* to come to Lexington once word got out about what was going on there.

Drug-testing subjects did not merely try out a mystery drug after thirty days on regular morphine. After the first Himmelsbach rating, they'd go back on regular morphine for another week, and then the placebo group would get morphine, the morphine subjects would get the mystery drug, the mystery drug subjects would get the placebo, and then once around again for another week of morphine, until everybody in the test group had taken all three preparations and eight weeks of morphine. Then, presumably, they all were detoxed.

Recruiting volunteers for a two-month stretch of daily morphine doses, to be broken twice at most by one-day episodes of withdrawals, was evidently not much of a problem unless the mystery drug turned out to be extremely unpleasant, like nalorphine or cyclazocine. Thankfully, both Lexington and Ft. Worth had a reservoir of "criminal" patients, who could be motivated to put up with a good deal of unpleasantness in the course of medical experiments, in the hopes of early parole.

Nalorphine and cyclazocine were very intensively studied in the late forties and throughout the next two decades. These bees had a highly intriguing variety of stings: They killed pain like any other opiates, but most addicts *hated* them. Rather than quelling grosser withdrawal signs, like cramps and anxiety, these drugs promoted them. (In 1953, after an ARC doctor discovered that overdose victims would almost instantly revive after an injection of nalorphine, this awful drug began saving lives by the score.) Best of all, if a subject were injected with nalorphine or cyclazocine, and then injected with morphine, the morphine would have no effect at all.

These agonist-antagonist opiates would, however, alter a person's consciousness, though not in any way that would conceivably promote drug-seeking behavior. In high or repeated doses, nalorphine and cyclazocine universally induced toxic psychosis: visual and aural hallucinations, insects in the flesh, distortions of subjective body image, and an overwhelming conviction of approaching nemesis.

As recently as 1965, ARC doctors were still devising protocols for detox therapies including nalorphine and cyclazocine. About that time, though, some ARC molecular biologists came up with a very advanced morphine molecule, designed to fit into human molecular opiate receptor sites and do nothing whatsoever. They called it naloxone, and sure enough, it blocked all the physical and emotional effects of heroin, with no side effects of its own. It didn't react with other drugs, and of course, it was nonaddictive. No sting at all, not even a bee. The trouble is, it only worked for a few hours at a stretch. So the ARC put together another version of it, modified to make it last in the body for three days straight, and today we have Naltrexone which is being touted—despite some salient drawbacks—as a powerful adjunct to detoxification aftercare.*

The Lexington addicts also tested methadone, although its advent in long-term addiction therapy was immoderately delayed. A U.S. Department of Commerce intelligence team discovered it shortly after VE Day in 1945, as they were going through the medical-experimentation records of I.G. Farbenindustrie. They were looking, of course, for Nuremberg indictment material—but if they came across an interesting pharmaceutical here and there, it turned up eventually on the patent list of some United States drug company. So when they came across a Farben chemical called Dolophine—named after *Der Führer* himself—it wound up in Eli Lilly, Inc., as AM 148, or "Ammidon," or

---

*Some neurophysiologists have speculated that long-term blockage of opiate receptor sites could result in permanent damage to the body's stress-adaptive mechanisms.

"Methodon." Germany had been starved of poppy but hideously afflicted with pain through the last few years of the war, so a good deal of rather rushed field testing already had been done on this petroleum-based opiate. It had dependable, uniform narcotic-analgesic properties in animals and humans alike, the Farben papers revealed. This expedited much of the basic research, so Abraham Wickler, Harris Isbell, Nathan Eddy et al. were able to complete their own human tests by late 1947.

Lexington patients who had completely detoxed accepted the offer of methadone readily enough. It took a good deal longer for the effects to be felt, compared to morphine, but once that happened, the addicts reported that it was "as satisfying" as their accustomed drug. Addicts going through withdrawals experienced complete relief from a dose of methadone, which was only one-quarter the amount of the last morphine dose they'd been given before the withdrawals started. Wickler therefore wound up ARC's 1947 methadone survey with a rather urgent recommendation that this drug be locked up tight. And so Dolophine remained a mystery drug until the 1960s.

When the ARC researchers weren't preoccupied with testing and evaluating mystery molecules for Lilly and Parke-Davis, they turned their energies to the problem of relapse which had been a stumbling block to the whole cure scheme for most of the century.

In 1942, just before the wartime research interregnum, Carl Himmelsbach had confirmed that the high spirits and moral determination exhibited by ex-addicts right after a thorough morphine detoxification was an unhappy illusion. This was only an initial, "biologically adequate" adjustment of the body's internal homeostatic apparatus to the abrupt absence of morphine, Himmelsbach concluded. Innumerable earlier studies of detoxed addicts—not to mention the embarrassing experience of all those pre-Lexington Cure specialists—universally showed that for at least a half-year after any sort of detox, people had a peculiar tendency to go back on the needle. After NIMH picked up ARC in 1946, Himmelsbach at last got to carefully observe this phenomenon in two groups of addicts: one group had detoxed and stayed drug-free at Lexington for months; the other group detoxed and then went back on stabilized daily morphine injections for two years straight. Sure enough, the "clean" subjects showed a heightened stress sensitivity and unusual emotional volatility for months after detox, while the maintained subjects coped with all sorts of aggravations and inconveniences—including bi-weekly electric shock pain-response aversion tests, nonsense-word memorizations, code-learning exercises, and other onerous and painful routines. They recognized pain and irritation as clearly as before they'd become addicted, but their response to it was characterized by uncommon *sang froid*. While the detoxed addicts, by contrast, even months after withdrawing from heroin, were overreacting to the least unpleasantness with uncalled for acuity, frustration and outright panic.

Significantly, relapsed addicts reapplying for treatment at Lexington always told the doctors when asked why they'd gone back on the needle, that they'd simply run into old addict friends on their return home, and wound up taking a shot with then. Further probing generally elicited the recollection that on first going back to the old neighborhood, the addict had felt inside a sudden turmoil of emotion, spilling out into occasional accesses of runny nose, stomach-rumbles, and anxiety. This surge of phantom withdrawals could often be forcibly suppressed, as long as it was just a matter of being around the old neighborhood. But then one's family and compassionate friends persisted (understandably) in treating one as an addict. And invariably the social stigma of having *been* an addict made it very hard to be treated like a human being by police, landlords and employers. Acutely susceptible in a *physical* way to frustration, the detoxed addict would begin suffering a runny nose, stomach-rumbles, and anxiety several times per week, or even every day. Forcibly suppressing such things can only take a person so far. Since the exact same physical symptoms would be elicited by the mere physical presence of one's addict friends—and since heroin was the *obvious* thing for alleviating these symptoms—it would be almost superhuman not to try a shot, just once, to get over the worst of it. Since no one at ARC (naturally) ever told them any better, most ex-addicts, in capitulating to their yen, would inject their accustomed pre-detox dose of heroin as a "taste"; those who didn't overdose on it, would instantly wind up with their predetox tolerance levels and overnight have to go back to hustling.

All this was solidly on record at ARC by the late forties, thanks to Dr. Himmelsbach, but there were disbelievers. Dr. Abraham

Wickler, for one, was determined to minimize the significance of those phantom withdrawals as much as possible. It was Wickler's conviction that these post-addiction abstinence flashbacks were almost entirely hypochondriacal in origin, a mere trick of the mind—"conditioned abstinence," the ARC behaviorists dubbed it. But in the end Wickler did a spectacular job of disproving his own assumptions and raising the whole level of addiction theory to a new plateau of complexity.

Wickler started out promisingly enough in the late forties with lab rats: male Wistar rats injected every single morning in the stomach with 200 milligrams of morphine per kilogram of body weight. After just a few days of this, of course, the rats would start withdrawing violently every afternoon—circling, jumping, gnashing their teeth, fur bristling, shaking like wet dogs, and squeaking piteously when stroked by attendants. After the dog-shakes and diarrhea subsided, they'd go back in the general cage with the control rats, who were only getting saline injections.

Each night the researchers provided two troughs offering liquid refreshment in the general cage. One trough was pure water, while the other was dosed with a weak opiate called etonitazine, and also with *anise*, a flavor which sugar-loving rats powerfully despise. And sure enough, while the control rats categorically shunned the drug-and-anise beverage, the test rats lapped up a little bit of it every night, despite the revolting taste; though their little bodies were pharmacologically detoxed by nightfall, obviously there was something in the etonitazine that made them feel better. At night when rats get frisky, convivial and horny, it became evident that these Wistar addicts had some special condition that was inhibiting their natural conviviality, but could be alleviated with a little taste of opiate.

It seems not to have confounded the ARC researchers that even after undergoing total addiction and cold-turkey withdrawal every day for a couple years (their time) the rodents still only lapped up just enough etonitazine so they could be naturally frisky, convivial and horny with their nocturnal chums.*

---

*Lab animals from rats to rhesus monkeys have been seen, over the years, to self-administer all sorts of dangerous and addictive drugs in preference to food. Researchers have had monkeys taking morphine, cocaine and even PCP to the point of outright starvation; of course that always makes terrific headlines.

So in 1979, researchers at a Vancouver university set up a veritable Elysian Garden

The point of the project, borne out satisfactorily, was this: long after the addict rats were taken off opiates entirely, they'd commence to leap, chatter, bristle, gnash and dog-shake every time they were put in the special withdrawal Skinner box. And what's more, every night they continued to lap up a little of that awful anise water, even though there was no longer any drug in it. This satisfied Wickler that postdetox withdrawal flashes were entirely psychic in origin, promoted by environmental cues which had previously said "dope" to the addict, when the addict was still enjoying illegal drugs. (No one ever bothered to ask the rats if maybe they'd just come to like the exotic *taste* of anise, drinking it every night for two years straight their time.)

At the same time as he was injecting the rats, Dr. Wickler was refurbishing the animal shed at Lexington and boning up on veterinary surgery. Wickler took pains with his animal shed. He had some exceedingly delicate "preparations" to maintain there.

Out of seventeen dogs lobotomized at ARC in 1952, only two survived, making them exceedingly precious. If a lobotomy was to be performed, it had to be done with a lethal suction-pump device dragging out every last nerve-bundle from the orbital frontal neocortex of the animal, while leaving all the biologically necessary brain structures intact. These preparations were *alive*,

---

for rats, a spacious, airy enclosure outfitted with pleasant bourgeois nest-burrows, race-cages, slides and ladders, public meeting-greens, secluded orgy groves, and romantically gloomy spots where the residents could simply squat and brood over their rodent philosophies and problems. The choice of beverages in Rat Park, as it was called, featured one trough of plain water, and another dosed with morphine so heavily sugared as to be irresistible to any curious, sweet-toothed Sprague-Dawley K-2.

Sure enough, everyone in the park gorged themselves on that delicious morphine trough—until they noticed that for hours afterward, they'd be dreary, associable, and unresponsive to flirtation from acquaintances of the opposite sex. Within a couple of weeks, the morphine trough was hardly being visited at all. Once in a while, some thrill-seeking soul *would* lap up a little morphine, obviously for the expected high, but none became addicted or overdosed.

In the meantime, the researchers had been keeping another batch of rats in typical research-lab Skinner cages, 2′ x 2′ x 1′, furnished with nothing but two drink dishes: water and plain morphine. The rats gradually began taking a little morphine every day to cut the boredom and depersonalization of solitary confinement. By and by, they were taking more as tolerance set in, and presently they were hooked.

After the solitary rats had worked up really enormous habits, the researchers liberated them and put them in Rat Park. Some had been addicted for the equivalent of human years on tremendous daily doses, so they had a tough time of it: dog shakes, leaping, walking around and growling, nothing more complicated than that. Assuming that all learning and conditioning in mammals is a function of neocortical activity, then these preparations would be immune to it. They would not be able to learn to fetch sticks or newspapers now; and if "drug-seeking behavior" was a conditioned response, you wouldn't be able to teach them to anticipate morphine injections either, no matter how heavily you might get them physically addicted.

The canine preparations were addicted to 25 milligrams-per-kilogram per day of subcutaneous morphine, four injections at regular six-hour intervals, with expected acute results: salivation for three to five minutes after injection, vomiting, then a lot of restless circling for ten minutes, succeeded by profound, immobile torpor until the dose wore off. Since the animal shed was confined, the preparations spent most of their time in a circular bin mounted on a rotating fulcrum. When they had an urge to get up and walk, the bin would rotate; the "distance" walked, and the time elapsed, would be recorded automatically. Before the addiction phase, the animals would just walk at odd times of the day. In the early part of addiction, as previously mentioned, they started walking ten minutes after every injection. As they developed tolerance, they were walking for a whole hour after every shot—and for an hour *before* every injection, too!

---

and gnashing. But within a month, every single one was entirely self-detoxed despite the open availability of this delicious morphine-trough.

Finally the researchers took away Rat Park's pure-water trough, and an addiction epidemic was forced on Utopia. And when pure water was restored, the rats promptly detoxed, and went back to robust rodent one-upmanship, con games, competitive athletics, adultery and transcendental meditation as usual.

The obvious parallel, drawn by the Vancouver people, is the experience of American GIs in Vietnam. By an understandably conservative U.S. Defense Department estimate, at least thirty thousand of them became addicted to China White heroin, courtesy of the very governments they were supposedly defending. So the flourishing Nixon-era drug war substance-abuse industry was anticipating a bumper harvest of candidates for methadone programs and therapeutic communities. Even though every serviceman whose urine sample turned up positive for opiates was accorded a short-term methadone step-down in a Saigon hospital before repatriation, it was predicted that the irreversible mechanics of prolonged abstinence would surely have them relapsing before they could even apply for their disability benefits.

To the astonishment of all, less than 8 percent of them ever readdicted. Once they were back in the United States—their own personal Rat Parks—these G.I. addicts became just like everyone else.

These unteachable preparations became most unexpectedly regular about their morphine. They "learned" the time of day, in effect, from the drug and its action in the spinal ganglia, stomachs, and pancreas. The inevitable implication of this was astonishing: the spine, stomach and pancreas must *learn*, with no original input from the brain. And the spine, stomach, and pancreas were somehow inextricably connected to the phenomenon of addiction. Further studies on chronic spinal dogs—brains intact but spines transected in the lower thoracic column—convinced Wickler that nerve cells *themselves* develop a resistance to morphine's depressant effects. Moreover, once the morphine has been discontinued, this "resistance" mechanism goes on for months, promoting hyperresponsiveness, before it actually subsides to normal. It would appear, he speculated, that there was a physical component in the phantom withdrawals which he himself had much derided. The more work Wickler did with these animals, the cloudier and more complicated became the purely psychological theory of addiction, withdrawal, and relapse liability. The Autotoxin was ominously rattling its chains in the austere belfries of Lexington by the early fifties.

It was left to Dr. William R. Martin to begin to make sense of all this. Though in 1957, when he did his principal work, the lock-and-key mechanics of drugs and hormones working on nerve-membrane receptor sites was merely an avant-garde theory, Martin deduced from Wickler's spinal dogs that morphine worked in individual nerve cells to block the transmission of certain electrical impulses from one cell to another. Since the nerve-hormone acetycholine (ACh) was known to facilitate the flow of interneural current, then inescapably, morphine had to block ACh. The longer an addict uses morphine, he reasoned, the more ACh is backlogged in his system, and once the morphine is discontinued, a surfeit of nerve-juice vengefully courses down the ACh channels, promoting sniffling, tearing, stomach knotting, and insomnia. During withdrawal, over a period of a few days, the ACh channels return to something like a normal state, but not precisely the same state they were in before the addict began to use opiates.

At Martin's urging (he became director of ARC in 1962),

researchers now took a closer look at the phenomenon of phantom withdrawals, and found some subtle physical symptoms they'd never observed before. For an average of six to seven weeks, they noted, "primary abstinence" signs are still fairly conspicuous: elevated blood pressure, temperature, and heartbeat; dilation of the pupils; and yawning. Then between the sixth and tenth weeks after detox, the body does a general but erratic flip-flop on all parameters: "Secondary abstinence," during which all vital signs that were depressed are now hyperactive, and those that were hyperactive are depressed. This secondary phase, the researchers found, could last up to thirty weeks.

These variations are not particularly extreme, measurable only by sphygmomanometer and electrocardiograms, but we know now that precisely such changes—even on a molecular scale—in the body can cause shifts in mood, so dramatic they could easily drive an addict who has been religiously drug free months after detoxification to once again seek drugs.

The tremendous breakthroughs that have occurred in research on the mechanics of endorphin, the body's own opiate (see Preface), have shed even more light on the secondary abstinence phenomenon, though the workings of our body chemicals are so subtle and complex that it may be years before researchers assemble an unassailable theory of addiction. However, it would appear from what we do know that cure specialists are now faced with the problem of how to cure secondary abstinence; and that is not likely to yield easy solutions. Short of locking addicts up for six months and checking them daily for blood levels of cortisol and norepinephrine, there's simply no way of baby-sitting with them until they come through it. Near the end of the third month, when the ex-addict metabolism is seesawing clumsily between hyper- and hypo-sensitivity, hormone levels might have to be monitored continuously; even if the technology existed to do that, treatment for it would be inconceivably complicated. Drug protocols for handling prolonged abstinence syndrome would make the Charles B. Towns cure look like a rational and straightforward common-cold remedy.

While a small number of addicts—never more than 15 percent during the hundred-year history of more and less responsible detox therapies—have been able to thread their way through this neurophysiological labyrinth, the inescapable conclusion of all this furious effort may well be that there is *no* universal cure after all, and that the most efficacious solution to the opiate-addiction problem is simply to give addicts opiates.

Methadone maintenance was really the first substantial diffusion of addiction control away from the narcotics farms. New York City, where it originated, had always been dissatisfied with the Lexington system. New York's slums and ethnic ghettos have always been something close to Skinner boxes, full of alienated, unacculturated individuals aware of the environmentally-enhanced Rat Park that comprises the rest of America, but unable to get out and frolic in it. Through the fifties, New York developed a sizable market for the opiate importers of organized crime which prompted no end of scandalous newspaper headlines, police crackdowns, police corruption, higher crime rates, higher prison populations, higher court costs, overdose incidents, hepatitis, and thunderous political diatribes by opposition politicians.

Lexington in the late fifties was strangely preoccupied, working with LSD-25 and chlorpromazine (Thorazine). Neither of these drugs has any addiction liability, but at that time the U.S. Defense Department had a project called MK-ULTRA, under which any sort of drug with theoretical "control" properties was being enthusiastically investigated. So while the doctors at Lexington played around with exciting new hormone systems like tryptaminergic space-out transmitters and phenethyaminergic "reward" loops, New York City set out to cleanse itself of filth.

In this they were greatly aided by none other than Dr. Lawrence Kolb, Lexington's Brahmin of addiction. In 1956 Kolb actually threw his weight behind a recommendation by the New York Academy of Medicine that emergency heroin maintenance should be instituted there, simply to drop the bottom out of street heroin prices. The heroin trade is a complex, delicate, over-extended industry, through which the seasonal output of poppy fields in remote corners of the globe has to be collected, refined, stored, parceled out, cut, and made available to every practicing addict on an implacably precise four-to-six hour schedule, several times a day, every day of the year. In 1956, if New York City had started distributing heroin for free to any certified addict who applied, the newly-developing international heroin trade would have been ruined. But naturally the Federal Bureau of Narcotics attacked the Academy's proposal with a vituperative smear campaign against the doctors involved, and invented for the alarmed press whole legions of child heroin addicts who turned out—once the maintainance proposal was tabled, and the press returned to its normal level of imbecility—never to have existed. Even Dr. Kolb couldn't pull that one out of the fire, so the heroin magnates profiteered amain.

By the early sixties, the New York heroin market was a national scandal, but with F.B.N. chief Anslinger retired, new action was possible. Two eminent New York addiction specialists, Dr. Vincent Dole and Dr. Marie Nyswander, took the long-lasting oral opiate methadone out of Lexington where it had been sequestered since 1947, and began giving it routinely to addicts at Rockefeller University.

Methadone is a rather disappointing euphoriant. Addicts detest it. For people with no established tolerance to opiates or alcohol, a single dose of methadone will get them "high," but it's not a particularly exhilarating feeling: the word most often used is "zonked," a thoroughly unappetizing suspension of interest in one's surroundings, and a definite revulsion to the idea of action until the drug's effects have dissipated. People who have developed a moderate tolerance to opiates hardly feel the "high" at all, just the lethargy. And people who are thoroughly addicted to heroin don't notice *anything*; they just don't start getting sick until the next day, instead of the usual five hours after the last dose.

The drop-out rate among new methadone clients is accordingly enormous. A lot of them—the younger ones especially—show up expecting to con free drugs out of the overly compassionate methadone administrators they've read about in the press. When they discover that methadone's no fun at all—and that it takes the fun out of taking heroin—they opt straight back to the street, sniffling and cramping for days while their habits subside to an affordable level. But they generally do come back again.

The idea behind methadone maintainance is primarily prophylactic. A client maintained on approximately 80 milligrams of methadone per day cannot get physically high on less than 240 mg of heroin. That would cost more than $300 at current rates for a *single dose*; hence, methadone cuts down one's illicit "drug-seeking" behavior by simple, undeniable economics.

Once drug-seeking behavior has been "extinguished" this way, inevitably the addict finds more worthwhile things than drugs on which to spend all his energy, affection, and cash. The number of methadone clients who drop entirely out of the street culture for bourgeois vocations and the nuclear family life-style is really astonishing.

Families everywhere benefit from methadone, which is the single factor that keeps the project afloat in the face of universal public opposition and the election-year posturings of opportunistic office seekers. After three years in a methadone program, any given client is 90 percent less likely to be arrested by the police than *before* entering the program. While on heroin, addicts tend to be arrested for theft, assault, drug sales, check-kiting, vagrancy, fencing stolen goods, petty fraud, public intoxication, prostitution, attempted suicide and comprehensive disorderly conduct. Almost *never* do any of these crimes, in dollar value, represent even half of what it costs to arrest, process, detain, arraign, defend, prosecute, and try the alleged perpetrator; in event of felony conviction, the additional cost of keeping an addict in jail for a long term, with the collateral medical fees it commonly entails, can easily surpass the sum an addict would spend on heroin during his entire career. It costs an average of two thousand dollars to maintain an addict for one year on methadone. After three years—seventy-three hundred dollars—that person's potential for ripping off the public trough has been reduced by a factor of 90 percent. This is what keeps methadone afloat.

The best cure for addiction, ever since Dr. George Calkins decided it was a "disease" a hundred years ago, has been to keep it out of sight, and raise as little fuss over it as possible. Addiction is not, after all, a particularly grave or even slightly debilitating condition, and it's patently noncontagious. The problem has always been with police, legislators, and compassionate souls who will insist on dragging addicts into the spotlight, so that a great fuss can be made over them: a lot more fuss than they require, and *infinitely* more than they deserve. Considering methadone's magic facility for straightening out addicts who are sick of the street hustle, and allowing them to pass among the rest of us undetectable, methadone's probably a much better cure than we could rationally have anticipated when all this nonsense began.

EPILOGUE
THE BUSINESS

I believe that most drug addiction today is due directly to the Harrison Narcotic Act, which forbids the sale of narcotics without a physician's prescription. Prior to the passage of this act, there was a limited number of addicts who went to their corner druggist for their day's or week's supply. They paid a moderate price for the then legitimate article of sale, and the druggist, upheld by professional traditions that are only too often scoffed at, would no more dispense heroin or morphine to a curious adolescent than the old-time bartender would sell whisky to a child, especially since the profit was small and the temptation, therefore not inordinate. But with the passage of the Harrison Act the old addicts were immediately cut off from their old source of supply. The demand remained, the supply was almost nil. Following inevitable economic law, illicitly-obtained drugs went sky-high, and the dope-peddler appeared upon the scene . . . But even he is not the prime mover in the tragedy. He is but the economic result of the unsound theories of our legislators. Jail him and a successor is always at hand to support him.

If the Harrison Act crackdown in the 1920s accomplished only one thing, it created a market for illicit opiates and a grand opportunity for black marketeers. This was already abundantly clear to Robert Schles, who penned the remarks above in an *American Mercury* article titled "The Drug Addict." The failure of federal measures to control the things people drank, smoked, injected or sniffed to get high, was already abundantly clear in the case of liquor prohibition. People were drinking more than ever in 1925, spending millions of untaxable dollars on bootleg booze. There were not enough federal agents to stop them, and the agents that there were—were extremely susceptible to corruption; rum running generated huge sums of money for graft. The inevitable economic outcome of the "noble experiment," Prohibition, then, was inevitably the splendid enrichment of Al Capone, Waxy Gordon, and Arthur Flegenheimer (better known as Dutch Schultz), and the genesis of organized crime as we know it today.

The seemingly spontaneous generation of an underground drug trade, in the wake of the Harrison Act, was just as predictable though somewhat less spectacular. It was as inevitable in 1925 as it had been twenty years before when, in the wake of the first federal drug ban on smoking opium, a thriving black market opium trade had sprung up in New York's Chinatown, to confound reformers and enrich the Mock Duck and On Leong tongs mightily. When police crackdowns and harassment followed, quite inevitably, the rival gangs merged to form the Kown Yick Tong, an even more efficient, profitable, powerful and impenetrable organization. "All of which goes to show," the *New York Times* sermonized in 1906, "that mergers are convenient and harmful competition to be deplored, even among Chinamen." The lesson wasn't lost on the organized crime entrepreneurs who built the drug trade into an efficient and profitable big business over the next fifty years.

It's an indisputable fact that since the days of the Kown Yick Tong, the opium business has become inextricably tied to the fortunes of its by-product, heroin. While poppies can be grown almost anywhere—India, China, Russia, Iran, Southeast Asia, Mexico, Turkey and even America*—commercial opium is dif-

---

*At least until the Poppy Control Act of 1942 made growing opium poppies illegal in America.

ficult to smuggle. Big, black slabs of seductively fragrant raw opium are back breakers to tote and a dead giveaway to nosy border guards and sharp-eyed narcotics agents. When you consider that the international laws enacted in the twenties and thirties made no distinction between opium and heroin, it's little wonder that organized criminals have concentrated on the pure acetylized alkaloid that's so exquisitely portable.

There's also the sheer economics of it. In the remote jungles of Burma, where much of the opium for illicit heroin comes from, a kilo of crude opium sells for twenty-five dollars. That same kilo will be 3.5 to 4.5 percent heroin by the time it reaches the streets of New York, and it will be worth more than $200,000. A cash turnover like that has, quite naturally, attracted a host of implacably ruthless businessmen.

Even so, the heroin trade remains a difficult, inefficient, and risky business. Raw opium must be purchased in the jungles and hills where it is grown, converted to heroin, and smuggled into the States on a regular basis—despite the efforts of Customs and narcotics agents—for the operation to work. After the Harrison Act was passed, it took organized crime forty years to make the drug trade viable, but today these heroin barons reap great profits.

From all indications, the first organized mobster to amass a fortune from illicit narcotics was Vito Genovese, whose territory during the 1950s included most of Manhattan. As Genovese built his heroin empire, Harry Anslinger, the head of the Federal Bureau of Narcotics, was devoting most of *his* time to a propaganda campaign accusing Communist China of being responsible for the rising amounts of heroin on the streets. He did so in collaboration with Senator Joseph McCarthy, while all the while supplying McCarthy—who was himself a morphine addict—with pharmaceutical narcotics.*

The F.B.N. during the three decades (1930–60) that Anslinger

---

*Former narcotics agents, who worked for the F.B.N. at the time, have recently disclosed that it was McCarthy whom Anslinger was referring to in an autobiographical book, *The Murderers*, wherein he describes his plight when he learned that "one of the most influential members of the Congress . . . was a confirmed morphine addict who would do nothing to help himself get rid of his addiction." The senator refused medical help, Anslinger tells us, and insisted that no one would be permitted to "interfere with him or

ran it never once indicted or, it would appear, even *investigated* organized crime and the drug trade. Instead Anslinger limited the Bureau's operations to the arrest and harassment of street addicts and street pushers. "Missionary work," he called it. In the end, it was organized crime itself that finally brought down Genovese and his heroin business.

Shortly after the ill-fated Appalachian Conference which Genovese had organized in 1957, (police raided the meeting of sixty of America's most powerful syndicate leaders at a quiet farmhouse in upstate New York), a rather inauspicious street-heroin peddler named Nelson Cantellops started singing a most interesting song to narcotics agents. Cantellops claimed to have been a courier for "Big John" Ormento, an important Genovese lieutenant, and that he had been present in a car when Genovese personally gave orders for his men to take over narcotics distribution in the east Bronx. Though there was no solid proof of Cantellops's story, it was finely detailed, well-informed and superbly rehearsed with the help, it is said, of underworld boss Frank Costello who wanted Genovese out of the picture. It worked: Genovese was convicted of narcotics smuggling and jailed for fifteen years.

Genovese's arrest, of course, did not stop the drug trade. Other less careless mobsters just picked up where he left off and by the late fifties the American addict population had doubled, from an all time low of forty thousand following World War II to some one hundred thousand.

Narcotics laws have not only benefited organized crime and criminalized addicts, they have also bred corruption in the ranks of those entrusted to enforce them. The very first narcotics commissioner, Col. Levi G. Nutt, was promptly retired after a federal grand jury disclosed in 1929, that his son, Rolland Nutt, a lawyer, had been working for Arnold Rothstein, an underworld figure who, even before Genovese, was enriching himself on the illegal

---

whatever habits he wished to indulge." Anslinger perceiving the senator's condition as "a grave threat to this country," leaving him vunerable to blackmail and propaganda attacks, arranged to have him pick up all the morphine he needed at a Capitol Hill pharmacy. "The lawmaker went on for some time, guaranteed his morphine because it was underwritten by the Bureau," Anslinger concluded. "On the day he died I thanked God for relieving me of my burden."

During the 1930s when this cartoon appeared, Harry Anslinger, head of the Federal Bureau of Narcotics, was claiming great success at dismantling America's illicit drug trade.

drug trade. The grand jury also heard allegations that narcotics agents had routinely taken bribes, lost evidence in important cases, and padded their accounts by adding narcotics arrests made by local enforcement agents to their own records in an effort to secure more federal funding. However, even in the face of the most blatant evidence that the law-and-order approach to addictive drugs and drug addicts was not working, the grand jury recommended that the F.B.N. be given more money, and that penalties for drug addiction be stiffened. This was done, with predictably disastrous results.

Attempts to legislate drug addiction out of existence have resulted only in *more* addiction, *more* profits for organized crime, and *more* police corruption. In 1970 the Knapp Commission, convened in New York City under United States District Court Judge Whitman Knapp to study allegations made by police officer Frank Serpico, concluded in part:

> Corruption in narcotics law enforcement has grown in recent years to the point where high-ranking police officials acknowledge it to be the most serious problem facing the Department. In the course of its investigation, the commission became familiar with . . . corrupt patterns including:
> - Keeping money and/or narcotics confiscated at the time of an arrest or raid.
> - Selling narcotics to addict-informants in exchange for stolen goods.
> - Passing on confiscated drugs to police informants for sale to addicts.
> - "Flaking," or planting narcotics on an arrested person in order to have evidence of law violation . . .
> - Storing narcotics, needles and other drug paraphernalia in police lockers . . .
> - Accepting money or narcotics from suspected narcotics law violators as payment for the disclosure of official information.
> - Financing heroin transactions.

Yet, even as the Knapp Commission was issuing these grim findings, President Richard M. Nixon was declaring a new "War on Drugs," and allocating unprecedented amounts of money for narcotics control. Ironically, it was the American involvement in Vietnam that was substantially to blame for a surge in the availability of illicit heroin during this period. The successive South Vietnamese governments of Ngo Dinh Diem and Nguyen Cao Ky had supplemented their war chests with profits from opium, which had been widely used in Vietnam since the mid-nineteenth century when French colonialists established an opium monopoly there. From 1965 to approximately 1970, then, to aid our allies, the American Central Intelligence Agency set up a charter airline—Air America—to transport raw opium from growing regions in the highlands of Burma and Laos to Saigon.* Of course, not all that opium stayed in Saigon. Much of it was transported to Marseille by Corsican gangsters to be refined into heroin and shipped to America by way of the famous French connection. The result was a full-fledged heroin epidemic. The United States addict population swelled to seven hundred fifty thousand, and there was a proportional jump in addiction-related crime, accompanied by *more* overcrowding in prisons, *more* stagnation in the courts, and *more* hepatitis and overdose deaths.

The epidemic subsided with the fall of Saigon, as heroin smugglers searched for a new source of raw opium. By the mid-seventies, they had found it in Mexico's Sierra Madre, and "Mexican Mud" substantially replaced "China White" heroin in the illicit street trade. This situation prevailed until 1978, when a program was instituted by the United States and Mexican governments to spray poppy fields with the defoliant Agent Orange. The eradication program has been termed a huge success, resulting in a substantial decrease in the amount of Mexican Mud on the illicit market; the costs in terms of environmental damage and the Agent Orange's effect on the health of the people living near the poppy fields has yet to be calculated.

No sooner, though, had the Mexicans begun eradicating the poppy than there was a new upsurge of Southeast Asian heroin; when that source dried up as a result of severe drought in 1978, the heroin barons found ample new supplies of opium in the

---

*The CIA with funds from USAID also helped Laotian General Vang Pao set up his own opium-moving airline, Xieng Khouang Air Transport.

Golden Crescent (Iran, Afghanistan, Pakistan), where political upheaval had removed any restraints on poppy cultivation.

All this was the inevitable result of unsound legislation, as Robert Schles foresaw back in 1925. When one source of opiates dries up, another replaces it; when one trafficker is arrested, a successor is always at hand. And so it goes, to the point where some law enforcement officials privately admit that there's simply no hope of ever containing, much less dismantling, traffic in narcotics. For some enforcement officials, this is not necessarily a bad thing. Superintendent David Hodson of the Hong Kong Narcotics Bureau:

> The question you're really left is, which is the best approach—to disorganize organized drug trafficking, or to leave organized drug trafficking organized and try to minimize it... Because whatever happens, you're going to have drug trafficking. As long as you've got drug addicts, you're going to have drug traffickers.... Of course the danger if you leave it organized and minimize it, is the problem of (police) corruption.... But if you disorganize it, you end up with probably a worse problem than you had in the first place, because it's much more difficult to control, to police disorganized drug trafficking than it is organized drug trafficking.

There are others, however, like Detective Sergeant William Gillespie of the New York City police narcotics division who, after considering the inevitable outcome of the current approach, wonder frankly if "maybe we should just give addicts heroin."

That, of course, would mean not only the loss of millions of dollars in profits to organized crime, but millions of dollars in enforcement agency budgets, so it is not an opinion very often voiced in law enforcement circles. Drug enforcement, after all, is also a big business.

And what does the American taxpayer get for all this money? At the present time, officials of the Drug Enforcement Administration (D.E.A.)* admit its agents are able to intercept only about *5 percent* of the illegal heroin coming into America. To

---

*The Federal Bureau of Narcotics was reorganized in 1960, after Harry Anslinger's retirement, into the Bureau of Narcotics and Dangerous Drugs (BNDD), which was in turn reorganized following disclosures of corrupt practices into the Drug Enforcement Administration in 1971.

their credit, the pressures narcotics enforcers bring to bear on smugglers tend to keep the quality of heroin low and the price high,* which certainly deters a few people from trying the drug and insures that addicts are not likely to overdose in alarming numbers. But such observations fall far short even of the goal of "minimizing" narcotics use in America. The seeming futility of enforcement in this area was summarized aptly in the title of a 1979 Government Accounting Office report critical of the D.E.A.: "Gains made in controlling illegal drugs, yet still the drug trade flourishes."

In addition to the millions of dollars spent on narcotics enforcement, with minimal results, millions more are spent on cures that don't work and education and prevention programs that are blatantly ineffective. In fact, from 1969 to 1979 America spent $52 *billion* on drug control. Of this amount, only $222 million went to those foreign places where poppies are lanced and squeezed of their juice; where the juice is dried in the sun to opium gum, where the gum is filtered through cheesecloth into morphine base, and the base carried to jungle labs where it's synthesized into heroin. Disrupt this laborious process at any point, and the whole rickety money train is derailed, and the poppy peasants migrate before they can plant a new crop. It would not cost much to do this—more than $222 million, but nothing like $52 *billion*. Instead, though, the heroin always gets manufactured, and the rest of the money is spent, as it were, trying to put the toothpaste back in the tube.

The remaining $51,775,000,000 in that lump of taxpayers' revenue was carved up in the seventies by various domestic enforcement and treatment personnel, and now those people *depend* on it. This is the very height of bureaucratic incompetence: a multi-billion dollar business, ostensibly created to stop people from taking opiates, which is positively dependent on opiates and opiate users for its survival. Meanwhile, the heroin is synthesized, shipped and distributed by modern-day robber barons, and everyone greatly profits.

---

*By the DEA's accounting, heroin street purity nationwide is currently only 3.5 percent, and is selling at $31.60 per 20 milligrams, an average addict's dose.

Everyone, that is, except for the peasant who grows the poppy, but he is blessed by being far away from this madness. In his thatched hut in the mountains of Burma he sits, turning his bamboo pipe over his flickering peanut-oil lamp. The opium bubbles, the smoke blooms, he inhales deeply, and gazes out the window. Outside, on the nearby hills, fields of poppies, white and pink, bend lazily in the moist jungle breezes.

New York City
March 1981

FOR FURTHER READING

PREFACE:
FLOWERS IN THE BLOOD

Colton, Walter. "Turkish Sketches—Effects of Opium." *Knicker-bocker*, April 1836.

Greene, Graham. "My Own Devil." *Vogue*, October 1973.

Judson, Horace Freeland. *Heroin Addiction in Britain*. New York: Harcourt Brace Jovanovich, 1973.

Snyder, Solomon H., and Matthysse, Steven. *Opiate Receptor Mechanisms*. Cambridge, Mass.: M.I.T. Press, 1975.

Nova. "The Keys of Paradise." Boston, Mass.: WGBH Educational Foundation, 1979. (Transcript available through: WGBH Educational Foundation, 125 Western Avenue, Boston, Mass. 02134.)

ONE: LEGENDS

Graves, Robert. *Greek Gods and Heroes*. New York: Dell, 1960.

Homer. *The Odyssey*. Translated by Robert Fitzgerald. New York: Anchor Books, 1963.

Kritikos, P. G., and Papadaki, S. P. "The history of the poppy and of opium and their expansion in the eastern Mediterranean area." United Nations *Bulletin on Narcotics*, Vol. XIX, No. 3, July–September, 1967.

Wasson, R. Gordon; Hofmann, Albert; and Ruck, Carl. A. P. *The Road to Eleusis*. New York: Harcourt Brace Jovanovich, 1978.

TWO:
DRUGS OF GOOD AND EVIL

Leake, Chauncey D. *An Historical Account of Pharmacology to the Twentieth Century*. Springfield, Ill.: Charles C. Thomas, 1977.

Rosenthal, Franz. *The Herb: Hashish versus Medieval Muslim Society*. Leiden, Holland: E. J. Brill, 1971.

THREE:
THE STONE OF IMMORTALITY

Haggard, Howard W. *Devils, Drugs and Doctors*. New York: Harper & Brothers, 1929.

Kramer, John C. "The Opiates: Two Centuries of Scientific Study." *Journal of Psychedelic Drugs*, April–June, 1980.

Lewin, Lewis. *Phantastica*. New York: E. P. Dutton, 1931.

Ross, James Bruce, and McLaughlin, Mary Martin. (eds.) *The Portable Medieval Reader*. New York: Viking, 1949.

Waite, Arthur Edward, ed. *The Hermetic and Alchemical Writings of Paracelsus*. Boulder, Colo.: Shambhala Publications, 1976.

FOUR:
THE BRITISH EXPERIENCE

Berridge, Virginia, and Edwards, Griffith. *Opium and the People: Opiate Use in Nineteenth Century England*. London: Allen Lane, 1981.

Ober, William B. *Boswell's Clap and Other Essays*. Carbondale, Ill.: Southern Illinois University Press, 1979.

FIVE:
THE DREAMERS

Abrams, M. H. *The Milk of Paradise: the effect of opium visions on the works of De Quincey, Crabbe, Francis Thompson, and Coleridge*. Cambridge, Mass.: Harvard University Press, 1934.

De Quincy, Thomas. *Confessions of an English Opium-Eater*. New York: Penguin, 1971.

Haytor, Althea. *Opium and the Romantic Imagination*. Berkeley, Calif.: University of California Press, 1970.

Le Febre, Molly. *Samuel Taylor Coleridge—A Bondage to Opium*. Briarcliff Manor, N.Y.: Stein and Day, 1974.

SIX:
CHINA: THE OPIUM WARS

Ching-Jen, Chen. "Opium and Anglo-Chinese Relations." *The Chinese Social and Political Science Review*, October 1935.

Greenberg, Michael. *British Trade and the Opening of China, 1800–42*. New York: Cambridge University Press, 1951.

Inglis, Brian. *The Forbidden Game*. New York: Scribners, 1975.

Le Fevour, Edward. "Western Enterprise in Late Chi'ng China: A Selective Survey of Jardine-Matheson and Company's Operations 1842–1895." Harvard East Asian Monographs. Cambridge, Mass.: Harvard University Press, 1968.

Morse, Hosea Ballou. *The International Relations of the Chinese Empire*. London/New York: Oxford, 1910.

SEVEN:
AMERICAN AFYON

Downs, Jacques. "American Merchants and the China Opium Trade." *Business History Review*, 42 (1968).

Porter, Kenneth Wiggens. *John Jacob Astor: Businessman*. Cambridge, Mass.: Harvard University Press, 1931.

EIGHT:
NERVOUS WASTE

Calkins, A. *Opium and the Opium Appetite*. Philadelphia: Lippincott, 1871.

Frisch, John R. "Our Years in Hell (American Addicts Tell Their Story) 1829–1914," *Journal of Psychedelic Drugs* 9 (1977).

Kane, H. H. *Opium Smoking in America and China*. New York: Putnam, 1882.

Ludlow, FitzHugh. *The Hasheesh Eater*. San Francisco: City Lights Books, 1979.

NINE:
YELLOW PERIL

Hill, Herbert. "Anti-Oriental Agitation and the Rise of Working-Class Racism." *Society*, January–February, 1973.

Szasz, Thomas. *Ceremonial Chemistry*. New York: Anchor Books, 1975.

Silver, Gary, and Aldrich, Michael. *The Dope Chronicles*. New York: Harper & Row, 1979.

**TEN:
THE FATHER OF AMERICAN
NARCOTICS LAWS**

Bruun, Kettil; Parr, Lynn; and Rexed, Ingemar. *The Gentleman's Club*. Chicago: University of Chicago Press, 1975.
Musto, David F. *The American Disease*. New Haven, Conn.: Yale University Press, 1973.
Taylor, Arnold H. *American Diplomacy and the Narcotics Traffic, 1900–1939*. Durham, N.C.: Duke University Press, 1969.

ELEVEN: HEROIN BOYS

Baily, Pearce. "The heroin habit." *The New Republic*, April 12, 1916.
Lindesmith, Alfred. *The Addict and the Law*. Bloomington, Ind.: Indiana University Press, 1965.
Street, Leroy. *I Was A Drug Addict*. New York: Random House, 1953.
United Nations. "History of Heroin." *Bulletin on Narcotics*, April–June, 1953.

TWELVE: THE CURE

Burroughs, William. *Junky*. New York: Ace, 1953.
———. *Naked Lunch*. New York: Grove Press, 1962.
Dole, Vincent. "Addictive Behavior." *Scientific American*, December 1980.
Levin, Gilbert; Roberts, Edward B.; and Hirsh, Gary B. *The Persistent Poppy*. Cambridge, Mass.: Ballinger, 1975.
MacFarlane, Peter Clark. "The 'White Hope' of Drug Victims." *Colliers*, November 29, 1913.
Waldorf, Dan; Orlick, Martin; and Reinarman, Craig. *Morphine Maintenance: The Shreveport Clinic, 1919–1923*. Drug Abuse Council Monograph. Washington, D.C.: Drug Abuse Council, 1828 L St., NW, 1974.
Annotated Bibliography of Papers from the Addiction Research Center, 1935–1975; Drug Addiction and the Public Health Service. Available through: The National Clearing House for Drug Abuse Information, Room 10A-53, 5600 Fishers Lane, Rockville, Maryland 20857.

EPILOGUE: THE BUSINESS

Cheshire, Maxine. "Drugs and Washington, D.C." *Ladies Home Journal*, November 19, 1978.

Government Accounting Office. "Gains made in controlling illegal drugs but still the drug trade flourishes." Washington, D.C.: Government Accounting Office, October 25, 1979.

Hammer, Richard. *Playboy's Illustrated History of Organized Crime.* New York: Playboy Press, 1975.

McCoy, Alfred W. *The Politics of Heroin in Southeast Asia.* New York: Harper & Row, 1972.

INDEX

JEFF GOLDBERG is best known as an investigator of psychoactive drugs and how they work in the brain. His first book, *Flowers in the Blood*, an in-depth history of opium, began while Goldberg was working as an editor at *High Times* magazine in the late 1970s. Goldberg's second book, *Anatomy of a Scientific Discovery*, an on-the-scene account of the discovery of endorphins also reissued by Skyhorse Publishing, established him as a leading science writer. His articles on science and medicine have appeared in *Life*, *Discover*, *Omni*, and other magazines internationally.

DEAN LATIMER is the former executive editor of *High Life* magazine. Born in Canton, New York, Latimer was an important figure in the flourishing underground press in the late 1960s, helping to originate the East Village Other, to which he contributed to politically, as well as to the *National Lampoon*. His articles have also appeared in *Oui* and *Penthouse*, among others.